Mission:

"A specific task

with which

a person

or a group

is charged."

MERRIAM-WEBSTER'S
2021 UNABRIDGED DICTIONARY

A Simple Structure for Missional Effectiveness

MISSION:
POSSIBLE
3+

Kay Kotan & Blake Bradford

Market
Square
BOOKS

Mission Possible 3+

A Simple Structure for Missional Effectiveness

©2021 Market Square Publishing, LLC
books@marketsquarebooks.com
P.O. Box 23664 Knoxville, Tennessee 37933
ISBN: 978-1-950899-28-9
Library of Congress: 9781950899289

Printed and Bound in the United States of America
Cover Illustration & Book Design ©2021 Market Square Publishing, LLC
Publisher: Kevin Slimp
Editor: Kristin Lighter
Illustrations: Kerri Bradford
Post-Process Editor: Ken Rochelle

Table of Contents

Acknowledgment

This book is dedicated to the hundreds of churches and pastors who have invited us into their ministry. Thank you for the opportunity to journey with you and serve alongside you. It is because of you that we have had the experiences to share with others so that they might benefit from your challenges and achievements.

Why Mission Possible 3+

We have been working with churches who have implemented the simplified, accountable structure for more than a decade. The first version of Mission Possible was an attempt to put together a "how to" manual for churches who were either considering the model or who had decided to move to it, and needed a handbook to understand the model, implement it, and use it as an on-going resource for the greatest effectiveness. In the second version, Kay invited Blake to collaborate as a lay-clergy team. We added many more resources, expanded both the "why" and "how-to" along with sharing our learnings since version 2.0 was published.

As more districts, conferences, and churches explored this model, we found that more trained coaches and consultants were needed to assist church leaders to implement the simplified, accountable structure. As a result, SAS[1] Coach Certification was introduced to equip coaches to assist churches how to discern this model, lead equipping workshops for local church leaders, and help churches in their implementation. In the first few months, more than a hundred participants engaged in the SAS Coach Certification.

It was through this training with others that we felt the need to add more information, reformat and reorganize the book into the three phases, offer more resources, and give the book more of a workbook look and feel. All of this is offered as our on-going commitment in providing the latest evolutions and learnings about this model *(see shifts in SAS on Page 282)* while continuously striving to provide the best possible resource for you and your church leadership. It is truly a labor of love with the desire to be helpful to churches to live out their mission more effectively for the best possible Kingdom impact!

---

1 Simplified, accountable structure

Introduction

I (Kay) have had the privilege of taking a few cruises in the past twenty years. They are always enjoyable. It is a great time of relaxation, sunny weather, and beautiful destinations. There are no worries. Someone else does the grocery shopping, plans the meals, prepares the meals, serves the meals, does the dishes, makes my bed, mops the floor, cleans my room, pilots the boat, manages all the port clearances, shuffles my luggage to my room, entertains me, etc. It is truly a vacation from reality. It is an escape! It seems so easy and carefree from a passenger standpoint, but there are hundreds of employees behind the scenes orchestrating this experience. There is a captain leading this cohesive team with a single focus working collaboratively to create this dream experience for all its passengers.

Now can you imagine that same cruise ship out in the Caribbean Sea allowing only the weather, wind, and tides to determine its destination? We would never dream of allowing such a thing to occur. There is no way anyone would allow a multi-million-dollar boat with thousands of people to toss aimlessly in the waves without a predetermined destination. Some passengers may have embarked the ship with a desire to go to Aruba while others had a desired destination of Alaska. Without a map, radar, established route, itinerary, or captain directing the way and the people aboard, the experience would be quite different. Yet, this is how many of our churches operate today. No one is directing the ship with a commonly understood destination, course, or purpose. People are busy doing "stuff," but we aren't going anywhere. The GPS is not engaged and certainly no one is watching the radar for weather conditions. We are simply being tossed about by the sea of life and culture, all while being frustrated that we are not getting anywhere. No one has their eye on the mission – making disciples!

While a simplified, accountable structure is not the answer to church transformation, it does set the table for transformation to occur. In our experience, churches moving to this model begin to shift their conversations and focus, release more people into ministry, and therefore have a much higher likelihood of a fruitful, vital ministry. Without this shift in structure and accountability, churches find it much more difficult to find the traction and focused purpose to revitalize their church.

Mission NOT Accomplished/Possible

W. Edwards Deming, a postwar engineer and scientist of manufacturing systems, proclaimed that "every system is perfectly designed to get the result that it does." The mainline churches' congregational governance structure was designed with multiple layers of checks and balances. Our inherited governance and leadership structure is a system built to maintain and preserve the ecclesiastical institution – to make sure that nothing too crazy (or creative) happens. While this may have been fine in the American postwar era of church growth and engagement, the missional church of the twenty-first century must be creatively and structurally enabled to make nimble changes in methods to fulfill its disciple-making mission.

The typical church structure is driving the mission rather than the mission driving the structure! We are simply not accomplishing the mission Jesus intended for our churches. Because of the way in which we are structured, the mission is sometimes not even possible. To make matters worse, most of us know this, yet many of us are not willing or able to change it. Our churches get mired down in the "way we have always done things" and find it difficult if not impossible to change the "way we have always done things." All the churches we work with desire to reach new people (of course, mostly young people with children). Yet, some are not willing to make the needed changes for this to occur. We cannot count the times churches "say" they want to reach people, but when it comes down to making the changes to actually reach new people, many dig their heels in and resist the change. Mostly this is because the changes will affect those resisting the change personally. If changes only affect others, the changes are acceptable. But once they become personal, changes are much more difficult to accept.

Do you believe the mission is possible? Do you want the mission to succeed? Do you *really* want the mission to succeed? If the answer is yes, we must align all that we do and all that we have as churches and individual disciples to the mission of making disciples of Jesus Christ for the transformation of the world. Yes, making disciples is the very reason each and every church exists. Jesus designed the church to continue His work in spreading the Good News. So again, do we want the mission to succeed? Really? I have always loved this quote from Tom Bandy about putting the very important missional question into perspective:

> *Are you prepared to stake **everything**, change **anything**, and do **whatever** it takes – even if it means altering long familiar habits, redeveloping precious programs, and redeploying sacred assets?*

Tom Bandy, from the foreword of Winning On Purpose

There is hope! There is another way forward. There are options where faithfulness for reaching the mission is more possible and likely than others. We must structure our churches today to be lean, effective, and efficient if we are to impact our non-church centric world. We can simply no longer function in our archaic structures and methods if we are to reach the people of today for Jesus Christ. The structure (the way we make decisions) in many of our churches is holding us back from accomplishing our mission. In some churches the current structure and methods do not allow us to keep our eye on the ball. We are so busy running our structure, that the structure is running us! Our mission is no longer our focus. And without focus, the mission will not succeed.

Our motivation for providing this resource is multi-fold. Kay has been working as a coach, consultant, and conference staff with churches and pastors across the country who are trying to make structural changes for over a decade now. In walking alongside thousands of leaders and hundreds of churches working to move to a simplified, accountable structure, we continue to evolve the model and best practices for effectiveness and efficiency. In addition to pastoral service in large and small churches, Blake has served on conference staff and as a district superintendent, which has afforded him the opportunity to see leaders and structures from a wide cross-section of contexts. The same pitfalls are observed repeatedly.

Our hope and prayer in providing this resource is to first help churches really understand what they are undertaking before deciding to move forward with changing their structure. Secondly, we hope this resource will help churches navigate the process with eyes wide open and the tools needed to do so. Thirdly, the pandemic created a new perspective on the need to make decisions quickly and be more adaptive and flexible in relating to a changing context. Churches in a simplified, accountable structure found themselves much more poised to respond with timeliness and innovative approaches than churches who were working in a traditional structure and decision-making model. And finally, we hope this resource provides the outcome of fruitful and effective ministries to reach new people for Jesus Christ.

This book will lead you through both the technical and adaptive shifts that will need to be addressed to align your church to the mission of making disciples. If you came to this book looking for only the technical "how to's" for moving into simplified structure so you can have fewer meetings, you may be a bit frustrated. Our intention is to challenge you to move beyond making this just a technical change, but to also move you through this very large adaptive change. It is in the adaptive changes that churches can create a whole new trajectory of vitality with a much deeper and transformational impact.

If you are ready to partake in a bold, brave journey for you and your church towards faithfulness in fruitful ministries, let the journey begin!

A Few Disclaimers

Terminology: Simplified vs Single Board

You might have heard what we are referring to in this resource as "simplified structure" referred to by others as the "single board model." Indeed, when I (Kay) first began to work with simplifying church structure, we referred to this practice as the single board model with accountable leadership. I try to no longer use the terminology of the single board. Here is my reasoning: When churches heard "single board," some interpreted that to mean that there were no other committees or teams except for the one leadership team. That misinterpretation solely based on the name led those churches in no longer having ministries teams or even a Nominations Committee. The churches simply stopped ministries and only had worship. This was a huge misunderstanding and was difficult to course correct. In fact, there was one particular church that almost closed due to this misunderstanding! No one wants that to happen, so we changed the terminology we now use to describe changing structure. We have also learned that moving only to simplifying structure without also practicing accountable leadership proves to be an uphill battle for missional effectiveness. For these reasons, we now refer to this model as simplified, accountable leadership structure.

Personal Interpretations

Provided herein is our own personal interpretation and application of the United Methodist Church's *Book of Discipline* (BOD) as it pertains to structuring a local church through our coaching and consulting in hundreds of churches. Refer to your district superintendent, cabinet, bishop, and annual conference for confirmation or local interpretations that might differ. Understand that your conference or district may also have additional policies that require modifying the advice or Disciplinary interpretations. Ultimately, this model is at the discretion and approval by your district superintendent. What we offer is the most up-to-date, practical, and experience-based model that is working best in local churches.

United Methodist Centered

Many times, the BOD is referenced in these writings and our experiences are mostly from United Methodist Churches. If you are not United Methodist, please make sure you apply your own church polity to these writings.

Keep it Simple for Christ's Sake:
Two Ecclesiastical Parables

It almost seemed like the system was designed to make sure ministry would not happen. A member had an idea: What if we converted our annual Easter Egg Hunt, a nice little gathering of our church membership's families, into an opportunity to meet more of the neighborhood, bless the families of the community, and perhaps get contact information that might be followed-up on as an act of evangelism? A ministry team was formed. The idea continued to hatch. A cookout and kids' fair was dreamed up and planned by the team. A member who was a grocer pledged to donate the food. The leader of the children's ministry and the pastor were fully on board and so was the Church Council. But a change to our normal way of doing things required some permissions to make sure no one would get upset. The Church Council wanted to make sure that the other committees of the church would not get upset by a usurpation of their power. First, the Trustees would need to get involved, since the idea included using the Church's front lawn at the center of town. Then, the team would need the finance committee to approve shifting the budgeted children's ministry funds from one line item to another. After those two committees met and each approved the plan, the Council would make its final determination. It is too bad that the series of scheduled meetings would require that the idea for an Easter event would receive its final approval in June!

Meetings are not ministry. The system of committee-based checks and balances that was suited for the days of mid-twentieth century Christendom is no longer an effective way to mobilize the people-power and resources of the church in our twenty-first century interconnected world in which the church is no longer at the center of community life. We need a nimble, mission-focused structure that can respond to fresh ideas and approaches to ministry. We United Methodists can, at times, get distracted by our desire for consensus and lose sight of our actual mission. Leaders (lay and clergy alike) need to be allowed and empowered to lead. Meetings need to actually matter and operate as moments for accountability and missional alignment.

A simplified, accountable governing structure makes it possible for your church to better focus on leadership equipping, missional alignment, and your next steps in ministry. Meanwhile, removing bureaucratic redundancies allows more members to spend their time in service as disciples who make disciples rather than sitting in unproductive meetings. By consolidating administrative functions into a single governing team, disciples can focus on using their spiritual gifts and passions for ministry to contribute to the vitality of the congregation as it seeks to reach the mission field.

So, let's imagine another story: A member is blessed with a great idea to connect to the community during the Easter season. A ministry team engages with the idea, improves upon it, recruits serving disciples to help, and a donation from a member is acquired to help offset a portion of the expenses. Staff rearrange their budgets under existing authority they have been given to accommodate the rest of the event expense. Because the change involves a huge cultural shift in the way the church has historically experienced the Easter season, the pastor asks the simplified structure Leadership Board to consider supporting the change. Since the change fits into the mission, vision, and evangelistic goals of the congregation, the Council celebrates the new idea and commends the ministry team leading the effort. Eight weeks later, at the new Community Egg Hunt and Cook-out, dozens of guests experience the relational hospitality of the congregation. Contact information is collected at an Easter Bunny photo booth for follow-up. New friendships are created and new disciples begin their discipleship journey through the ministry of the church.

Structured to Thrive

It is for the sake of Christ and the Great Commission that our congregations exist. By simplifying our church structures, we are creating an environment where ministry can thrive. Vital and fruitful churches must be governed and led in new ways today so that Christ's mission for us can be fulfilled! The disciple-making mission which Christ has given us is too important to let bureaucratic redundancies distract us from our work. For the sake of Christ's mission and our mission fields, many churches are discovering that there are simpler ways to provide governance and strategic direction so that the congregation can be unleashed for ministry.

Resource Layout

Unlike previous versions of *Mission Possible*, you will find this resource offered in four primary sections. The first three sections reflect the three phases of moving to a simplified, accountable structure. The first phase is that of **discerning**, followed by **equipping** in the second phase, and finally **implementing** in the third. Each phase involves different players (leaders) and different seasons. By dividing the process and this resource into the phases, it allows the different players to more closely focus on their particular phase involvement. Please note: This does not mean we recommend only reading one particular section of the resource. Rather, it is our hope that each leader will digest the whole resource and also be able to more easily refer back to this as a resource to be used as needed while progressing in the process, as well as for helpful reminders along your journey.

The fourth section contains information and **resources for judicatory leaders** such as district superintendents, presiding elders, cabinet members, congregational developers, directors of connectional ministries, etc. Because these leaders play a role in the approval of the local church structure, it is important that we all are on the same page. This is especially true of district superintendents. This section provides checklists, recommendations, and specific resources to use for church and charge conferences in relationship to local churches moving to a simplified, accountable structure. This section is a brand-new addition to the resource from previous versions.

In addition to these four sections, you will find a **Resource** section at the back of the book. These are resources for the existing Church Council, the new Leadership Board, the Committee on Nominations and Leadership Development, judicatory leaders, and Certified SAS Coaches. They include over twenty resources such as a sample leadership application samples, a checklist for discernment, organizational charts, FAQ's, and sample guiding principles to name just a few.

Unlike the previous two versions of *Mission Possible*, this layout was created so this resource could be used as both a workbook and a resource. You will find pages where there are guided questions and exercises to help steer you through decisions and steps along the way. During the various leadership seasons, you will want this resource handy as a reference, too, to remind you of those best practices and recommendations. This resource was not meant to be read once and then placed on the bookshelf to collect dust. Rather, it was written with the intent to be close at hand for Leadership Board members, pastors, coaches, and judicatory leaders as a guide, resource, reference, and tools for simplified, accountable structure.

Brief Overview of Simplified, Accountable Structure

If this is your first introduction to the church leadership structure we have come to refer to as simplified, accountable structure or if you are trying to explain what it is to someone, this section is for you!

In the United Methodist Church (UMC), our polity has historically called for four administrative committees to care for the "business" of the church. Those four committees are the Trustees Committee, Finance Committee, Pastor-Parish Relations Committee, and the Church Council. These committees usually consist of 6-12 people serving three-year rotating terms. In addition to these generalities, each committee has its particular nuances and requirements as outlined in our *UMC Book of Discipline* (book that constitutes the law, polity, and doctrine of the United Methodist Church). While the structure and numbers vary from church to church, the average congregation has somewhere between 25 to 75 members tied up in serving on these four administrative committees.

While the predecessor bodies that constitute our denomination have approved a *Book of Discipline* for two hundred years, the first edition of the *United Methodist Book of Discipline* originated in 1968 when the UMC was formed through the union of the Evangelical United Brethren Church and the Methodist Church. In 1968, the church's primary responsibility was to receive the continuous flow of people coming in the door from a church-centric culture and make them official members. Designed for continuity and stability, the legacy committee structures we inherited were simply not designed for the complexity and rapid changes of our modern era. In the 21st Century, simply adding names to the membership roll is not the primary responsibility of the administrative committees since culture is no longer church-centric (in fact, the church is counter-cultural) thus resulting in the church needing to structure differently for a shifting time and focus.

In the latest edition (2016) of the *Book of Discipline* ¶247.2, the church, with approval of the district superintendent, is provided the opportunity to restructure in order to be more missionally focused. While the *Book of Discipline* describes in great detail how the four administrative committees are formed, this latest paragraph is quite general and flexible in nature. In working with hundreds of churches and thousands of leaders over the past decade (plus), we (Kay and Blake) have continuously massaged, tweaked, and improved a simplified, accountable structure model for local congregations to adopt. This model has now found its way into churches across the country in multiple conferences. It is now referred to the simplified structure model generally accepted by district superintendents, cabinets, and bishops (with some districts and conferences requiring their own particular nuances).

This paragraph was introduced for the primary benefit of small churches who were struggling to have enough people to fill the four administrative committees as required by the traditional structure. However interestingly enough, it was the larger churches who were some of the early adopters. They quickly identified the efficiency and effectiveness in the model.

We are often asked about the effectiveness of simplified, accountable structure for the various size churches in the various church settings (rural, suburban, urban). In our experience, this model can (and does) work in any size church. Of course, there are nuances in the various settings, but the overall number of board leaders and accountability are static. The nuances occur in such things as the structure of staff and ministry teams according to church size, whether the church has a daycare or preschool, and how to operate in a multipoint charge. Further nuances occur in the guiding principles, leadership covenants, and the nominations process. The bottom line is that a simplified, accountable structure can work for any size church in any setting.*

*Note: There is only one circumstance that is an exception to this statement. If a church is unable to fulfill the requirements for a simplified structure (nine unrelated people), this is not an issue around structure (although small churches often seek out this model as the answer to the problem). Instead, we believe there is a need (and perhaps responsibility) to be asking different questions and looking at other options. If the minimum legal and polity requirements can't be met by a church, is it time to consider becoming a house church, a society, band or class model, merge with another church, close, etc.?

To simplify church structure, the four administrative committees (trustees, finance, staff-parish relations, and council) cease to exist as we know them, and they are replaced by one new Leadership Board of nine people with three year terms. This new board is nominated by the Committee on Nominations and Leadership Development and voted on by either the church or charge conference. Rather than holding four separate meetings of the four previous administrative committees, there is now one board meeting where the leaders are able to practice a healthier and more holistic approach with missional focus and direction. Technically, and in fulfillment with the requirements of the *Discipline*, all four committees still exist, but they exist as a single unified Leadership Board, with all of their responsibilities, qualifications, and authority of each administrative committee located in the simplified board. The new Leadership Board is the Church Council, and it is also the Trustees, which is the Finance Committee, and is the Staff Parish Relations Committee.

When simplifying the structure, accountability must be a deeply integrated and highly accepted component of simplification. Without accountability, simplification is not recommended! When transitioning to accountable leadership, the new Leadership Board shifts from *managing* the church to *governing* the church. This is a significant shift that should not be minimized or glossed over. While simplifying is a technical shift, accountability is an adaptive shift which takes longer and is a harder turn to make for most churches. Thus, this is not the "easy fix" some churches might think or even desire.

Accountable leadership changes not only the agenda, but also the conversations, focus, and priorities at the table. The nominations process is adapted, too, in this model. The role of the pastor will likely need to shift and sometimes staff roles will, too. While the new Leadership Board governs in the model of accountable leadership, the pastor leads, the staff (paid and unpaid ministry leaders) equips and coordinates ministry, and the congregation is released to be in ministry.

The primary purposes and benefits of simplified, accountable leadership are:

- Removes bottlenecks in the decision-making process (i.e. time, energy, resources, multiple committees/layers, silos, disjointed focus and priorities, etc.)

- Systems, procedures, and policies in place that are flexible and adaptable

- More people released and available for ministry

- Leadership Board responsible for church's faithfulness to The Great Commission (making disciples)

- Leadership Board aligns church resources to the mission and vision

- Guiding Principles in place for efficiency and permission-giving within healthy boundaries

- Leaders are held accountable at all levels

- Leadership Board is responsible for focusing on the areas of stewardship, strategic alignment, generative future-focus, and accountable leadership

- Missional focus, priority, and alignment are non-negotiables.

Remember, this explanation is provided for your convenience as a general overview of simplified, accountable structure. It is not intended nor recommended to be a substitute for digesting all of this resource and the additional training and recommendations covered herein. Rather, it is simply a quick overview provided for a basic understanding of the model. This resource lays out the three phases of leading with the simplified, accountable structure (discerning, equipping, implementing) in detail, along with tools and samples to ease the transition and encourage clarity as your congregation begins operating with this powerful and effective model of leadership.

THE DISCERNING PHASE

What is this phase?

The Discerning Phase is the first step in considering the adoption and implementation of the simplified, accountable structure. We have found it to be foundational in the process. This phase covers starting the conversation in the local church to explore, the request of the district superintendent to explore, the information and communication with the local congregation regarding the model, and ultimately the discernment of the congregation and its leaders if this is the right model in the right season for the church.

Who is involved in this phase?

The phase is led by the council chair, lay leader, and pastor initially with a SAS Discernment Team being added along the way. Your congregation's leadership will need to consult with your district superintendent, and some conferences may have SAS certified coaches to journey with you in your process.

What is the timing of this phase?

Ideally this phase is started in the first quarter of the calendar year if it is the intent of the church to move to the model the following January 1. This phase should not be rushed and will be approximately three to six months in duration.

CHAPTER D-1

Starting the Discernment Phase

The way God designed our bodies is a model for understanding our lives together as a church: every part dependent on every other part, the parts we mention and the parts we don't, the parts we see and the parts we don't. If one part hurts, every other part is involved in the hurt, and in the healing. If one part flourishes, every other part enters into the exuberance.... You are Christ's body – that's who you are! You must never forget this. Only as you accept your part of that body does your "part" mean anything. You're familiar with some of the parts that God has formed in his church, which is his "body":

apostles

prophets

teachers

miracle workers

healers

helpers

organizers

those who pray in tongues.

But it's obvious by now, isn't it, that Christ's church is a complete Body and not a gigantic, unidimensional Part? It's not all Apostle, not all Prophet, not all Miracle Worker, not all Healer, not all Prayer in Tongues, not all Interpreter of Tongues. And yet some of you keep competing for so-called "important" parts.

But now I want to lay out a far better way for you.

1 Corinthians 12:25, 27-31

Moving to a new structure is, potentially, a transformational change. Consideration of converting your leadership structure into a simplified, accountable structure is no exception. Too often leaders learn about the model, get excited, and then rush to get through the local church and district approval process. When the proper prayer, communication, information, and process are rushed or short-changed, the new leadership model starts off on the wrong foot from the very beginning. Likely, it has created a lack of trust both for the model and in the new leadership. Because we have seen this happen way too often, we have created a step-by-step process to help churches discern this model in a healthy, transparent method. Following these steps provides the church the opportunity to launch this new structure with a strong foundation rather than a shaky foundation fraught with mistrust, anxiety, and mystery.

At the end of this chapter, you will find a quick overview of the steps in the Discernment Phase. You will also find the overview in the **Resources Section** on Page 233. Refer to the list often to ensure each step is covered and in the proper order.

The four chapters of this first section of the book cover the entire Discernment Phase. These four chapters appear in the order in which they would be implemented. It is important to understand the whole Discernment Phase as you start this journey. At the same time, it is essential that you not rush the process or skip steps. Trust us here, please! Too many churches never give themselves a fighting chance for this model to work because they rushed to implementation.

The Discernment Phase may feel like it slows the process down (and it does), but it provides such a healthier process that is so worth the investment long term. I (Blake) have assisted in leading a few church building programs over the years. Every time, I am amazed how long it takes for the construction team to complete site work and pour a slab to begin building. I'm not a particularly patient person, so I just want to see steel and masonry going up, drywall hung, and fixtures installed. But we all know that excellent foundation work will ensure that the building will be there for generations of ministry. Likewise, a leadership structure needs time spent on its foundation if we expect it to hold up well to the challenges and tensions of ministry in today's world.

Here is a checklist for the initial steps in the discernment phase. You will find a step by step guide for all 12 steps in the discernment phase later in this chapter. This is merely a checklist as you take the first steps in determining if SAS is even the right model for your church. Come back to this checklist often so you don't miss any important steps as you begin this journey.

Checklist for Discernment

- Read this entire resource before making a decision

- Complete your SWOT analysis of your current governance compared with a change to simplified, accountable leadership structure. Consider how you might mitigate the risks and costs involved in a change while still remaining focused on your congregation's mission.

- Know your *why*: Build a clear case for a change using each of the four driving motivators:

  - Efficiency – Our churches must be structured so that leaders can lead, not simply maintain the status quo. Moving toward a permission-giving culture with less meetings and more leaders involved in direct ministry!

  - Alignment of people, funds, facilities, programs, and other resources

  - Missional focus – Moving from self-focus and institutional survival toward incarnational ministry in the lives, neighborhoods, communities, and the larger world.

  - Accountability – When "everyone" is in charge, no one is actually held responsible. Our structure should enable leaders to hold themselves and others accountable for missional fruitfulness.

  - Adaptability– Creating experiments to meet the needs of a changing landscape.

- Undergird the discernment phase in prayer at all levels. We suggest a Prayer Team be created early in the process.

- Lead with transparency and layers of conversations and communications for all

- Provide plenty of time for this phase. Don't rush it. Start the process 9-12 months in advance of rolling out the new structure.

Starting the Journey

Typically, someone discovers the simplified, accountable structure (SAS) from another church leader, attended a workshop or webinar, or read some information or a book on the subject. This leader begins to share their curiosity and/or excitement about the model with other leaders. Before long it comes up in some meeting (staff-parish, council, finance, trustees, or nominations) and those who have more information and have had more time to think about it are trying to convince others it is the best thing since sliced bread. Often there is some deadline coming up like fall charge conferences that make for a rushed decision. Let's stop right here and redirect!

The conversation for discernment needs to typically start in the first quarter of the fiscal year (typically also the calendar year). This allows the appropriate time for healthy discernment, information sharing, and equipping for the normal fall charge conference rhythm. In addition, the conversation needs to be housed in the proper body. Since this again is a big change for congregations, the process needs to go to the appropriate leadership body which is the Church Council/Board. While conversations might have sprouted in another group, the Discernment Phase needs to be owned and implemented by the Church Council.

The first step in the Discernment Phase is:

Determine why a structure change is needed or desired. Church Council votes to explore SAS after assessing the why.

The first step the Church Council needs to be taking is not voting on approving the structure. NO! STOP! The Church Council needs to be presented with enough overview information (i.e. the Overview of SAS in this book or overview videos of SAS on kaykotan.com or blakebradford.org) to understand the general concepts of the model.

Once there is a general understanding of the model, it is now important for the Council to explore why this change of structure is needed or desired. The desire to get to the implementation of a change often skips us right to the what, but the *why* is the most important factor for considering the change. Not spending the discovery time for the *why* is like pouring the concrete for a foundation without first placing gravel and rebar. The foundation will not provide the appropriate support for the structure built on it and will likely crumble and crack.

Discerning the Shift

Fewer people making decisions is NOT the goal of moving to a simplified, accountable leadership structure. The goal of any change in structure must ultimately be about successfully implementing the mission/purpose of the organization. For churches, that mission is the making disciples of Jesus Christ to transform the world. You need a governing and strategic structure that will help make this holy mission a reality. Some seek this change in governance because the number of active members is not sufficient for filling all the Disciplinary committees as separate entities/committees. While a simplified structure may help to solve that dilemma, it should never be the ultimate purpose. Simplifying your structure in partnership with accountability is not about consolidating power, it is about making the congregation's decision-making nimbler and unleashing lay leadership for more ministry!

Often when we teach church leaders about simplified, accountable leadership structure, someone in the crowd will share a metaphor about moving deck chairs on the Titanic. There is a truth in the statement: it is certainly correct that a change in structure will not fix relational dilemma or missional apathy. Simplified, accountable leadership structure could, however, create clarity in roles, connect responsibility and authority, and bring missional focus to your congregation and its leadership. To return to the metaphor about deck chairs on the sinking ship: a simplified, accountable leadership structure isn't about the deck chairs, it is about the leadership. It is the Titanic's captain, its officers, and its owners who ignored the radio warnings about icebergs, failed to provide lookout officers with binoculars and searchlights, turned the ship the wrong way, decided to travel full-speed through icy waters, and under-equipped the ship's lifeboats. The deck chairs were fine. It was the folks on the ship's bridge that caused the trouble. Simplified, accountable leadership structure is about who is on the "ship's bridge" and how they are empowered (and held accountable) to lead the church in fulfilling its disciple-making mission.

We also offer a warning that we shared in our book *Impact! Reclaiming the Call of Lay Ministry,* "Changing the number of people around the leadership table without also changing the leadership culture will only result in an isolated and ineffective board."[2] The 21st Chapter of the Gospel of John is instructive here. After the resurrected Jesus had appeared to Mary, the gathered disciples, and Thomas in John Chapter 20, Peter went back to what he knew best – fishing in Lake Galilee. He even went back to fishing on the same comfortable side of the boat. And they were catching nothing. It took another appearance of Jesus for them to try fishing from the other side of the boat. And this time their net was filled to capacity! It was so filled that they couldn't even haul their net into the boat! After a meal with the Risen Christ, Peter and Jesus had some words, including Jesus' imperative: "Follow Me!" Peter couldn't go back to comfortable habits and remain fruitful in Christ. He had to change to become the disciple Jesus needed him to be to fulfill God's mission.

That is why your why is so important. We have both seen many churches that changed their structure, but they did not change their behaviors: They continued to use the same

---

2 Kay Kotan and Blake Bradford. *Impact! Reclaiming the Call of Lay Ministry.* Market Square Books Publishing, Knoxville. 2018. p 114-115.

agenda. The same decision-making processes. And, therefore, they kept on having the same conversations at the table. After becoming frustrated, they either reached out for help or scrapped the whole process. A clear why moves a structural change from just being a technical modification into being an transformative opportunity.

Who Are We Now

In order to get to your deep why for a new structure, you and your fellow church leaders need to fully understand and be able to describe the structure of your current leadership system. How does your church make decisions and set goals now? Does your official nominations report submitted and approved at Charge Conference actually reflect your system of governance, or are there unwritten rules or unelected people, such as a matriarch or patriarch, that have a de facto veto power over all your church's decisions? Also, be honest with yourselves as a church. If your congregation has lingering issues of mistrust or a history of power-grabbing cliques, then a change in governance structure will not be a magic wand. Instead, it will probably deepen and intensify your internal mistrust. Congregational health and a re-focus on Christ's mission for the church must come first.

As you consider your current leadership structure, think in terms of it as a system. Often when we work with congregations to articulate a description of their current structure, especially in smaller churches, we are told about the people and their relationships to each other. While relationships are vitally important in ministry, now is the time to think systematically – roles, responsibilities, limits to authority, policies, and committee job descriptions.

In preparation for discussions of a structure change, perform a leadership inventory and analysis:

Step 1.

1. What is the total number of elected leadership positions in your church, compared to total active membership? What is the percentage of active members who are in elected leadership? (We have seen churches where 90 percent or more of the congregation is in elected leadership, which might be understandable in very small congregations, but it is a recipe for leadership inertia in mid-size churches. If everyone is in charge, then actually no one is in charge. If everyone is in an elected leadership role, then who is left to actually do the ministry?)

Total Number of Active Members	
Total Number of Elected Leadership Positions	
Percentage of Active Members in Elected Leadership	%

2. How many leaders are currently in administrative/governance leadership (finance, trustees, SPRC, administrative board) versus the number of members in programmatic/ministry leadership (worship, evangelism, etc.)?

Number of Administrative Positions	Number of Members in Program/Ministry Positions

3. How many leaders sit on more than one committee? _____

4. Think through the past few years and consider two or three large projects that your leadership had to approve. In those cases, how many committees were required to be involved to make a decision? How long did the entire approval process take, from conception to implementation to writing the thank you notes?

PROJECT 1

What Committees were Required for Approval:

❑ Administrative Board/Church Council

❑ SPRC/PPRC/Personnel

❑ Trustees

❑ Finance

❑ Other: _____

❑ Other: _____

❑ Other: _____

Number of Weeks for Approval	Number of Weeks for Implementation

PROJECT 2

What Committees were Required for Approval:

- ❑ Administrative Board/Church Council
- ❑ SPRC/PPRC/Personnel
- ❑ Trustees
- ❑ Finance
- ❑ Other: _____
- ❑ Other: _____
- ❑ Other: _____

Number of Weeks for Approval	Number of Weeks for Implementation

PROJECT 3

What Committees were Required for Approval:

- ❑ Administrative Board/Church Council
- ❑ SPRC/PPRC/Personnel
- ❑ Trustees
- ❑ Finance
- ❑ Other: _____
- ❑ Other: _____
- ❑ Other: _____

Number of Weeks for Approval	Number of Weeks for Implementation

5. Looking at your answers from questions 1-4, share what you have discovered about how your congregation currently deploys disciples for leadership? What surprised you? What challenged you?

6. How does your existing structure, both in reality and in written Charge Conference submissions, conform to the requirements of the *United Methodist Book of Discipline* (or other denominational book of policy standards for our non-UMC readers)? Identify and record any areas that are out of conformant or requirements.

Your answers to these questions will give you the contextual background information you will need as you consider a new way of leading your congregation. Now you are ready to begin considering *why* a new structure might enable your congregation to be more intentional in your discipleship processes, to focus more on creative opportunities beyond your walls, and to more effectively manage the fiduciary responsibilities of the congregation.

The Why

Before making any change, whether it be in governance or in implementing a new ministry, we must first begin with the *why*. So many times, when organizations go through changes, we lead with the "what" and the "how." We communicate what we desire or what steps we need to accomplish. However, it is most helpful to lead with the *why*. In other words, *why* is this change needed? *Why* will this change make a difference in the life of the congregation? People are often more motivated by the *why* than the "what." In our experience, when we lead with the what, people come to their own conclusions about the *why*. These self-conclusions are often misled because they were not well-informed.

At this point in your discernment, describe your initial *why* for a change in structure:

To help with determining the *why*, you might even think about using a SWOT analysis for communicating the need for change. A SWOT analysis is a strategic planning technique that includes a study of the internal strengths and weaknesses of the organization, mapped out in comparison to the external opportunities and threats the organization faces.

Begin with describing all that is going well in the church (strengths) and consider how your current structure is using your resources including leaders, their spiritual gifts, their energy, and their time. Next, describe the motivating factors that created the conversation about a possible change. Describe the obstacles and challenges that keeping your current structure will create or sustain, along with an honest evaluation of the costs of making a structural change (weaknesses). Then, it is time to look beyond your walls and stained-glass windows to external factors. Start by imagining the way a new structure will enable the congregation to make faster and more holistic decisions on behalf of the church to make disciples and impact the world (opportunities). Finally, explain the possible outcome for the church's mission if the change is not made (threats).

Complete your SWOT analysis in a group or committee setting and take notes using the blank chart provided.

SWOT Analysis for a Structure Change

	Strengths	Weaknesses	Opportunities	Threats
Assess your Current Leadership Structure	What is working well? What is the best part of how you are currently using resources and people?	What isn't working so well? What are your motives for keeping the current structure? Are the motives missional or for other reasons, such as protecting "turf" or entitlement?	How does your structure respond to new ministry ideas or creative solutions? How proactive is your current Leadership Board in actually looking for opportunities, taking risks, and setting the strategic direction of the congregation?	How will your congregation make disciples of Jesus Christ to transform the world in our complex, fast-changing culture that is very different from the one in which our structure was built?
Imagine a new Simplified, Accountable Leadership Structure	How might a change be a better use of resources and people?	What are the costs of shifting to a new simplified, accountable leadership structure, particularly in the area of relationships and trust? How might you mitigate the negative effects of the change, especially among those who feel a loss of power?	What opportunities are you missing, either because of the lack of alignment or the overworking of the same people for multiple committees? Imagine how the well-aligned and nimble board might be able to claim opportunities.	How do you imagine the simplified, accountable Leadership Board will be able to engage our complex and fast-moving world differently to lead the church in fulfilling our mission?

SWOT Analysis for a Structure Change

	Strengths	Weaknesses	Opportunities	Threats
Assess your Current Leadership Structure				
Imagine a new Simplified, Accountable Leadership Structure				

Motivating Factors

Most churches we work with find one or more of the following five elements to be the driving motivators in considering structure changes: efficiency, alignment, missional focus, accountability and adaptability.

Efficiency: In its traditional structure, many church decisions must run through multiple committees. Not only are there multiple stops on the permission train, but the train schedule is not efficient! One must sometimes wait a month or more for the next scheduled meeting on the permission train schedule. Those trying to work the process often find themselves discouraged, frustrated and may even give up! Many times, churches also have their congregation tied up in administrative tasks and committees leaving no one to do the ministry! I (Kay) once worked with a church with about 100 in worship attendance and had nearly 130 committee seats to fill. In the Arkansas Conference, one of our key points of the Bishop's Mission Plan is to "Unleash Lay Leadership". The more time that disciples are dealing with administrative issues, the less time they have for ministry in the neighborhood. By simplifying governing structures, more leaders can then put their spiritual gifts to work in ministry, not time spent in meetings.

Alignment: Most churches find themselves working in silos. One team or committee has no idea what the other is doing. Sometimes scheduling or resource conflicts arise. There is internal competition for people power, funding, and staff time. The Trustees move along a maintenance plan without talking with the SPRC that is responsible for budgeting for custodial staff. The Finance Committee creates a budget without taking into consideration the new priorities of the Church Council. Groups do not seem to all be pulling in the same direction for a common purpose or focus. Some churches often operate as multiple mini-churches or groups within one church. Alignment with the mission and vision is about being faithful to our purpose – it is not about reaching a consensus. Alignment to our mission and vision needs to be non-negotiable.

Missional focus: It still astonishes us that if you were to ask the average person in the pew why the church exists, they would most likely give you an answer something like, "to serve me," "to help me grow in my faith," or "to provide pastoral care to the flock." While those are all great benefits for members, it is not the foundational purpose of the church. Somewhere along the line we have lost sight of our purpose. We have become a nation of churches where so many have an internal focus of being served rather than an external focus of making disciples. A change in structure to fulfill a missional focus usually helps us shift more time, energy, resources, and disciples into ministry and fewer used in administration. In my

(Blake's) conference, we describe this as "unleashing laity for missional leadership." The more leaders and time we are spending on governance and strategy, the fewer leaders are available for the impactful work of forming, equipping, and sending disciples.

Accountability: For some reason, there is a belief that because the church is made up mostly of "volunteers," no one can be held accountable. (As an aside, we never use the term volunteers, and instead prefer the term serving disciples). Think about that for a minute. If this life is preparing us for eternal life, where did we ever come up with the idea that accountability for fruitfulness in the life of the church and as a disciple is not reasonable? Should this not be the place where we are held most accountable? We are Wesleyans, and Methodist Christians have accountability hard-wired into us from our history of class meetings and the early societies and conferences. We need to reclaim this missional accountability today.

Please, heed this WARNING. If you are considering simplifying your structure but are unable or unwilling to also begin practicing accountability, don't move into simplification. All churches could (and we would suggest need to) practice accountable leadership. Some churches could shift to simplified, accountable leadership. No church should move to simplified, accountable leadership without accountability. Time and time again, churches who have moved into simplified structure without accountable leadership practices have had severe issues with push-back, conflict, decline, and flat-out ugliness. It is all but impossible to hold a committee accountable. Individuals are held accountable. Accountability keeps us from falling into the traps of being pastor-centered churches, churches of silos, churches who hoard resources, or churches of controlling cliques. Also, be honest with yourself about your motivations. If the motivation for seeking this change in structure is a pretext or passive-aggressive attempt to get a particularly difficult member off a committee, hit the brakes. In those cases, the congregation needs to work on communication, healthy boundaries, and accountability. No structure, no matter how simple or elegant, can fix problems of relational health. Don't use a *Discipline* ¶247.2 response to a Matthew Chapter 18 problem. We will share much more about accountable leadership in Phase Two: Equipping.

Note of One Exception: The ONLY time simplified structure without accountability makes sense is when a church is in its final life stages. The church has consciously and intentionally made the decision to live out its limited final days caring for themselves and their facilities. The church has made the choice to enter "hospice." The church is sent a "hospice" chaplain to care for the small remnant congregation, hold their hands, and conduct their funerals. A small team of lay leaders is needed to fulfill fiduciary responsibilities and to ensure that a legacy is left to launch new faith communities.

Adaptability: For years, most of our changes in congregations were technical. We had tried and true tools and methods at our disposal. Innovative and resourceful congregations tested solutions to ministry problems and provided roadmaps for other congregations to follow their recipes for success. Most of these recipes have broken down due to the sheer magnitude and speed of changes over the last decade or two. Adaptive leadership is about creating solutions and experiments where no roadmap or recipe is yet available. Rapid cultural change is not going away. Adaptability calls for us to regain our pioneering roots that Jesus modeled, and Wesley reinforced. We must forgo our habits of being settlers in pews and once again use our pioneering roots to be a movement. For lay leadership to thrive, nurture creativity and innovation, maintain accountability, and be nimble, simpler structures must be enthusiastically invited into our congregations.

At this point in your discernment, rate (in order) which factors are part of your discerned reasons for simplifying your structure, then describe your why for a change in structure as it has evolved:

_____ Efficiency

_____ Alignment

_____ Missional Focus

_____ Accountability

_____ Adaptability

Your *why*:

Once the *why* has been identified and communicated, the church needs to consider the process to further explore a new structure with accountable leadership through prayer, discernment, and congregational conversations. This is a process that should not be rushed. Sometimes leaders are anxious to "get going" and rush through to the execution. This is a fundamental mistake! You are better off to slow the process down. Be intentional and thorough in walking the congregation this important time of discernment. Clear, complete, and patient preparation will pay generous dividends as you proceed in the process. This intentional process of discernment continues in the next chapter.

Church Council Vote to Explore

The Church Council's first decision point is to determine if they desire to enter into the Discernment Phase of SAS and explore the model with their congregation. That's it. No decision to adopt the model. It's too soon. There is not enough known or understood to adopt let alone implement SAS. It is simply the time for a decision to enter into a season of prayer and discernment exploring the model.

Once the Church Council has taken adequate time to understand the key factors of simplified, accountable structure and explore the motivating why to consider simplified, accountable structure, it is only then that the Church Council is ready to vote on their decision on whether this is the right season and model for the church to explore in dialogue with the entire congregation.

The second step in the Discernment Phase is:

Letter from council chair and/or lay leader and pastor to the district superintendent seeking permission to explore the SAS model

Step, 2,

If after faithfully exploring the model, the why, and a positive vote by the Church Council to explore is obtained, you are now ready for the next step. The next step after a vote to proceed to explore the model is for the pastor and Council Chair and/or Lay Leader to write a letter to the district superintendent to formally ask permission to explore the SAS model of leadership structure. Simplification of the structure outside of the four administrative committees of traditional structures is allowed by the *UMC Book of Discipline* in ¶ 247.2 in partnership with the district superintendent. In the letter include the missional purposes for moving to SAS (your why). A congregation can move to simplification of structure only in partnership and with approval of the district superintendent.

In my district, I (Blake) actually require a letter from the Pastor, Lay Leader, and Church Council Chair so that I know these steps have been followed and there is some buy-in from key leaders. You may proceed in exploring the model only after receiving permission to do so from your district superintendent. Below is Blake's form he uses with churches exploring SAS in his district for purposes of both documentation and ensuring all bases are being covered in the process. This form can also be found in the **Resource** section on Page 284.

Initial Consultation with Your District Superintendent

Share your motivations and reasons (your why) for a potential structure change.	
List the names and roles of lay officers involved in the discussion up to this point.	
Share which Disciplinary administrative committees you believe will be incorporated into the governing Leadership Board. While this may, of course, change as your church leadership wrestles with the possibilities and options, the DS may have particular recommendations or requirements so that your church's structure may be approved.	❑ Church Council/Administrative Board ❑ Council on Ministries ❑ Staff-Parish Relations Committee ❑ Board of Trustees ❑ Finance Committee ❑ Endowment Committee ❑ Other _____ ❑ Other _____ ❑ Other _____
Share your possible timeline for the structure change. Use the Discernment Steps.	Discernment Steps:_____ Consultation with the DS: _____ Contact SAS Certified Coach: Congregational Vote: _____ Nominations Work: _____ Charge Conference Elections:_____ New Board Begins Service:_____

Following is the complete set of steps for moving from the legacy committee structure into simplified, accountable structure. These steps can also be found in the **Resource** section on Page 233.

12 Steps to Discerning and SAS Transition

1. Church Council votes to explore SAS after assessing the why

2. Letter from Council Chair and Pastor to DS seeking permission to explore

3. Approval from DS to explore and assignment of SAS Coach

4. SAS Coach works with leaders to establish a SAS Prayer Team and SAS Discernment Team to lead in learning, organizing, and communicating the SAS discernment process

5. The SAS Discernment Team implements communication and information plan

6. Based on congregational feedback and leadership discernment, the leaders submit letter to DS to approve moving to (or not) SAS

7. DS reaches out to coach for feedback and makes decision

8. DS approval via letter (church conference timing)

9. Coach begins to work with Nominations and continues to work with leaders on communication strategies (see Equipping Phase)

10. Church Conference to approve SAS model

11. Nominations completes their work

12. Church/Charge Conference to approve Nominated Leaders

Note: After completing the Discernment Phase, move into Phase Two: Equipping and then onto Phase Three: Implementation.

We highly recommend partnering with a SAS certified coach through all three phases for the most effective and healthiest outcome!

CHAPTER D-2

Discernment Team & Plan

*James and John, Zebedee's sons, came up to him. "Teacher, we
have something we want you to do for us."*

"What is it? I'll see what I can do."

*"Arrange it," they said, "so that we will be awarded the highest places of honor in your
glory – one of us at your right, the other at your left."*

*Jesus said, "You have no idea what you're asking. Are you capable of drinking the cup
I drink, of being baptized in the baptism I'm about to be plunged into?"*

"Sure," they said. "Why not?"

*Jesus said, "Come to think of it, you will drink the cup I drink, and be baptized in my
baptism. But as to awarding places of honor, that's not my business. There are other
arrangements for that."*

*When the other ten heard of this conversation, they lost their tempers
with James and John. Jesus got them together to settle things down. "You've observed
how godless rulers throw their weight around," he said, "and when people get a
little power how quickly it goes to their heads. It's not going to be that way with you.
Whoever wants to be great must become a servant.
Whoever wants to be first among you must be your slave. That is what the Son of Man
has done: He came to serve, not to be served – and then to give
away his life in exchange for many who are held hostage."*

Mark 10:35-45

You figured out your *why* – your purpose in making a structural change. Amen! Hopefully your why goes well beyond simply having less meetings, and instead is about leading your congregation to impact your mission field. Your district superintendent has approved your exploration of the simplified, accountable structure model by entering into the Discernment Phase. Now you and your fellow leaders will need to enter a period of continued discernment and intentional communication.

I (Kay) have a confession to make. When I first started working with pastors and churches, simplifying the church structure (how decisions are made) seemed to be a no-brainer. After all, I had lived this model in corporate America and in my own business. Why would not each and every church be running towards moving to this structure? I had also lived through the pains and struggles of navigating a cumbersome structure in my own church as a layperson. Again, I could not for the life of me understand why churches were not sprinting to their district superintendents' offices to gain permission to move into this structure. And then it happened…reality check! What I have come to understand is that this is a very difficult shift for most churches. It is difficult for a host of reasons. Through my coaching and consulting, I have discovered those reasons include lack of trust, fear of change, misunderstanding of the model, misunderstanding of the purpose, lack of transparency, lack of leadership adaptability, unwillingness for leaders to give up their seat, fear of the unknown, and the perception of the power of the church being in too few of hands. Because of all these potential or existing barriers, a church must spend time discerning, preparing, teaching and communicating about this possible shift of structure FIRST. Believe me, trying to do this after the new structure is in place is not a good idea and will likely end in a disastrous outcome.

As a district superintendent, I (Blake) have a few additional reasons to ask that leaders take the transition process patiently and intentionally. As readers of this book and (I'm sure) a researcher of different models of church structuring, you and your team have spent hours poring through the BOD and downloading charts and lists. You have discerned your why, and you understand the governance architecture of the structure you are building. However, your average church member has not done this homework. While they may trust you enough to vote their approval of a new structure, a problem shows up a year or two later, after the first set of leaders rotate off the board, or when your pastor is appointed to a new congregation. Then the church is left with a governance system that nobody understands or knows how to run. I have spoken with congregational leaders who have then inherited a "sports car of a structure," but nobody in leadership knows how to drive a stick.

So, be intentional and patient in communicating the shift to a simplified, accountable leadership structure. We offer the continued steps in the Discernment Phase to assist you in considering this transition. You are now ready for the next step.

The third step in the Discernment Phase is:

Approval from DS to explore and assignment of SAS Coach

It is our hope and desire that your district superintendent has a ministry partner who has become a Certified SAS Coach. If this is the case, the district superintendent will dispatch a SAS Certified Coach to assist your congregation through the Discernment Phase. Consider your SAS Coach as a ministry partner just as the coach is a ministry partner with your district superintendent. If your District does not have a Certified SAS Coach, check to see if perhaps your Conference might have a Certified SAS Coach. If your Conference does not have a Certified SAS Coach, feel free to contact Kay (Kay@KayKotan.com) to provide you with a list of Certified SAS Coaches nearest you.

A WORD OF CAUTION ON COACHING

Your authors, while by no means experts, do have some of the deepest and longest-tenured experience in the simplified, accountable structure leadership model. It has become a focus of our ministry and therefore a great deal of time and energy has been and continues to be invested in equipping leaders in the model and paying attention to where congregations most struggle so that tools or resources can be developed to assist. More importantly, we have continued to invest, learn, and evolve the model over more than a decade. As we (Kay and Blake) continue to invest in SAS with hundreds of churches and thousands of leaders across the country, several evolutions and best practices have evolved (and continue to evolve) over the years.

Unfortunately, not everyone who claims to coach in the simplified structure has kept up with the evolution, latest resources, and most up to date best practices. Some may not even be familiar with this resource. This is why we have launched a certification process and coaching community and network for SAS Coaches. Coaches are certified for a period of one year at a time after extensive training and coaching with one of us. As a Certified SAS Coach, the coach has access to the latest resources, a community of coaches to bounce ideas off or ask questions, quarterly calls with the authors for further training, emerging topics and latest learnings from the mission field, and updates on best practices. Churches that invest in Certified SAS Coaches by and large have a significantly healthier experience, launch SAS with greater effectiveness, and avoid common potholes other churches encounter. We HIGHLY RECOMMEND a CERTIFIED SAS COACH. It is well worth the investment to partner with a coach. We just felt it was important to offer a word of clarification and caution about your coach selection.

SAS Discernment Team

The next two steps of the Discernment process are:

4. SAS Coach works with leaders to establish a SAS Prayer Team and SAS Discernment Team to lead in learning, organizing, and communicating the SAS discernment process

5. The SAS Discernment Team implements a communication and information plan. Ensure the congregation is prepared for an accountable leadership model of governance. Prepare for and lead congregational conversations about potential changes utilizing two-way communication. Lead with the why and then follow with the "what" and "how". Create a draft timeline and plan for discernment, communication of the proposed change, congregational votes, and launch.

With the help of your SAS Coach after approval to explore SAS from your district superintendent, it is now time for you to assemble a SAS Discernment Team. This team is a work team with no Disciplinary authority, so it does not need to be nominated officially through your Nominations Committee. The SAS Discernment Team is generally a team identified by the Pastor and Council Chair and/or Lay Leader. A team size of approximately five to seven people is generally adequate. Those serving on this team will be ones that have a good grasp on the SAS model, clearly understand the motivating *why* the Church Council voted to explore the model, be good communicators, are respected by your congregation, and are people you can depend on to follow through on a plan in a timely manner. Keep in mind the need to assemble a team that can communicate with the variety of people and groups within your congregation.

The SAS Discernment Team will be tasked with developing and implementing a plan of discernment for the congregation. This plan will include prayer, communication, information, conversations, timelines, and feedback loops. The Certified SAS Coach is the resource person and accountability partner for the team. The SAS Discernment Team is typically doing this work in the second quarter of the year.

Following are the steps for the SAS Discernment Team to include in the SAS Congregational Discernment Plan:

- A paragraph or two overviewing the why which the Church Council articulated that led them to their recommendation to enter this Discernment Process.

- Communication identifying the decision to enter into the Discernment Process was a Church Council decision brought by a vote after careful consideration and conversation.

- Make it abundantly clear that this is a time of exploration. No decision to adopt the model has been made. The congregation's members will have a chance to make that decision with their vote at a Church Conference IF the congregational discernment time leads them to requesting the vote and the DS approves calling a Church Conference to take a vote.

- This is a time of prayer and discernment. We suggest a SAS Prayer Team be created to help keep the focus on the missional impact of the church. Prayers will be lifted asking for guidance and clarity on the model and the timing. Ask God to provide wisdom and clarity if this model will help the church be more faithful and effective in its mission of making disciples.

- Share an overview of the SAS model. Feel free to use the "SAS Overview" provided in the beginning section of this book. You are also welcome to use the SAS overview videos (5-minute or 20-minute) that can be found at KayKotan.com.

- Create a plan to have multiple conversations to share the why and overview of the model with groups within the congregation. We have found it to be most effective to gather people in their existing small groups (i.e. Sunday school classes, existing small groups, choir, United Methodist Men/Women, etc.) for sharing information, answering questions, and receiving feedback. Invite all active attenders and members that are not in existing groups to be a part of a conversation to learn about the model. Make sure everyone is invited and has had the opportunity to be part of a conversation. Host multiple rounds of conversations if needed. This builds transparency and trust.

- While it is important to share information during these conversations, it is just as important to ask what questions or concerns they might have. Also inquire how they think this model might be helpful for the church. Offer additional follow up conversation if people have other questions later or have additional feedback. The SAS Discernment Team should keep track of the feedback it is receiving from these important conversations: common questions, concerns, and what about the model excites members.

- Create additional communication avenues outside the conversations to share information and methods for people to contact the SAS Discernment Team for questions or comments. This can include newsletters, email, texts, Facebook posts, bulletin insert, and other means your church normally uses for congregational communication. Over communication is all but non-existent, so err on the side of over-communicating!

- Consider a small group equipping experience for those desiring to take a deeper dive into understanding SAS using Mission Possible as a resource. The Church Council might even want to consider participating in or leading this equipping opportunity to further understand the model and aid in their discernment process. Your SAS Coach may also be willing to help with this equipping piece.

- Create a timeline for the conversations, additional congregational communications, equipping, and the deadline for the Church Council decision.

- Continue to be in conversation with your SAS Coach with any questions and updates on progress.

- Keep in contact with the SAS Prayer Team. Provide the team a schedule of the conversations so they can be praying for that particular gathering specifically. Receive feedback from the SAS Prayer Team.

- Challenge the congregation to be in prayer during this Discernment Phase for a faithful next step.

- Provide a summary of the conversations and feedback for the Church Council to inform their discernment and decision on whether to recommend adoption of the SAS model.

Once the SAS Discernment Team has completed the steps in the Congregational SAS Discernment process outlined above including the completion of their summary report/ presentation, the SAS Discernment Team has completed their work. Thank them for this hard work! The SAS Discernment is now back in the hands of the Church Council. Proceed to Chapter D-3 for the next steps in SAS Discernment.

CHAPTER D-3

Discernment Completion & Next Steps

Trust God from the bottom of your heart;

don't try to figure out everything on your own.

Listen for God's voice in everything you do, everywhere you go;

he's the one who will keep you on track.

Don't assume that you know it all.

Run to God! Run from evil!

Your body will glow with health,

your very bones will vibrate with life!

Honor God with everything you own;

give him the first and the best.

Your barns will burst,

your wine vats will brim over.

Proverbs 3:5-10

The SAS Discernment Team has completed their work and delivered the congregational feedback and their summary to the Church Council. The SAS Prayer Team has been praying for the congregational and leadership discernment as well as clarity around whether SAS is the right model and the right season for the congregation. We hope the members of the Church Council have also been in an attitude of prayer of discernment in this season.

The next step in the Discernment Phase is:

Based on congregational feedback and leadership discernment, the Church Council votes to request adopting SAS. If a favorable vote results, the Pastor and Council Chair submit letter to DS to approve moving to (or not) SAS

It is now time for the Church Council to make their decision. Here are some questions you might consider as you prepare to make this important decision

- Is simplified, accountable structure the right model for the church?
- Is this the right season to move to this model?
- Do we understand that fewer people will be in administrative leadership so that more people can be released for the most important work of the church - ministry?
- Are we prepared for the hard work of learning the new model and leaning into accountable leadership?
- Is the congregation generally supportive and trusting of such a structure change?
- Was the congregational discernment process thorough and did we receive the feedback needed to make the decision before us?
- Are we facing this decision being fully informed with our eyes fully open to the pros and cons for both staying in our current structure and shifting to a structure of SAS?
- Are we willing to invest in leadership and coaching if we decide to move forward with SAS to set ourselves up for the best possible outcome?
- Is this the next faithful next step for our church?

It is now time for the Church Council to vote on whether to move to the next step and request permission from the district superintendent to officially move to a simplified, accountable structure.

Formal Request to the DS

If the Church Council vote is favorable to request approval to move to a SAS structure, the Pastor and Council Chair and/or Lay Leader will write a letter to the district superintendent formally requesting to move to a simplified, accountable structure through a called Church Conference. In the letter to the district superintendent include the following information outlined below. Use the boxes below to help draft the content of the letter. This can also be found in the **Resource** section on Page 285.

1. A request for approval of a modified organizational plan, based on ¶247.2 of the *Discipline*	
2. A listing of the committees that will be combined in the new Leadership Board	❑ Church Council/Administrative Board ❑ Council on Ministries ❑ Staff-Parish Relations Committee ❑ Board of Trustees ❑ Finance Committee ❑ Endowment Committee ❑ Other _____ ❑ Other _____ ❑ Other _____
3. A brief overview of the discernment process used by the congregation to come to their recommendation.	Discernment Team study: Initial Consultation with the DS: Congregational Feedback Methods: Work with SAS Certified Coach:
4. A copy of the resolution that will be used to transition to the new structure	See the Resources Section, Page R-9 for a sample resolution.
5. A request for further consultation and feedback with the district superintendent, as the superintendent feels necessary.	
6. A request to convene a charge conference as a ¶248 Church Conference in order to encourage the broadest support and participation of the congregation for the change.	

We are often asked, "Why require a *church* conference, not a *charge* conference?" I thought we were trying to make things simpler?" We recommend that the meeting to make the transition to a new structure be a church conference because we believe that as many people as possible need to be involved in a vote of this magnitude. A lot of people are about to be removed from elected office in the church. A church conference allows every professing (baptized and confirmed) member, not just the board, to make the decision. There needs to be a clear sense that this change was never pushed through by a small minority of the leadership to cling to or gobble up power for themselves. A church conference provides the greatest participation and opportunity for transparency in the decision-making process. Of course, any calling of a Charge or Church Conference must be done in consultation with your district superintendent or presiding elder, but we highly recommend a churchwide vote to utilize this model to increase transparency and accountability, and to ensure the new Leadership Board's legitimacy.

Next step in the Discernment Process is:

DS reaches out to SAS Coach for feedback and makes decision

Once the letter is received, it is our recommendation that the district superintendent consult with the SAS Coach for feedback of the process. The district superintendent may also consult with the Pastor, Church Council chair, Lay Leader, and/or SAS Discernment Team leader. Again, the district superintendent has full authority to approve or decline the request. Keep in mind that your district superintendent might have information that your congregation does not that might affect the decision (i.e. appointment change).

Next steps in the Discernment Process are:

DS approval via letter (including church conference timing)

Coach begins to work with Nominations Committee and continues to work with leaders on communication strategies

What's Next?

If the district superintendent approves the request, there are four next steps to take right away:

- Inform the congregation of the decision for the Church Council to request approval and the district superintendent's approval to move to SAS.

- Schedule the Church Conference with your district superintendent and provide notice to the congregation.

- Inform your SAS Coach of the approval so the coach can begin to work with the Committee on Nominations and Leadership Development.

- Decide on the name that will be used to identify the new structure. We use the name of a Leadership Board in this resource. You can use whatever name your Church Council decides to use. However, we highly recommend not using the same name you currently use for your leadership team, which is typically something like the Ad Board, Church Council, Administrative Council, etc. Change the name to remind the congregation and the leaders that this structure is new. It's different. There are new expectations. Decisions will be made differently. If you choose to use something other than "Leadership Board" for the name of your new SAS structure, be sure to update the name in the Resolution to be used at the Church Conference and the Formal Request to the DS introduced earlier in this chapter. Both of these can be found in the **Resource** section on pages 285 and 256. There is much more information about the Resolution in the next chapter, D-4.

While we fully understand the discernment process has not been easy, it's important to remember your work has just begun. To finish up this Discernment Phase, move to the final chapter in this section where we will walk through preparation for the Church Conference when church members vote on the adoption of the simplified, accountable structure leadership model.

Every step taken during this Discernment Phase has been intentional to create trust, transparency, and congregational buy-in so that when the new Leadership Board takes shape and begins to guide the church, they are leading from this strong foundation.

CHAPTER D-4

The Big Vote

The rest of the people, priests, Levites, security guards, singers, temple staff,
and all who separated themselves from the foreign neighbors to keep The Revelation
of God, together with their wives, sons, daughters – everyone old enough to
understand – all joined their noble kinsmen in a binding oath to follow The Revelation
of God given through Moses the servant of God, to keep and carry out all the
commandments of God our Master, all his decisions and standards.

Nehemiah 10:28-29

The district superintendent has approved your Church Council's formal request to move to a simplified, accountable structure. You are now entering the final stages of the Discernment Phase. This final stage is the ultimate discernment of your congregational members as they vote to approve (or not) the SAS model.

The next step in the Discernment Process is:

Church Conference to approve SAS model

This is no time to let up on the communication strategy. Be sure to keep your congregation informed:

- What is the date and time of the Church Conference?

- Where will the Church Conference be held (i.e. sanctuary, fellowship hall, etc.)?

- How does voting at a Church Conference work? (i.e. only members present can vote)

- Will the vote be by ballot or show of hands?

- Who will preside at the Church Conference? District superintendent? Presiding elder?

- Be clear that this will be the only item to be voted on at the Church Conference and no other agenda items may be considered or added.

- Members will vote to approve the structure only. The new leaders will be nominated by the Committee on Nominations and Leadership Development during the regular fall Charge Conference if/when the structure is approved.

Other Preparations and Considerations

This part of the Discernment Phase is likely to be completed in the summertime. This assures the previous steps of informational conversations, feedback loops, council vote, and DS approval have had plenty of time, but still leaves time for the Nominations Committee to be equipped for their new work before the fall charge conference to vote on the nominated leaders for the new SAS structure.

We recommend that either the Pastor or Church Council Chair work with the DS on the preparation of the process and the Resolution to present to the congregation for the vote to move to SAS. A sample Church Conference Resolution for Structure Transition can be found in the **Resource** section on page 256.

Please note that we ***strongly recommend*** a two-step process for the approval. The first step is for a Church Conference to approve transitioning to a new structure model. The second step is approving the people nominated to serve on the new Leadership Board. There are two very important pieces of this recommendation to notice. First, we recommend a Church Conference (congregational members votes) rather than a Charge Conference (specific leaders only vote) because, as we stated in the last chapter, this helps with the trust and transparency of the process and the transition. If only a small portion of the congregation were to make such a huge decision, members often feel like they did not have an adequate voice or vote, and therefore the decision was made heavy-handed. Second, we recommend that only the new structure itself be considered at the Church Conference. It is seen as presumptuous if both the new structure and the names of the new leadership are presented at the same time. Voting on both at the same time also does not give the appropriate time for the Nominations Committee to be trained in the new model.

Keep in mind that each district superintendent has their own unique experience and understanding of SAS. This is dependent on how wide-spread SAS has been implemented in the District/Conference as well as their personal experience in local church leadership. Also know that each district superintendent has to work with dozens of different local church structures in their district. So, be clear and concise as to your plans, ask plenty of questions during the consultation meetings with your DS, and ensure that the congregation and the DS are both sharing the same plans and expectations.

We recommend that the Resolution for the structure change be made ava[...]
of time for members to review. This might provide the opportunity to answe[...]
ahead of time and clear up any mis-perceptions. If it is not made available a[...]
consider whether the members will be provided a copy of the Resolution, or i[...]
superintendent or presiding elder will read the Resolution. Here is a suggested text for a
resolution, also found in the **Resource** section Page 256:

The Church Council moves the Charge/Church Conference adoption of a resolution
to modify our organizational plan of governance, utilizing the simplified, accountable
structure:

Sample Resolution to Change Congregational Organizational Plan to Simplified, accountable Governance Structure

WHEREAS, ¶247.2 of the *2016 Book of Discipline* for the United Methodist Church allows
alternative models of governance; and

WHEREAS, the simplified, accountable leadership structure is utilized as an
alternative model throughout the denomination and fulfills the provisions of ¶ 243 of the
2016 Book of Discipline for the United Methodist Church; and

WHEREAS, the Church Council of _____ United Methodist Church
prayerfully voted on (date) to explore the simplified, accountable structure for local
church governance; and

WHEREAS, the congregation provided feedback concerning a potential change in
governance structure on multiple occasions; and

WHEREAS, the congregation was motivated to convert for reasons of efficiency,
alignment with our mission and vision, accountability, and missional focus; and

WHEREAS, the Church Council, Committee on Nominations and Leadership
Development, [the task force on governance], and the pastor, after months of
discernment, have crafted an alternative organizational for _____ United
Methodist Church and offered this proposal to the district superintendent for approval;
and

WHEREAS, the district superintendent approved the alternative organizational plan on
(date); and

NOW, THEREFORE, BE IT RESOLVED THAT:

1. On January 1, 20____ the Disciplinary authority and various responsibilities of the Church Council, Staff Parish Relations Committee (SPRC), Finance Committee, Endowment Committee, and Board of Trustees, will be combined into a single body called the Leadership Board. Existing elected leadership of all classes of all constituent committees that make up the new Leadership Board will conclude their terms of service on December 31, 20__, as the church transitions to the new organizational plan.

2. The Committee on Nominations and Leadership Development of _____ United Methodist Church is directed to submit a list of officers and members of a simplified, accountable structure known as the Leadership Board and a Committee on Nominations and Leadership Development, divided into appropriate three-year classes, as outlined in the *Discipline*, for election by the Charge Conference. All members of the Leadership Board and the Charge Conference will be professing members. The Chair of the Board of Trustees will be elected from among the voting Trustee members of the Leadership Board in the first board meeting of each year, in accordance with the *Discipline*, and s/he may be the Leadership Board Chair.

3. On January 1, 20____, the Charge Conference of _____ United Methodist Church will be composed of the members of the Leadership Board, appointed clergy (ex-officio), together with retired ordained ministers and retired diaconal ministers who elect to hold their membership in our charge conference, Lay Members of Annual Conference, the Lay Leader, Treasurer and Finance Secretary (if non-staff), and the elected membership of the Committee on Nominations and Leadership Development.

4. The Lay Member of Annual Conference and Lay Leader are ex officio members of the Leadership Board, if not already elected into a membership class of the Leadership Board.

5. All Disciplinary requirements and qualifications for each of the constituent committees (Church Council, SPRC, Finance Committee, and Board of Trustees) will continue with the combined Leadership Board, including Trustee age of majority qualifications and SPRC household membership limitations.

6. All references to the Church Council, Board of Trustees, SPRC, and Finance Committee, in all existing church policies, as of December 31, 20____, shall be understood to refer to the Leadership Board beginning January 1, 20____.

7. The Board of Trustees is directed immediately to make appropriate amendments to the congregation's bylaws to reflect the new plan for organization and submit an update to the Secretary of State's office in a manner defined by state law for nonprofit corporations.

8. In service to our common mission to make disciples of Jesus Christ for the transformation of the world, all existing ministry teams will be accountable to the Pastor and Leadership Board in administrative matters and in fulfillment of ¶243. The Weekday Child Care Ministry Advisory Board (¶ 256.2c) will be amenable to the Leadership Board in all matters, and is responsible for regular reporting to the Board. Alternative: If the Weekday Child Care Ministry is not a separate 501(c)(3), this Advisory Board will be a ministry team and accountable directly to the Pastor.

9. The Leadership Board will abide with existing financial, child protection, building use, and personnel policies along with the inaugural Guiding Principles. The board will create a Leadership Board Covenant. The Leadership Board is empowered to amend these policies, principles, and covenant. The Leadership Board shall share updated Guiding Principles with the charge conference annually.

APPROVED, _____ (date).

_____   _____
Secretary, Charge Conference   Presiding Elder

We also recommend that any entities associated with the church that are not separately incorporated be brought into the new structure. For example, if the endowment is not a separate 501(c)(3) foundation, the endowment is now part of the responsibility of the new leadership structure. This allows the best alignment, flexibility, and focus. Another example might be a daycare or preschool that is not separately incorporated. Again, if this is not a separate legal entity, this ministry is under the authority and responsibility of the SAS leadership team and should be aligned as such. While advisory teams can always be created to assist in their leadership, this is the time to clean up these governance silos and align for accountability.

Important Reminder: As stated at the end of the previous chapter, it is time for your SAS Coach to start working with the Nominations Committee. While the new leadership does not need to be nominated ahead of the Church Conference vote on structure, this committee will need plenty of time for learning a new approach to nominations, discern the contextual steps in their new process, create the new process, and implement the new process with prayer and discernment.

The Big Vote

The day has finally arrived. The day of the Church Conference. The decision is in the hands of the members of the congregation as presented through the Resolution. Make sure the SAS Prayer Team has been in prayer during the week leading up to the vote. You might even have someone from the SAS Prayer Team offer a prayer for the congregation before the vote with permission of your district superintendent.

The vote will be taken using the method (paper ballot or raising on hands) based on the decisions you made in collaboration with your district superintendent. For the Resolution (unless otherwise stated) to pass, the count to approve the simplified, accountable structure needs to reflect a simple majority of those members who are present to vote. The district superintendent generally reports the outcome of the vote on the spot as soon as the vote is counted.

Once the vote is completed, be sure to communicate the vote results to the congregation. Again, this not only lends to the spirit of trust and transparency, it also informs those members who were not present for the vote. If the vote was favorable, the work is now in the hands of the Committee on Nominations and Leadership Development.

If the vote did not pass, the Church Council might have a conversation about the underlying reasons for the vote and discern what might need to be worked on as a result. Are there trust issues that may need to be resolved? Is there some congregational conflict that needs to be resolved? Were the communication, information, and feedback loops inadequate to fully prepare the congregation and receive feedback? Often the underlying problem is not about the structure, it is instead about our relationships.

As you move from the Discernment Phase into the next, the final step of the Discernment Phase is on the horizon:

Church/Charge Conference to approve Nominated Leaders

The Discernment Phase is now almost complete. If your church voted to adopt SAS, you are now ready to move into the next phase, Equipping Phase. Just before we can take this final step in the Discernment Phase, we must simultaneously begin the next one, the Equipping Phase. The Equipping Phase begins with the SAS Coach training the Committee on Nominations and Leadership Development. We do hope you follow the recommendation and start this work right after the new structure is recommended by the Church Council and approved by the district superintendent. This provides more time for the Nominations Committee to be trained and coached before actually starting the discernment work of nominating new leaders to the new SAS structure. Let's transition into this next phase together now.

THE EQUIPPING PHASE

What is this phase?

The Equipping Phase is the second step in the process following the Discerning Phase. This phase is the training of the Committee on Nominations and Leadership Development members and the Leadership Board members to prepare and support them in their leadership roles in the simplified, accountable leadership.

Who is involved in this phase?

The Certified SAS Coach first equips the Nominations Committee in their work for the adaptive approach in discerning the new leaders for the Leadership Board. Once the Leadership Board is elected, the Coach will work with the members of the Leadership Board to begin to equip them for their new role.

What is the timing of this phase?

This Equipping Phase begins as soon as the simplified, accountable leadership structure is adopted by the Church Conference. Ideally this is mid-year when the Nominations Committee's equipping begins. The Leadership Board's equipping is generally in November or early December so they are ready to start on January 1. Remember, each year a third of the members roll off the Board and the Nominations Committee, so on-going, annual equipping is crucial!

CHAPTER E-5

Structuring the Leadership

Jethro, Moses' father-in-law, brought a Whole-Burnt-Offering and sacrifices to God. And Aaron, along with all the elders of Israel, came and ate the meal with Moses' father-in-law in the presence of God. The next day Moses took his place to judge the people. People were standing before him all day long, from morning to night. When Moses' father-in-law saw all that he was doing for the people, he said, "What's going on here? Why are you doing all this, and all by yourself, letting everybody line up before you from morning to night?"

Moses said to his father-in-law, "Because the people come to me with questions about God. When something comes up, they come to me. I judge between a man and his neighbor and teach them God's laws and instructions."

Moses' father-in-law said, "This is no way to go about it. You'll burn out, and the people right along with you. This is way too much for you – you can't do this alone. Now listen to me. Let me tell you how to do this so that God will be in this with you. Be there for the people before God, but let the matters of concern be presented to God. Your job is to teach them the rules and instructions, to show them how to live, what to do. And then you need to keep a sharp eye out for competent men – men who fear God, men of integrity, men who are incorruptible – and appoint them as leaders over groups organized by the thousand, by the hundred, by fifty, and by ten. They'll be responsible for the everyday work of judging among the people. They'll bring the hard cases to you, but in the routine cases they'll be the judges. They will share your load and that will make it easier for you. If you handle the work this way, you'll have the strength to carry out whatever God commands you, and the people in their settings will flourish also."

Exodus 18:12-23

It was a meeting like most church board meetings. You walk into the room, pick up your copy of the minutes and finances and take a seat. The pastor opened in prayer. Then the reporting started … it seemed like it would never end. There were endless reports about what we had already done being read directly word for word from a report that would become part of the minutes. If there were no real decisions to be made, it was more of a process of the proverbial "rubber stamp." No one was quite sure who really had a vote, so everyone voted, and obviously therefore everyone had a voice. There was never a mention of how the church was aligning itself (or not) to the mission of disciple making. There was no mention of annual goals and progress. No one had a clue if there were any baptisms or professions of faith. We were simply there to hear reports and rubber stamp any decision brought before the group. Some leave the meeting feeling like it was a big waste of time. It seemed like we were just going through the motions. If real conversations were had, they were conducted in the parking lots after the meeting. And the meetings have gone this way for decades … or more. Does that sound like any church board meeting you have ever attended? If so, allow us to give you hope that there is another way, and what we believe is a more faithful and effective method to lead churches.

Most churches have traditionally been structured with four administrative committees. Those four committees include finance, trustees, staff/pastor parish relations committee (S/PPRC), and the board/council. Each team functions separately. The interesting part is the difference from church to church in how the committees relate (or not) to one another and how they relate to the pastor. Those differences would denote how the structure functions and the chain of command. This is commonly demonstrated in an organizational chart. When consulting with congregations, it is always a fun exercise to ask the leaders of a church to sketch their organizational chart. First, most churches have never really considered mapping their structure, let alone creating an actual chart on paper or virtually. Secondly, most times there are a variety of charts presented to us. Most often, we are handed at least six to eight different and conflicting charts from the same church. Sometimes leaders report not even knowing where to start. No wonder we struggle with our current structure! We must have a common understanding as to how each committee relates to each other, who is responsible for what, how we function together and separately, and how the pastor relates to each committee or team.

In addition to all the challenges mentioned above, another challenge is when a church finds itself with a huge number of positions to fill, but a limited number of people to fill them. Once all the official administrative committees are filled (or perhaps filled partially), there is simply a small number of people to fill the ministry positions. We seemed to place a higher emphasis on filling the administrative positions first, thus leaving a small percentage of leaders to guide ministries. Through this practice, we tend to focus on our internal affairs more than we focused on doing ministry to reach new people for Jesus Christ – our very mission! This is one of the many reasons why we have an abundance of internally focused churches struggling to be vital and are disconnected from their communities. It is because of the confusion, the common likelihood of silo-ing committees, the complexity, and the cumbersome nature of operating in the structure created in the 1960's that more and more churches are moving to a leaner, streamlined, effective, and efficient structure. While the restructuring option was provided as an opportunity to streamline for small churches, large churches were among the first to adopt the simplified structure.

In the United Methodist Church's *Book of Discipline* (BOD), there is a provision to structure your church uniquely for missional purposes. Below is an excerpt from ¶ 247.2 in the *2016 Book of Discipline*:

> *The charge conference, the district superintendent, and the pastor shall organize and administer the pastoral charge and churches according to the policies and plans herein set forth. When the membership size, program scope, mission resources, or other circumstances so require, the charge conference may, in consultation with and upon the approval of the district superintendent, modify the organizational plans, provided that the provisions of ¶ 243 are observed.*

And paragraph 243 reads:

> *¶ 243. Primary Tasks – The local church shall be organized so that it can pursue its primary task and mission in the context of its own community – reaching out and receiving with joy all who will respond; encouraging people in their relationship with God and inviting them to commitment to God's love in Jesus Christ; providing opportunities for them to seek strengthening and growth in spiritual formation; and supporting them to live lovingly and justly in the power of the Holy Spirit as faithful disciples.*

A church must still fulfill the requirements for the responsibilities of finance (dollars), trustees (property), and staff-parish relations (personnel), as well as the board/council. However, the way those responsibilities are fulfilled can be accomplished in more effective and efficient methods that reflect more modern systems and practices.

Because of the generalized wording in the BOD ¶ 247, there are a variety of ways to streamline structure. There is no one way that is right or perfect. But as we have walked alongside hundreds of congregations to implement this, we will share best practices based on the collection of those experiences. You will need to take local context and values into consideration when establishing the new structure. Our recommendation, whenever possible and as a best practice, is to do a pure, full model of simplification. This means that all four administrative teams would be rolled into one single board of nine members (plus the pastor acting in an executive capacity). Technically, the trustees, finance committee, and S/PPRC all still exist in function, but they exist as one combined team taking on the responsibilities and authority of one administrative team we refer to as the Leadership Board.

Leadership Board = Council + Trustees + Staff-Parish Relations + Finance

However, there are times when this full-model simplification is just not possible. (see caution below.) For example, sometimes there is just too much of a political powerhouse in place with trustees, and so the trustee committee may need to operate separately for a while until more trust can be built up. Similarly, some congregations have an endowment committee that reports to their church council or to the trustees. Endowments often have complex governing documents that may require multiple steps to include their functions in a simplified governing board. Therefore, it may be best to simplify the rest of the functions and have a timeline to include the endowment responsibilities in the future. Meanwhile, the endowment committee would report to the new Leadership Board. If the endowment is not a separately incorporated entity, as a best practice we **highly** recommend disbanding the endowment committee and bringing this responsibility under the umbrella of the governing board.

A Word of Caution

"Do not allow complicated politics to keep you from moving forward" is what we wrote in our second edition of Mission Possible. Now, with even more opportunities to work with congregations and leaders across the country, we would amend that statement. Instead, we would suggest to be cautious in proceeding if complicated politics, lack of trust, or high conflict are in play in your local congregation when considering SAS. It is best to work on creating a healthier culture **before** introducing SAS. SAS works most effectively and efficiently when it is rolled out in a fairly healthy church culture. Rolling the model out in a less than healthy congregational culture will only make the implementation more difficult. It is often best to slow the process down and address the underlying issues first before adopting SAS. Other congregations with issues of trust or conflict choose to gradually move into complete simplification over a two or three-year period. The primary drawback to this "step-in" method is that it creates a large amount of role confusion on the part of the leaders as well as the congregation. The church has to be very intentional to maintain Disciplinary-approved processes during the transition and often find it difficult. In addition, this step-in model does not usually support or promote accountable leadership nor the needed adaptive changes. It's another likely example of moving the chairs around on the Titanic.

How to Structure

First, a common mistake in describing simplified, accountable structure is that "we got rid of all of our committees." Actually, all your administrative committees still exist, and, in their combined form, all their combined responsibilities constitute the authority of the new Leadership Board. In other words, the Leadership Board IS the Finance Committee and IS the Staff/Pastor Parish Committee and IS the Trustees and IS the Church Council. Nothing in the *Book of Discipline* is ignored or removed. Instead, the functions, roles, and responsibilities of each of the constituent committees are all placed upon your new Leadership Board.

To move into the most simplified structure, you will need nine members. Because nine is the standard sized committee required by the BOD for trustees, finance and SPRC, this is the recommended size for a simplified structure. There are ways to have a larger Leadership Board, but it involves adding a lot of complexity, with only a certain limited number of members being "on the SPRC" or as voting "trustees." If your church has a chartered United Methodist Men or United Methodist Women and someone from those groups requests to be on the Leadership Board, you may (depending on politics) need someone from those groups serving on the new structure. You will also need a youth, lay leader, lay member of Annual Conference, and chair. Keep in mind, a single individual serving on the new structure can serve in multiple roles (more on this and our recommendations later), such as UMW and as Lay Leader. This single committee then serves all the functions listed in the BOD for the Committees on Finance, Staff Parish Relations, Trustees, and Council.

The Organizational Chart

Following you will find an example of the recommended organizational chart that outlines a simplified structure with accountable leadership. This chart illustrates clear lines of authority, responsibility and accountability. It provides clarity for who reports to who and the role for each.

Organizational Chart

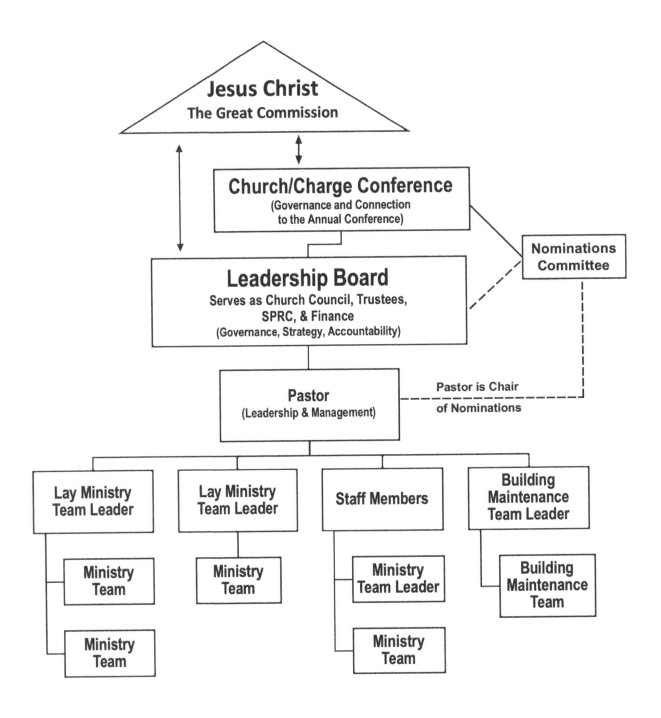

Study the chart. What shifts will need to be made to live into this new structure?

What communication needs to occur between levels?

Identify potential learning curves at all levels. What resourcing is needed to overcome those learning curves?

What training and coaching is needed for the new Leadership Board?

What training and coaching is needed for the Ministry Team Leaders?

What training and coaching is needed for the Pastor in this structure?

SAS and Ministry Teams

Dan Entwistle, the Managing Executive Director for Programs and Ministries at the United Methodist Church of the Resurrection, uses the excellent metaphor of a bicycle to describe the difference between the strategic work of a governing board and the mobilization work of ministry teams. Imagine a bicycle; there are two major points of interaction with every bike. You have your handlebars and your pedals. The handlebars are for steering – through the handlebars, you set the direction you want to go. The pedals are for locomotion – to create the power that takes the bicycle where you are steering it. A bike with no pedals goes nowhere. A bike without a working set of handlebars will land you in a ditch. The Leadership Board's job is to do the **steering** – to set the direction via strategic visioning, mission alignment, accountability, and administration. For ministry **mobilization** – to actually get to the place Christ is calling your church – you are going to need some pedals. Mobilization is the work of ministry teams.

Members of ministry teams are not nominated and elected for specific terms like the members of a council/board. Instead, they are identified based on their gifts and passion for a particular area of ministry with no predetermined length of service. They are identified, recruited, and equipped by staff (paid or unpaid), team leaders, and/or the pastor, and then deployed into ministry. Teams may last only as long as a particular project (i.e., Fall Neighborhood Festival ministry planning team), or may serve on an ongoing basis (i.e. hospitality team), with members joining and moving off the team throughout its life. They could be led by a serving disciple (aka as unpaid staff) or a paid staff member and should ultimately be accountable to the oversight of the pastor. It is suggested that a move to simplified structure include changing the names of assorted ministry committees, such as "Worship Committee", to a name that more appropriately describes a ministry team's defined work such as Worship Planning Team, Worship Design Advisory Team, Praise Team, or Worship and Hospitality Team. This helps to define the expectations for team members and also brings clarity to the differences between the governance of committees (steering) versus the ministry of teams (mobilization).

The Building Maintenance Team is different than the Board of Trustees

Let us take a moment and talk specifically about trustees and building maintenance. This is another area where churches get tripped up in moving to the simplified structure. In many churches, trustees have been tapped, practiced or labeled as being the people who perform the actual hands-on work to the building and grounds. They maintain the grounds, change the light bulbs in the sanctuary, and fix the running toilet. They certainly take care of the fiduciary responsibilities of the trustees (such as property insurance, facility policies, lease agreements, filing bylaws and articles of incorporation with the state). But in most cases the majority of their time and energy is spent on building and parsonage repairs and maintenance. By and large, they have become great stewards of the facilities. And we thank God for these people!

We believe this is actually the intentional function for trustees even in the traditional structure. The trustee committee was given the authority and responsibility to oversee and maintain property and conduct the legal affairs of the church. They were given the responsibility, but nowhere does it state an expectation of the trustees as being the committee to "do the work." Like the other administrative committees, there was a sense and purpose that these administrative teams had governing responsibilities, but not management or hands-on responsibility. This shift just evolved over time and the lines became blurred. The facility management became the most consuming and demanding of the trustees' time and attention causing this shift from a fiduciary/governing focus to one of management.

Maintenance needs obviously do not go away in the new model. Our church property still needs to be maintained. To use the bicycle metaphor, there is still pedaling needed. In our experience, the people who enjoy hands-on work, do not necessarily enjoy the fiduciary and strategic work and attending meetings. The hands-on work is their ministry using their gifts, experience, and passion! Our recommendation and experience as a best practice is to have a Building Maintenance Team. Give this team the authority and responsibility to care for repairs and maintenance within healthy parameters set by the board (*see suggested sample Guiding Principles in the Resource Section, page 262, for examples of parameters*). This practice allows this team to go about the business of building maintenance without being bogged down in the administrative and fiduciary responsibilities that are now being handled by the board, such as handling matters of policy and insurance. When creating a

Building Maintenance Team, you will want to select a trusted team leader and give her or him some authority to select team members as needed. This is a ministry team and would most likely report to a staff person or to the pastor. You will also want to specify the limits of the teams spending authority in your Guiding Principles (*see Chapter E-6 for more on Guiding Principles*).

Keep a Separate Committee on Nominations and Leadership Development

The Committee on Nominations and Leadership Development nominates members of only two committees: the Leadership Board and the Nominations Committee itself. The BOD does not allow the duties of the Nominations Committee to be rolled into the new simplified council/board, so it will continue to exist and serve as an independent body. For the most part, these will be the only two standing committees with governance responsibility. The only exception for this would be if there is a separate legally chartered church entity such as an Endowment Committee. Note: If the Endowment Committee is not a separately chartered entity, the responsibilities will roll into the board's responsibilities and governess eliminating the need for a separate Endowment Committee.

The Committee on Nominations and Leadership Development is to have no more than nine members, not including the pastor, who is the chair of the committee, and the lay leader. Members are placed in three classes.

Remember, ministry teams are recruited and equipped by the pastor and staff/ministry team leaders. The ministry teams are all "pedaling together" to accomplish the objectives driven by the church goals. Ministry teams are created and discontinued as needed to accomplish the goals. There is no need for standing teams in name only (like we practiced in the old model of structure) whose membership is elected as an annual slate proposed by the Nominations Committee. Of course, you will still need some standing teams for on-going ministries such as hospitality, children/youth ministry, missions, evangelism, building and grounds, and worship design.

Create Clarity of Charge Conference Membership

Who serves on the Charge Conference? We have seen all sorts of assumptions in our work with congregations. Some describe it as just the church council. Many invite everyone elected or selected for a church office to be voting members. The *Book of Discipline* is somewhat vague, with a floor being set as follows:

¶246.2. The membership of the charge conference shall be all members of the church council or other appropriate body, together with retired ordained ministers and retired diaconal

ministers who elect to hold their membership in said charge conference and any others as may be designated in the Discipline. If more than one church is on the pastoral charge, all members of each church council shall be members of the charge conference.

Because we have stretched the membership of the Leadership Board in the modified structure we call simplified, accountable structure, and in the interest of providing accountability and Charge Conference oversight of the Leadership Board, we suggest a description of the membership of the Charge Conference in our sample Resolution *(see the full Resolution sample in the **Resource** section Page 256* that creates a congregation's change in structures:

> On January 1, 20__, the Charge Conference of _____ United Methodist Church will be composed of the members of the Leadership Board, appointed clergy (ex-officio), together with retired ordained ministers and retired diaconal ministers who elect to hold their membership in our charge conference, Lay Members of Annual Conference, the Lay Leader, Treasurer and Finance Secretary (if non-staff), and the elected membership of the Committee on Nominations and Leadership Development.

We include the Nominations Committee because the committee will be offering names annually for the board, officers, and the Nominations Committee itself. Also, we have seen examples of congregations who, in opposition of our suggestions and the rules in the *Discipline*, fail to rotate board membership, making it an insular and isolated board. Simplified, accountable structure gives a lot of responsibility and authority to the Leadership Board. An accountability check on that power is in the Charge Conference, which elects Leadership Board members.

Structuring for a multi-site congregation

We are seeing many congregations discover the benefits of becoming multi-site. This word encompasses a variety of models including (but certainly not limited to) multiple worshiping campuses, fresh expressions, "mother-daughter" configurations, and resourceful congregations that have been handed the keys of closing churches and are attempting to re-brand and relaunch as multi-site. We believe simplified, accountable structure is especially important in these complex congregations because there is an inherent challenge of bringing missional alignment to multiple worshiping communities. When a multi-site congregation uses the legacy structure of multiple committees with assigned "representatives" from each campus, it creates silos within silos and missional integrity and alignment is usually the first victim.

There are contextual concerns that will greatly influence the design of your simplified, accountable leadership structure in multi-site congregations. First, if a congregation has been asked to take responsibility for a closed church or merge a church about to close into a larger church, there will be some voices asking (and occasionally demanding) that the remnant from the merging congregation have representatives on the receiving church's governing committees. We know of a large congregation, with thousands of members who automatically delegated one or two seats on every board to the worshipers of a declining church who had under 50 members when it closed. The new committee members were used to a family-sized church and had never had to lead in a church system as complex as the receiving church, with dozens of staff, multiple clergy, and hundreds of small groups and ministries. Designating these seats did harm to the congregation's trajectory and harmed the leadership development pathway of the congregation.

We understand the human need to be included and hope that the remnant will be welcomed, discipled, and cared for as valued members of the receiving congregation. However, this welcome does not need to include a precious seat on the Leadership Board. We therefore recommend no automatic ex officio seats be designated to the congregation that is closing. The receiving congregation needs to be able to focus on its mission and vision. Including members on the Leadership Board who have not bought into the vision and have not been enculturated and equipped by the congregation's leadership development pathway will damage the church's ability to be fruitful.

In congregations that have an intentional multi-site strategy, we recommend that the Nominations Committee consider campus location along with other diversity factors in trying to build a healthy, diverse Leadership Board. That means identifying the best leaders with an eye for including leaders beyond the "home campus." This may evolve over time. Since the lead pastor works with the congregation's Leadership Board and (ultimately) oversees all the campus pastors, accountability runs through the congregation's Leadership Board through the lead pastor and to the campus pastors. The Leadership Board will also need to be intentional about listening and ensure that their two-way communications opportunities include the campuses.

Staffing in Multi-sites

When it comes to the various staff in a multi-site, there are several things to consider. First there will likely be "executive" staff that are in roles that support and equip all ministry sites and settings. This might include a business director who has responsibility for finances and facilities, a director of ministries who is responsible for an overall ministry approach at all levels at all campuses that might also include some supervision of staff, and other key positions such as a directors of communications and director of technology. In some cases, the campus pastors are a part of the "executive team," but in other structures, the campus pastors report to one of the other executive team members. The executive team members traditionally report to the senior pastor directly. It is a common senior management practice not to have more than about five direct reports to the senior pastor.

For staffing at the various campuses, some senior pastors prefer to have the key staff at campuses report to the campus pastor. In other cases, campus staff report to someone on the executive team or someone who is a director of a niche ministry such as children, youth, or worship. Whichever of the two options you choose the most important part to remember is for everyone who leads needs to understand how decisions are made, who has the authority and responsibility to make what decisions, and the organizational chart clearly indicates who reports to whom. There can't be accountability through the flow of decision-making and reporting without this type of structural clarity.

As perhaps a side note, but relatable to accountability, structure, and alignment, we would like to offer a recommendation and caution regarding campus pastors. From Rev. Dr. Ken Nash's book in The Greatest Expedition series, *Expanding the Expedition Reach through Multi-site*, he offers these wise words:

> *A pastor who is suitable for a church plant or even for the revitalization of a dying congregation looks very different from a pastor in a multi-site ministry context. Nothing would be worse for the campus pastor, new campus, or sending campus to have a pastor gifted as a revitalization pastor to take the role of a campus pastor in a multi-site context or vice versa. Ideally, the best-case scenario is to train up a campus pastor from within the existing staff. This preserves the church constants and vision while maintaining established expectations and work habits that are a part of church culture.*[3]

If you are a multi-site ministry, there are lots more gems of wisdom in Nash's book, so we highly recommend you pick up a copy as a resource and guide for multi-site ministry. Nash has personally led two large multi-site ministries and has successfully coached dozens of churches in launching their own multi-site ministry.

Too often in our United Methodist appointment process, pastors are appointed as a campus pastor for a multi-site church without a real understanding of the different gifts and leadership styles needed as a campus pastor. The campus pastor needs a buy-in to the mission and vision of the multi-site ministry and has no need/desire to be the senior pastor. While this is an appointive issue, it is important for the sake of accountable leadership and simplified structure to be aware of this potential pitfall. This awareness may be helpful in asking more questions and deeper discernment for leadership and accountability in multi-sites.

---

3   Ken Nash, *Expanding the Expedition Reach through Multi-site*. Market Square Books Publishing, Knoxville, 2021.

Structuring for a Multiple-church-point Charge or Cooperative Parish

In the United Methodist Church, smaller congregations are often linked together as a multi-point circuit, a cooperative parish, or as a single charge. In cases where your congregation is considering moving toward a simplified, accountable leadership structure, but you are linked with a congregation that follows a more traditional structure, be sure to include your district superintendent in the conversation about the conference's expectations for sharing the work of the staff/pastor relations committee (S/PPRC).

If the churches are considered to be a single charge (station church), it is appropriate to have a single S/PPRC made up of members from each church to represent the interests and ministry of all congregations. One solution is for the nominating committee to assign a few members from your Leadership Board to be representatives on the combined Charge S/PPRC (including the lay leader) and to have those assignments approved as part of your charge conference.

In Cooperative Parishes, wide latitude is provided for structuring the relationship between multiple congregations. Your Leadership Board may serve as the congregation's S/PPRC and relate to the other S/PPRCs in the parish, or a separate Parish S/PPRC may need to be created by your Charge Conference. Your district superintendent will certainly have some expectations around these options. Additionally, in some flavors of cooperative parish, there are options to create a single parish or charge council to oversee the ministries of all the worshiping and ministry locations.

In all these options, a multi-point charge or cooperative parish will want to ensure representation from all the congregations. For instance, if three congregations of similar size are on a charge together in a cooperative parish model, then the Parish Leadership Board of nine people would be made up of three people from each congregation (preferably one from each class).

You will note that, in the diagram below, each congregation has a local Board of Trustees. It can be small, with a minimum of three people in successive classes. Because of legal concerns and property issues, local churches will need these separate Boards of Trustees. However, if all the constituent congregations have experience in the simplified, accountable leadership structure and are willing to share a combined board of trustees made up of members from each local church, you may decide to take the final step in simplification where the entire parish has one single governing board with accountability and one nominating committee that is made up of members from all the ministry sites.

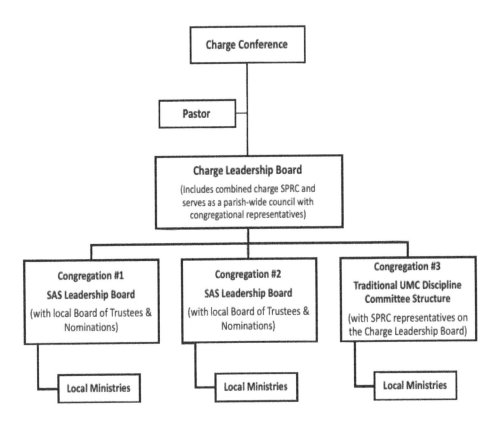

Specialists or "Representatives"

In the early years of churches converting to the simplified structure, a common procedure was for the nominating committee to assign board leaders titles of specialists, which were sometimes called "representatives." In those early days, we both taught the common wisdom of the day that specialists were an optional part of the model, believing that it might ease the transition into the simplified structure. Those shifting to this new model, have trouble envisioning how the work of the traditional structure administrative teams would be accomplished in the simplified structure. By having these titles assigned, it gave relief to know that the particular area of ministry would still have a point of contact and point people to perform the tasks associated with the old four-committee administrative structure.

While some still appreciate issuing titles and certain areas of responsibility for the areas of finance, trustees, and SPR, we *no longer recommend* this practice. The problem we discovered over the last decade is that assigning these titles of "representatives" or "specialists" was corrosive to the accountability of the Leadership Board because the Board, over time, ceased to retain responsibility and authority over the work of the specialists. The specialists became mini-committees often making decisions or taking actions without authority, fighting turf wars against the rest of the board. There is a reason we call the model simplified, *accountable* structure. While we **strongly no longer advise** using these specialist titles, so many congregations have used it as a part of their system that we feel it necessary to explain their use and offer some advice on how to interpret their role. *(see the recommended alternative option later in this chapter on Work Teams.)*

There are pros and cons for titles or designees. The pros for giving members a title (for example "Trustee Representative") is assigning specific and direct responsibility over a given area. There is then a go-to person as the congregation is accustomed to having. This is less of a learning curve for most congregations. The cons of having titles is the three people having these titles many times still act as their own separate committee. Therefore, three people end up making important decisions in their work area that they have no authority to do. It creates or reinforces working silos. Accountability and adaptive change is harder to instill. This also makes it difficult for the congregation to make the adaptive shift to a different type of structure and accountability.

A common mistake is if the "representative" or "specialist" title is given to certain people on the Leadership Board, there is a misperception that the sub-group of the Board of those three representatives or specialists are now a mini trustee, finance or SPR team. The BOD requires a minimum number of people for these administrative committees. So not only are the three people working as the committee against the rules of the *BOD*, but only three people making decisions is not healthy for the church overall.

In working with numerous congregations and pastors, **we highly recommend simplifying all the way** (without specialist titles) if at all possible. In our experience, the churches that keep titles find it more difficult to operate in a renewed mode. By keeping titles, members of the new simplified board arrive to the meeting table envisioning their role as the "representative" for a set of issues (property, finances) or a particular committee (that no longer exists) instead of arriving at the meeting table as the gathered leaders of the entire congregation seeking to engage the mission field for Jesus Christ. With titles they are likely able to make the technical change of having fewer people at the table, but they are unable to make the adaptive shift to change the conversation and focus at the table with a holistic approach. Old habits are not broken and instead it perpetuates business as usual.

For there to be a real, adaptive transformation towards effectiveness, efficiency and faithfulness towards the mission, the focus and conversation must typically change to live into the accountable leadership model. So, while your church may decide to have individual members of this committee serve as specialists or have particular assignments, please be sure to enforce the rule (polity) that only when the whole Leadership Board meets together can it serve the fiduciary responsibilities as the church's board.

PROS of Having Specialist Titles:	CONS of having Specialist Titles:
• Assigning specific and direct responsibility over a given area creates an identifiable go-to person for members. • There can be less anxiety for simplified, accountable structure for some congregations.	• The three people having these titles many times still act as their own separate committee, but now with only a couple of voices, robbing the larger Leadership Board of their responsibility and accountability. In these situations, three people end up making important decisions in their work area that they do not have any authority to do, which is also a violation of the *Discipline*. • It creates or reinforces working silos. • Leaders and the congregation do not adapt to new structure and accountability. • The specialists sometims undermine the work of the larger board, undermining alignment. • Accountability and adaptive change is harder to instill.

Because we highly recommend no longer using these titles, we do believe there is a healthier approach to accomplish the same outcome. We call this the Work Team approach and is now our recommended practice.

Work Teams

Please note that we consider the use of work teams to be an entirely different and much healthier approach than assigned specialists or representatives. Leadership Boards are encouraged to create work teams as needed to complete specific tasks or assignments within a certain time frame and bring back to the board. We recommend shifting the people and work involved amongst the different Leadership Board members. Otherwise we find, for example, that one or two people become the de facto "finance specialists" because they are always called upon to lead budget writing.

Work teams are assigned "projects" by the Leadership Board Chair when the need arises. The Chair calls on one person from the Leadership Board to take responsibility for the project. That Board Member is responsible for completing the project but can delegate or collaborate as s/he sees fit. The Board Member assigned the project can pull another leader or two from the Leadership Board or, better yet, pull people from the congregation to assist with the project. This allows others to be involved, expands the pool of resources available, and enables those who are unable to make a longer-term leadership commitment to still serve in a shorter-term capacity. Even members of the community may be pulled into a work team to share their expertise, knowledge or experience related to the project.

Work teams do not have authority to make decisions. They work within the confines of the assignment and disband once that project is completed. Work teams are not standing teams. They are assigned a project, they complete the project, and then disband. Work teams may be together for a few days to a couple of months, but typically it is a very short-term project window.

What types of "projects" are assigned to work teams? This will vary from congregation to congregation and for the various seasons of the year, but here are a few examples of the typical types of projects work teams are assigned:

- Create a rough draft of initial guiding principles

- Review the personnel handbook and provide suggested edits and additions

- Research and provide information on the new subdivision being built in town

- Create an initial budget draft

- Put the final touches on the goals from the Strategic Ministry Planning Retreat and ensure they are SMARTER goals. Present the final draft for review of the Leadership Board

- Create an initial draft of technology and security policies

- Explore the possibility of a multi-site ministry

Work teams allow for the most efficient use of time during Leadership Board meetings while still keeping forward momentum. Often drafts of projects being developed by work teams can be shared electronically between meetings for Leadership Board's input so progression is not stalled. In addition, there are times when projects are assigned and finished in a shared document and never have to come back to the table or agenda of the Leadership Board if the scope of the project is created with this intention.

We believe that work teams more readily function in the method that we initially envisioned the specialists or representatives were intended to function. However, by eliminating the titles and not assuming spheres of responsibility, it becomes much clearer for the leaders and congregation alike that all nine Leadership Board members have full responsibility and authority for the combined four administrative functions. We have found that using work teams does not promote the resulting confusion for both leaders and the congregation that using the 'specialists' titles created. Work teams allow for much more effective and organic use of time, energy, experience, and passions of the Leadership Board members, as well as those in the larger congregation and community who might be pulled into a work team. We will share more about using work teams.

Associated Ministries or Nonprofits

In today's complex world, congregations often relate to a host of related organizations. As a district superintendent, I (Blake) have felt, at times, that I spend as much time helping church boards/councils relate to their childcare ministries as I do in pastoral placement in appointments. Because the answer is foundational to the whole process of identifying the relationship of the childcare ministry to the church, one of the first questions I ask is rather blunt: "If there is a problem and an attorney sues, who will be served?" The following illustrates the SAS organizational chart that shows chartered ministries such as UMW, work groups, and a childcare program that operates under the legal umbrella of the congregation (the childcare and the rest of the church share an IRS employer identity number (EIN) and the childcare operates under the legal incorporation of the church:

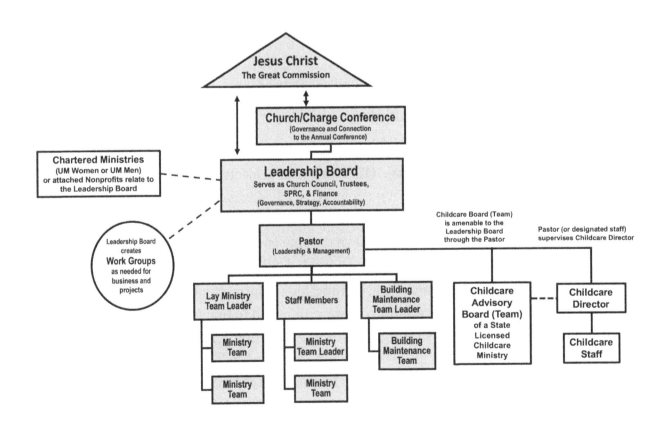

In most cases the ministry is operating under the legal umbrella of the church, so despite all the bureaucratic layers and advisory boards, the answer is simple: "the Board of Trustees." Here are some of the related organizations and groups to whom your Board may have to articulate (and sometimes negotiate) your relationship:

- Daycares, Preschools, Mother's Day Out programs, and other types of state-licensed weekday childcare programs.

- Endowment or Church-related Foundations

- Cemetery Associations

- Property Management Corporations

- Church-related Missional Nonprofits

- Scouting Ministries

- Hosting and/or leasing space to outside ministries, nonprofits, and for-profit organizations.

In cases where the associated ministry is operating under the legal umbrella of the church, I (Blake) have a saying: "Your Leadership Board can delegate responsibilities but can never abdicate them." If a ministry is utilizing the facility, utilizing church resources, or overseen by church paid or unpaid staff, the Leadership Board ultimately has some level of fiduciary relationship with the ministry that it cannot set aside because it is inconvenient or too time-consuming.

> Your Leadership Board can delegate responsibility, but can never abdicate responsibility.

Some of these types of ministries are covered by the *Book of Discipline*, but some require much more investigation to strike the right relational clarity. A perfect and common example is a weekday childcare program. If the program operates under the 501(c)(3) status of the church, and the teachers and church staff are all paid under the same IRS Employer Identification Number, the program is ***not*** a separate entity. The program may carry additional liability insurance, send money to help with church expenses, and even run a separate set of books with a separate bookkeeper, but it is still a part of the church and the childcare program is a ministry of the church. Its weekday ministry board would be an advisory board that is under the educational ministries of the church, and the board would be fully amenable to the church's Leadership Board in its capacity as the SPRC, Trustees, Finance Committee, and Church Council. *Book of Discipline* ¶256.2c covers this type of ministry:

c) Weekday Ministry Board – The term weekday ministry applies to any regularly planned ministry for children. When appropriate, one or more weekday ministry boards may be organized to oversee the weekday ministry programs of the congregation. The board's membership should be mostly professing members of the congregation, with parent, church staff, and weekday ministry staff representatives. The board will set policies consistent with the congregation's policies, state mandates, and sound business practices. The board will guide weekday ministries as appropriate opportunities for faith development, mission outreach, Christian education, evangelism, and safety. They will advocate for inclusion of children from various socioeconomic, cultural, and racial/ethnic backgrounds. Weekday ministry board(s) accountability should be placed within the local church organizational structure with consideration to the group responsible for the congregation's education ministry. (The Book of Discipline of the United Methodist Church, ¶ 256.2c)

When a weekday program operates as an extension of the congregation's ministries and under the nonprofit status (and liability) of the church, the program (no matter how large) needs to be governed as a church ministry. The program's director and staff are under the supervision (or delegated supervision) of the senior pastor. The weekday ministry board, in its advisory role, is delegated a span and scope of its work by the Leadership Board, and it should regularly report its finances and actions to the board. In many ways, the weekday children's ministry board is an advisory board, relating similarly to a ministry team through the pastor. The church and its Leadership Board is legally liable for what happens at the child care, and so paperwork should always list the Leadership Board of the church, in its role as the trustees and legal board of directors as the responsible party in all state accreditation and health department documentation.

If the childcare program is a separately incorporated 501(c)(3) nonprofit organization, then the relationship between the church and the board is completely different. The childcare program is more of a tenant with a lease agreement, and the childcare may have a very different mission than that of the congregation. Here is a chart that shows the relationship:

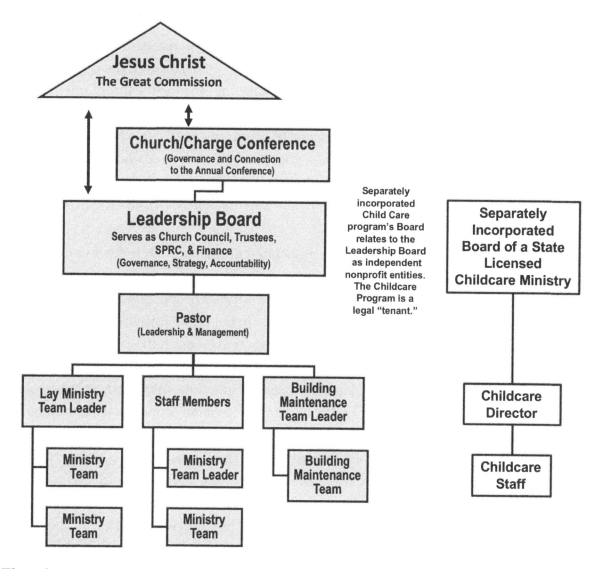

The relationship between the separately incorporated childcare board and the church's governing Leadership Board will need to be outlined clearly in its bylaws. This includes how childcare board members and officers are elected, if board members are to be congregation members, the expectations about ex officio board members (including the pastor and representatives from the congregation's Leadership Board), and what say the congregation's Nominations Committee and Charge Conference have in board membership. Some sort of lease agreement will need to be defined and approved by a Charge Conference, the pastor, the district superintendent, and the district board of church location and building (*The Book of Discipline,* ¶ 2540-2541).

Finally, much work will need to be invested in making clear the supervisory relationship (or lack thereof) between the pastor and childcare director. Otherwise, both leaders will be destined to collide in destructive ways. While many people over the years have advocated for separate incorporation of childcare centers for legal reasons, let's just be honest: If a childcare center is hosted at a church, the community sees the ministry as a branch of the church. A problem at the childcare center can cause enormous reputational damage at the church. The childcare may be separately incorporated, the congregation's Leadership Board may have no legal governance role, and the pastor might not supervise any of the staff, but any legal separation seems inadequate and meaningless if a problem at the childcare center ends up on the news or in a courtroom. We (Kay and Blake) believe that if a church is wanting to have a childcare *ministry (rather than a tenant)*, it ought to be a ministry within the church's structure and it should be aligned to the congregation's Christ-centered mission. Otherwise, it is more of a distraction and a drain on time and resources.

A childcare is one of the most common associated ministries, but today's churches (particularly in dynamic and innovative congregations), are pursuing alternative economy solutions to fund ministries. Congregations may own rental property leased out to for-profit or non-profit organizations or to private individuals to help fund ministry. Kay and I have seen congregations buy (or build) a strip mall and then lease out half or more of the property to pay the mortgage and facility expenses, letting ministries flourish through tithes and offerings. Church endowments would usually operate out of the simplified, accountable structure Leadership Board (perhaps with the assistance of an annual work team), but if the church creates a separate foundation (*The Book of Discipline*, ¶ 2535), then a separate (but interwoven) board is required by *Discipline* and state law. In all these formats and permutations, we strongly suggest that the congregation consult with their judicatory official (such as a district superintendent) and hire an attorney to make sure that governance documents are filed, the plan fits the requirements of their denominational polity, and questions of liability and insurance are appropriately addressed. If there is a change in the relationship, or if the associated nonprofit decides to discontinue its business, an attorney should be involved in making sure that the nonprofit is closed legally, and all debts and obligations are addressed, or the host church could find itself responsible.

Your Leadership Board needs to explore the practical and legal relationship between the church and the associated ministry:

- Describe the Associated Ministry:

- How does the purpose and vision align with the mission, vision and goals of the congregation?

Congregation	Associated Ministry
Mission:	Purpose:
Vision:	Vision:
Strategic Goals	Goals:

- What is the legal relationship between the church and the ministry?

  ❑ SHARED LEGAL STATUS: The church and the ministry share a 501(c)(3) status, incorporated status, and IRS Employer Identification Number (EIN)

  ❑ SEPARATE LEGAL STATUS: Separate nonprofit status and EIN

- Is the associated ministry operating under the auspices of the denominational polity of the church (UMW, UMM, Scouting)? If so, how is the relationship and responsibility defined in the *Discipline*?

- How (and by whom) are associated ministry board members chosen and elected?

- How are associated ministry staff supervised? What is the staffing relationship and the payroll relationship between the church and the associated ministry staff?

- How is the ministry covered by liability insurance?

- Who is responsible for performing and supervising background checks for those serving in the ministry?

Your Leadership Board: What's in A Name?

To help the entire congregation understand there is a new structure, we strongly suggest changing the name of the board/council. For example, if you currently refer to your governing board as an Administrative Council, change the name to the Church Board. Some other commonly used names for the new structure are: Vision Team, Strategy Council, Ministry Table, or Leadership Board. Changing the name helps draw a line in the sand that the church is doing a new thing and leading in a different way!

If you are leaning heavily in articulating the difference between a committee/board (elected with a term of office) versus a team (selected and evolving participants with no particular term of service) using the language from earlier in this chapter, you will want to use Leadership Board or some other language that specifies that the governing board is an elected committee and not a ministry team. And remember, the Committee on Nominations and Leadership Development is still required and is elected.

On the following page, you will find a reminder list of the polity and rules to remember when using the SAS model. This list can also be found in the **Resource** section on Page 244.

SAS Rules to Remember

All the Disciplinary requirements and limitations of each of the new Leadership Board's constituent committees remains in effect. Rules to remember:

1. A separate Nominations Committee, chaired by the Pastor, is required because the Leadership Board cannot self-nominate, and they have responsibility for leadership development

2. You will need nine members. Board members serve a three-year term. The Lay Leader and Lay Member of Annual Conference are exempt from the three-year term (and you may decide, although not recommended, to include them separately from the 9 rotating members). After being off the Board for a year, the person can roll back onto the Board if elected. SPRC and Trustees have minimum and maximum limits on the number of members, so (depending on your Leadership Team's size and composition), a few members of the Leadership Team may be barred as voting members of some of the constituent committees. For instance, there is a limit of 9 on Trustees; there is also a limit of 11 on SPRC, counting Lay Leader and a Lay Member of Annual Conference. It is because of the resulting complexity of exceeding nine that we highly recommend keeping the board at nine total members.

3. Pay attention to Disciplinary conflicts of interest. Household members cannot serve on the Board together. If it cannot be avoided, the family members may need to excuse themselves from the room or not vote on issues with potential conflict of interest. Staff and family of staff cannot serve on the Board because of SPRC membership restrictions (plus it is simply good ethics!).

4. Trustee Requirements: At the first meeting at the beginning of each new year, the Leadership Board will elect a "Trustee Chair" to satisfy the corporate resolution requirement. It is recommended the Board Chair serve as the Trustee Chair, if the Board member is one of the Trustees. The Leadership Board, serving as the Trustees, is also the legal Board of Directors. All Board members who serve as "Trustees" must be over 18. The Trustee membership rule of minimum 1/3 laymen and 1/3 lay women remains in effect. The Pastor cannot be a Trustee.

5. Even though the restructuring occurs, ministry teams are still needed and in place. Fewer people on the Leadership Board means more people are available to do ministry. Simplifying structure is the combining of the four administrative teams of the Council, Trustees, Finance and SPR Committees. The teams such as nurture, outreach, and witnessing ministries continue their disciple-making work as ministry teams and not elected committees.

6. The concept of a Leadership Board is designed to increase accountability and alignment for the whole church towards its holistic mission, not be a place for ministry representatives to negotiate "turf." Members of the Board only represent and lead the whole church, not a particular interest group or ministry.

7. If the Leadership Board has designated specialists (such as finance specialists) from the membership of their Board, the whole Board, in total, serves as the finance committee, Trustees, etc., not just the designated specialists. Reminder: We HIGHLY RECOMMEND moving away from this practice for the reasons stated in this chapter! Instead the Work Teams provide a much healthier approach.

8. The small number of governance officers on the Leadership Team requires huge trust and congregation-wide accountability. It is HIGHLY RECOMMENDED that you describe your future Charge Conference as being "The Leadership Board, Nominations Committee, and all clergy who hold their charge conference in the congregation" and it would also greatly help build trust, accountability, and transparency if your governing documents adopt a requirement that asks the district superintendent to convene all Charge Conferences as Church Conferences to allow all professing members to vote on matters. This allows the larger congregation to have a say in nominations and hold the Leadership Board accountable in the Board's role as the Charge Conference's executive committee.

9. Churches on multi-point charges will particularly need to take care to support and respect the organizational structure and ministry of one another's churches.

Structuring the Leadership

Moving to a simplified, accountable structure model (consolidating the four administrative committees into one) is only a portion of the decisions you will need to carefully discern in terms of structure. You will need to make additional decisions such as deciding on whether you will adopt the recommended 9-member Leadership Board, how UMM and UMW affiliation will be handled, the role of youth on the Leadership Board, how staff associate with the lead pastor, if the Chair will also be the Lay Leader, etc. This is yet another reason to have a Certified SAS Coach alongside you on this journey to help you navigate the decisions that are best for your congregation and your context.

- Take the time to carefully discern your structure for your context. All the Disciplinary requirements for all the committees apply for your new Leadership Board, which means that you will be flipping through multiple sections of the *Book of Discipline*. Structure by photocopy is not enough preparation. You will need to understand and communicate the mechanics of your new structure.

- Begin the transition towards creating a building maintenance team to handle day-to-day facility issues. This shift also includes moving this work from an administrative function to a ministry team. Empower this team through the guiding principles and assign this team to report to the current trustees (while still in the traditional structure before transitioning to SAS) as an interim step towards future simplification.

- Ensure you have a separate Committee on Nominations and Leadership Development. Train them on the principles of simple accountable leadership. Help them with the shifts in their discernment process for nominating leaders to the new Leadership Board.

- Bring clarity of governance and supervision to any associated ministries or nonprofits.

- Choose an appropriate name for the newly formed Leadership Board. Changing the name helps leaders and congregation alike to recognize the new structure with its new function.

CHAPTER E-6

Selecting Leaders

During this time, as the disciples were increasing in numbers by leaps
and bounds, hard feelings developed among the Greek-speaking
believers – "Hellenists" – toward the Hebrew-speaking believers because their widows
were being discriminated against in the daily food lines. So the Twelve called a
meeting of the disciples. They said, "It wouldn't be right for us to abandon our
responsibilities for preaching and teaching the Word of God to help with the care of
the poor. So, friends, choose seven men from among you whom everyone trusts, men
full of the Holy Spirit
and good sense, and we'll assign them this task. Meanwhile, we'll stick
to our assigned tasks of prayer and speaking God's Word."

Acts 6:1-6

We have been there, and we are sure you have likely been there, too. You have attended meetings that seem like an absolute and complete waste of time. You have likely also attended very important meetings where people seemed to be elusive, unplugged or maybe even absent. There are other times when people take offices so they can have the title but have no interest in doing the work. Other times we might have experienced where on occasion people have a seat at the committee table because it is one of honor or prestige rather than responsibility. You may have even worked on committees where committee members bring personal agendas to the table or feel that their job at the leadership table is to "fight for their constituents" (a particular ministry team, the quilting circle, scouts, their beloved Sunday School or worship time, the endowment) when it comes time to prioritize staffing and finances. We have been there, and we have done that – served on dysfunctional committees. Changing the structure is only part of the solution. We must also re-consider how we choose the people sitting at the table.

Preparing the Nominations Committee

We (Kay and Blake) both teach workshops to help congregational teams in transitioning from their inherited complex committee structures into a simplified, accountable leadership structure. In those workshops, we usually start by doing a reality check. We ask, "How many people in your congregation are members of a governing (administrative) committee?" We get answers from 25-50 to even 100 folks as members of governing boards! I (Blake) have seen a congregation with 50 worshiping members have over 50 leadership and committee positions. It is a part-time church with a bi-vocational, quarter-time pastor. All she has time for is sermon writing and attending redundant meetings.

Your Nominations Committee will need to let go of some expectations. I (Blake) have chaired many nomination committees over the years in which we completed a 10-page long nominations report for charge conference, with dozens and dozens of slots to fill every year. The Nominations Committee needs some internal preparation to look at a single page nominations report with a couple officers and two committees (only the governing board and the Nominations Committee itself). At first, there will be a mixture of relief and fear: relief that dozens of slots don't have to be filled and then fear that so many people will be "left out" of leadership.

While your Nominations Committee could look at a simplified Leadership Board and think that it shrinks the pool of involvement and leadership, actually the reverse is true. We believe that people (especially new disciples) are not looking to fill a slot. Disciples are seeking to have lives of meaning and make an impact in the world for Jesus Christ. Keeping a chair warm on an administrative committee which has no real responsibility or authority does not bring meaning into their life and neither does a cumbersome decision-making process. If it takes too long for a ministry idea to become a ministry reality, today's leaders will drop out. Twenty-first century disciples want to be able to see how their participation in ministry is actually growing new disciples or changing lives. Actually, this was always the case.

By making leadership service real and meaningful, the pool of possible leaders actually increases. Using the bicycle metaphor from the last chapter, by shifting more leadership from committees who steer to teams who mobilize ministry, your church is actually enlarging the pool of leaders who can guide impactful ministries. Steering does not create ministry and missional momentum. Only pedaling (ministry mobilization) creates momentum.

To understand the reality of the change, we ask the Nominations Committee some of the same questions we asked the governing board in our discernment section:

- What is the total number of elected leadership positions in your church, compared to total active membership? What is the percentage of active members who are in elected leadership? (We have seen churches where 90% or more of the congregation is in elected leadership, which might be understandable in very small congregations, but it is a recipe for leadership inertia in mid-size churches – if everyone is in charge, then no one is in charge)

Total Number of Active Members	
Total Number of Elected Leadership Positions	
Percentage of Active Members in Elected Leadership	%

10. How many leaders are currently in administrative/governance leadership (finance, trustees, SPRC, administrative board) versus the number of members in programmatic/ministry leadership (worship, evangelism, etc.)?

Number of Administrative Positions	Number of Members in Program/ Ministry Positions

11. How many leaders sit on more than one committee? _____

The answers to these questions will help your Nominations Committee grasp the enormous changes coming in the new structure. You may be wondering what happens to all the leaders if they are not nominated and elected for specific terms as members of a Leadership Board. They certainly don't disappear. Instead, ministry teams should flourish, and these teams will need dedicated lay leaders to organize and coordinate their work. Once again using the bicycle metaphor, we need a lot more peddlers mobilizing ministry than we need folks with their hands on the steering wheel. Begin planning now how you will encourage leaders to rethink their ministry when their former role disappears.

Too Many Committee Meetings, Not Enough Ministry

AKA: "But I'm Always on a Committee"

I (Blake) once met the chair of Trustees at a large church who had served in that position for thirty years, succeeding a fellow that served as chair multiple decades before him. The church was large enough (over 2000 members) that there were plenty of high-capacity leaders who could have stepped into that important role. Pastors came and went, but the Trustees membership was eternal. Over the decades, even the thought that he would rotate off became verboten – it was almost seen as treason. As your congregation seeks to create a simplified and accountable leadership structure, challenges such as these will show themselves. In our *Greatest Expedition* series, Blake wrote in the *Strengthening Decision Making* volume:

> *This concept is difficult for a member whose identity -- sometimes their sense of self – might be wrapped up in holding the same church office for decades or who doesn't feel particularly gifted in leading ministries and prefers the administration of the church (I would actually call that a spiritual issue). When churches hand out offices and roles to placate certain families or constituencies, it distracts from the difficult work of servant leadership. Bob is not on the Leadership Board to represent the choir. And Bob, along with every member of the board, is responsible first to the mission of Jesus Christ. The Leadership Board should represent the entire church as it seeks faithfulness and fruitfulness in this mission.*

> *While one could look at a simplified board and think that it shrinks the pool of involvement and leadership, actually the reverse is true. I believe that people (especially new disciples) today are not looking to fill a slot. Disciples are seeking to have meaning in their lives and make an impact in the world for Jesus Christ. Keeping a chair warm on an administrative committee which has no real responsibility or authority does not bring meaning into their life and neither does cumbersome decision-making processes. If it takes too long for a ministry idea to become a ministry reality, today's leaders will drop out. Twenty-first century disciples want to be able to see how their participation in ministry is actually growing new disciples or changing lives. Actually, this was always the case.*

All the people currently on administrative committees will not have a place on the new Leadership Board, but everyone will have a place to serve. Over time, mainline churches have lifted up administrative committees as the place of "real power" and "where things really happen." We (Kay and Blake) have seen too many congregations that vetted leaders for administrative committees, but let anyone who could pass a background check run the church's missions and ministries. Frankly, that is upside down, backwards, and wrong-side out! We need creative, talented, spiritually gifted leaders coordinating ministries, leading small groups, and forming disciples! These are our highest impact areas!

We hope (and recommend) that the Nominations Committee will look beyond the membership of the congregation's current administrative committees when recommending a new slate of leaders for the Leadership Board. Having all the old leaders govern in a new board will waste an opportunity to add new people with fresh eyes and innovative ways of leading.

A Note of Warning: Please don't utilize the nominations process to deal with interpersonal issues. Blake often exhorts congregational leaders to avoid using the *Book of Discipline* or a SAS restructure to solve a Matthew 18 problem. Reading this book, we know that a few readers will have a particular difficult person in mind and imagine using simplification to finally remove that annoying leader from office ("Sorry, Ralph, I suppose your position was just eliminated; oh, well"). Using the transition to simplified, accountable structure for these purposes will poison the entire foundation of the process. Instead, follow Jesus' plan for disciples to engage other disciples with accountability and reconciliation as found in Matthew 18. Talk with your "Ralph" honestly and don't use the restructure as a tool for punishment or favoritism. Let's keep our eyes solidly on the Great Commission and Kingdom impact during this transition and leave all the other agendas on the curb.

As your congregation lives deeper and more adaptively into SAS, there are a couple of other reminders. First remember that the Committee on Nominations and Leadership Development is also responsible for leadership development. With this in mind, potential leaders after the first year will have participated in a leadership development process. Following this intentional leadership development process, there will be discernment required on both the part of the potential leader as well as the Nominations Committee members to determine if this is the right season and the right person for church leadership and for which role.

Secondly, it is highly recommended that part of the leadership development process includes learning and resourcing Peter Scazzero's materials in *Emotionally Healthy Spirituality* and/or *The Emotionally Healthy Leader*. Third, the Nominations Committee will want to create an on-going intentional leadership development pathway. Check out *Launching Leaders* by Kotan and Schroeder as a guide for creating a process, leadership and spiritual habits, and starting pathway for leadership development.

What Are you Looking for in Board Members?

Acts Chapter 6 and Paul's letters to Timothy and Titus offer some examples of qualifications for church leadership. Notice that the biblical qualifications focus on some timeless qualities like "full of the Spirit and wisdom," experience in personal "household" management, being "above reproach," and practicing self-control in behaviors and relationships. Before anything else, church leaders need to be disciples of Jesus Christ. Church Nominations Committees often try to build committees for reasons unconnected to fulfilling the mission of Christ, such as attempting to please different constituencies, or out of concern that a wealthy member not feel excluded from decisions. While we understand the political realities of leading a mostly "volunteer" institution, know that every person included on the Leadership Board for non-missional reasons will distract your Leadership Board from doing God's business. Even deeply devoted disciples may not be right for governance board work if they are unwilling to see beyond the ministry they are personally leading. For instance, I (Blake) remember working with a passionate leader of a feeding ministry. The leader raised thousands of dollars each month in in-kind gifts from grocery stores for distribution and worked with nonprofits and churches throughout the city. But the leader was so passionate about her ministry that other ministries and groups, such as youth and children's ministries, were often pushed out of the way and their storage space "borrowed." This leader was so focused on one aspect of the church's ministry, the other areas were considered less important. This is why we recommend that Leadership Board members are not also leaders of ministry teams. While we hope and pray that Leadership Board members will continue to be active participants in small groups, growing in their own discipleship and active in missional ministries, this three-year season of churchwide leadership is a great opportunity for you to hand off the ministry team leadership baton to another leader.

In business management, there is a metaphorical concept of leaving the frenetic activity of the dance floor and moving to the balcony where leaders can better see all the dynamics and figure things out (*see Ronald Heifetz and Marty Linsky's article "A Survival Guide for Leaders," in the June 2002 issue of the Harvard Business Review*). So, instead of getting a Leadership Board filled with representatives of different groups or ministries, many of whom may wish to prioritize their own ministry above others, your Nominations Committee is seeking to identify, recruit, equip, and deploy leaders who can see the church from this "balcony perspective".

Your Board leaders need to be completely dedicated to Jesus Christ, be growing as disciples, and be personally invested in the church's mission. This is often a completely different process of identifying leadership than the practices we have inherited in church leadership. We can find experts in building, banking, human resources most anywhere. But to lead a church, it is most important to have our most mature disciples at the table. I (Kay) once was working with a church who had a finance chair who did not attend worship, a small group, or any other ministry and gave absolutely no dollars to the ministry. I am still baffled how that type of thing can happen. A simplified, accountable leadership structure also has no spaces left over for honorific positions. All Leadership Board members are working members of the board and the whole board must be committed to the church's mission. Church members may be extremely effective in business, pillars of the community, and show all the outward signs of "success," but if they are not dedicated disciples of Jesus Christ, then they need to keep on growing as disciples and not serve as leaders on your simplified, accountable structure board.

Take some time to consider the type of leader the church needs at the table. Think through some of these questions and discuss them in your Nominations Committee meeting:

- What are the characteristics, expectations and behaviors that would be beneficial?

- Is there expectation that members of the board would be regular worship attenders, participants in a small group, serving periodically, have a regular prayer life, and a proportional giver (i.e. living and modeling their faith)?

- How will you ensure diversity amongst board members? Including members from different racial and cultural backgrounds, long and short tenures, age diversity, and socioeconomic backgrounds will all produce better conversations around the table and help the new Leadership Board avoid "group-think."

- Is there an expectation that leaders would be available to attend most all Leadership Board meetings?

- Would there be an expectation that leaders check their personal agendas at the door?

- Would there be an expectation that Leadership Board members would be able to hold confidential information?

- Would the board member be able to openly support and authentically communicate the decision of the Leadership Board regardless of their personal feelings about the decision?

- How will the Nominations Committee gather recommendations and ideas about potential members as the nominations slate is created? One method is to create an online recommendation form for members to submit candidate recommendations (along with rationales) for potential board members. How could your team get the entire congregation involved in the nomination process?

- How will the Nominations Committee gather information to make faithful decisions? One method is to interview (discernment conversation) potential leaders to better understand their hopes, dreams, and desires along with their spiritual development and practices of being a disciple.

In addition to the people in your leadership pathway, the creation of a new leadership structure is an excellent opportunity to invite leaders who have been sitting on the sidelines. For many high-capacity leaders, the cumbersome old structure seen in most churches is a repellent. High-capacity leaders want to be challenged and make a difference, but the endless reports from endless committees was not attractive. A simplified and accountable leadership structure may be catnip to these high-capacity leaders. So expand your search beyond the usual suspects and have meaningful conversations with these potential leaders. Whatever appropriate characteristics, expectations, and behaviors are named; potential leaders will discover these in the leadership development process. It is always best to be upfront with people rather than asking them to serve and then sharing with them in arrears the Leadership Board member expectations. Set the standards and expectations upfront prior to inviting leadership commitments.

Organizing the Initial Leadership Board

The chair of the Leadership Board will be elected by the Charge Conference (we recommend they be nominated by the Nominations Committee). To ensure alignment and role clarity, it is recommended that the Leadership Board member elected as the chair of the Leadership Board also be elected as the trustee chair at the board's initial meeting each January (there are legal and Disciplinary rules that require this to be a separate vote of the board itself). Likewise, we recommend the Leadership Board Chair be named by the Nominations Committee as the staff/pastor parish relations liaison to the district superintendent. This recommendation comes from some difficult experiences when the Leadership Board Chair was not the district superintendent's contact. As a DS, I (Blake) have gotten conflicting requests from a Leadership Board Chair and a separate SPR liaison, which muddied up the *Disciplinary* waters, legally speaking. Information was coming in from someone on the board rather than the chair and information was not necessarily shared or disseminated with the rest of the members of the committee. In yet another example, I (Kay) was working with a church where the SPR liaison received the pastoral consultation form from the district office, pulled in two other SPR "Reps" to complete the form, and submitted it to the DS without any conversation or consultation with the Leadership Board who had a different recommendation for the pastoral appointment that the SPR liaison and her cohort had reported. Therefore, it is deemed a best practice for all outside coordination or correspondence be done through the Board Chair, serving in her or his capacity as the S/PPRC chair.

We recommend that part of the Nominations Committee Report to the Charge Conference make it clear that the Leadership Board Chair fulfills all the presidential functions, and that your Leadership Board makes it a custom to elect the Leadership Board Chair to be the chair of the Trustees. In addition to electing the chair of trustees, the Leadership Board will also need to select a secretary of the Board of Trustees from its membership. While note-taking may be passed around, the roles of Trustee chair and Trustee secretary have legal implications, especially if the congregation buys property or is registered with your state's Secretary of State as a nonprofit corporation.

The Nominations Committee can use notations to show particular roles of committees for individual members, such as the Lay Leader or the Lay Member of Annual Conference. Note that youth under the 18 are unable to serve on the Board of Trustees. The Leadership Board will also need to comply with the Disciplinary Board of Trustees requirement that at least one-third of the members be men and at least one-third be women.

To comply with the BOD and to keep the team fresh and accountable, you will still need to place members into three classes (i.e. Class of 2022, Class of 2023, Class of 2024). Once the membership of the new Leader Board is decided, the Nominations Committee will need to divide the initial group into three classes to begin a series of rotations. We (Blake and Kay) have seen the simplified structure quickly go off track when congregations, fearful of losing the wisdom of the initial class of leaders, decide to ignore the rotating class system and either push back rotation dates or immediately "re-up" those who served only one year for another term.

Don't fall into the trap of thinking the church "can't do without" a certain leader of the board. Succession classes are important for your Leadership Board's accountability and for your future leadership development. With classes in place, one-third of the board will then rotate off each year and new people will be seated. This allows for continuity, historical preservation, and the important work of on-boarding and equipping new leaders each year.

Finally, take the time to carefully discern your structure for your context. All the Disciplinary requirements and qualifications for all the committees apply for your new

Leadership Board, which means that your Nominations Committee will be flipping through multiple sections of the *Book of Discipline*. Structure by photocopy is not enough preparation. Your Nominations Committee will need to fully understand and be able to communicate the mechanics of your new structure.

Example of a Leadership Board roster:

Class of 2022

John Jones, T/F/SPR

Carol Clark, T/F/SPR/LM

Yolanda Youngperson, F/SPR/Y

Class of 2023

Sue Smith, T/F/SPR/UMW

David Dent, T/F/SPR/UMM

Maria Martínez, T/F/SPR

Class of 2024

Jennifer Jackson, T/F/SPR/C/LL

Ben Black, T/F/SPR

Larry Lewis, T/F/SPR

Key

T-Trustee	C-Chair of the Board
F-Finance	Y-Youth
LL-Lay Leader	LM-Lay Member to Annual Conference
UMM-United Methodist Men	UMW-United Methodist Women
SPR – Staff Parish Relations	

In addition to this example, you can find a complete nominations report in the **Resource** section on Page 250.

The Annual Nominations Process

So, it is time for the annual gathering of the *Committee on Nominations and Leadership Development* to meet to decide who should serve on which committees. Maybe your experience is different than ours, but most times it goes something like this: "Okay, so where is the latest copy of the church pictorial directory? Let's look through the pictorial to see if it will help us think of some new people. Who can we coerce to say yes? Who from the Nominations Committee should call so the nominee will most likely say yes?" That inherited process is more about filling spots with bodies. It is time for a new day with a new process for a new outcome!

A healthy nomination process actually starts months before the nominations begin. Notice, the official title of this committee is the Committee on Nominations **and Leadership Development**. We must have an intentional process of developing leaders. When churches have a leadership development process, it feeds the nominations process. I (Blake) have spent a couple of decades attending Nominations Committee meetings. I quickly realized that there is a big difference between nominations meetings where we are all staring into the ceiling trying to conjure up a name versus nominations meetings where we have profiles of engaged disciple-leaders on the table in front of us. Our job is to strategically discern and manage the process of bringing leaders onto the team so we have a variety of gifts and perspectives in our most mature disciples.

In the leadership development process, potential leaders are invited into a several weeks to a several months' time to journey with other potential leaders. This will be a time of discernment, faith development, gift assessment led by the pastor and Nominations Committee. Remember, as the Nominations Committee, you are seeking to raise up three or four leaders for the leadership board each year to fill vacancies for classes rolling off. In order to have these leaders prepared and ready for a commitment, you will likely need eight to ten leaders in the leadership development pathway. Some leaders will discern they are better suited to lead ministry teams rather than be a board member. Others might realize the timing for such a leadership covenant is not quite right. You might even have some go through the process that either do not finish and/or the pastor discerns is not quite ready or equipped for leadership. The leadership development process helps prepare leaders and set expectations of leadership in the various areas of leadership.

When it comes to the question of using assessments in the leadership development process, there are a few different schools of thought. On one hand, using assessments might shed light on someone's leadership style and strengths for the first time. Others may have already encountered this in their work life. I (Kay) like to use assessments such as DiSC,

Strengths Finder, and Enneagram. I find them to be great coaching tools. Self-awareness is critical in being an effective leader. If a person is not self-aware, assessment might be a great tool to help build this awareness and identify their leadership style.

It might be helpful to use assessments as a springboard on helping leaders understand how to work with other leaders who have different leadership styles in a team or board setting. Learning how to work effectively together as a team that is trusting, accountable, vulnerable, and transparent can be challenging, but can be very rewarding with fruitful results. In addition to self-awareness inventories to equip individual members, there is also work to be done in building healthy team processes. Building team processes for meetings and decision-making that encourages everyone to engage the individuals to fit into preconceived inventory-based roles. Examples of this type of group equipping include Edward DeBono's old-but-relevant Six Thinking Hats parallel thinking system and the Harvard Business Review's question-based meeting agenda.

Assessments might be a great tool for leadership development, but don't use them as the sole tool for selecting people for leadership nominations. For example, you would not want to only nominate leaders who are a "D" in the DiSC assessment for the Leadership Board. Having a mixture of leadership styles within the Leadership Board who have the skill and self-awareness of their own leadership style, but also know how to team well with others will bring about a much richer and more favorable leadership outcome.

In a reverse of the normal "fill the slot" mentality of many churches, some forward-thinking congregations even have a Nominations Committee application and interview process in place for those seeking possible Leadership Board membership. We will cover this in more detail later in this chapter. There are samples in the **Resource** section on Pages 246-248 of the application and the interview questions.

In Kay's book, *Gear Up (Abingdon Press 2017)*, you will find more resources and information on leadership development as well as the book she co-authored with Phil Schroeder, *Launching Leaders: Taking Leadership Development to New Heights*. Both of these books are great resources on helping develop a leadership development process. *Launching Leaders* also has a ready-to-go leadership development process you can start using right away until you develop one specifically for your context. Also check out our first book together, *IMPACT! Reclaiming the Call of Lay Ministry*. Future board members will need to understand that the goal of the Leadership Board is to lead the church in impacting the mission field, not simply to maintain the institution and keep their fellow Sunday school members happy.

Leadership Covenant

Chapter E-7 provides directions on creating a leadership covenant for the Leadership Board which serves as a clarifying document that offers board members guidance on expectations and relational boundaries. While your board will probably be drafting a new covenant each year, the board's existing covenant may be a great tool for the Nominations Committee to identify future leaders and explain the expectations of board members.

Board Member Candidate Interviews

We have seen several congregations flip the script on their nominations process. Instead of selecting leaders based on the best guesses of the Nominations Committee, or even taking recommendations from the congregation, they are discovering that passionate disciples are actually seeking out an opportunity for servant leadership and shaping their process toward this goal. Usually a process that takes a few years to fully enculturate, the Nominations Committee can seek out applications and hold "job interviews" or better referred to as Discernment Conversations for the few precious Leadership Board positions every year. In this process, the Nominations Committee and pastor can discover the right giftedness to build the team needed for the upcoming season of ministry. The interview/conversation will not only focus on what skills and giftedness the person can bring to the leadership table, but also be used to share the purpose of the board and expectations of members. This will also be a time for the potential leader to share about their faith journey and their practices as a disciple. There is a board application and a set of recommended interview questions in the **Resource** Section on pages 248-249.

An application and interview process is not without risks. Before a congregation considers it, the overall relational health of the church must be excellent, the mission and goals crystal clear, and an intentional leadership development pathway be ongoing. Otherwise, the only people who "send in an application" might be wanting to join the Leadership Board may be seeking to bring their own agenda. For instance, when I (Blake) was serving as a local church pastor, I was always concerned when a member constantly asked to be put on the staff parish committee so "the church could start acting like a real business." I wasn't quite sure what that meant, but I could tell enough that his agenda had little to do with our congregation's stated mission, vision, and strategic goals. Some churches start using an application process a year or two into the new structure, when the identity of the board is established, and the church's leadership development pathway is on track. Other churches choose to make this adaptive change upfront clearly indicating there are changes in leadership discernment and expectations.

An Invitation to Lead

Your members have been burned before. A pastor or a Nominations Committee member has called them, sharing that "We need you on the _____ committee. No one else would say yes, so I need you to agree. Don't worry, it won't take up too much of a time. It's really just a committee on paper. There isn't any outside work to do, so all you will need to do is show up at the quarterly meetings." Well, we suppose some folks may jump at that incredibly compelling opportunity to serve Jesus, but perhaps a bit more thought and preparation is required! When we have low expectations of leaders, we will get low-quality investments from our leaders. While some faithful, gifted, and talented leaders may say "yes" to such an invitation, the committee will always be on their back-burners. High-capacity leaders will instead channel their God-given talents to other pursuits where they feel valued and where they can bring value and have impact.

With your change to an accountable and simplified Leadership Board, you have the opportunity to invite high-capacity leaders to REALLY make a meaningful impact both inside and outside the church. This won't be a committee on paper that meets a few times a year to write a report. Your Leadership Board will be filled with agents of transformation, listening to the Holy Spirit, discerning God's vision, and guiding the congregation into the mission field in the name of Jesus Christ. So, make sure your invitation is personal by connecting the requirements and expectations for Leadership Board members to the gifts you see in the invitee. Share last year's board covenant so the expectations are crystal clear. Before prospective board members say "yes," they need to know that board service will require work: preparation before meetings, task assignments between meetings, difficult conversations about mission and accountability, the shouldering of risky ministry experiments, and bold leadership. Along the way, Leadership Board members will learn, they will pray (A LOT), they will actually be able to make decisions instead of recommendations to yet another committee, they will receive encouragement and discover personal growth, and (most of all) they will have the opportunity to serve Jesus Christ, our Risen Savior, by steering the congregation toward a trajectory of reaching new people and disciple-making. Now, THAT's a compelling invitation!

- Think back to when you received a compelling and a less than compelling invitation to serve. What made the difference? How did the invitation affect your service?

CHAPTER E-7

Tools for the Leadership Journey

If anyone wants to provide leadership in the church, good! But there are
preconditions: A leader must be well-thought-of, committed to his wife
cool and collected, accessible, and hospitable. He must know what he's talking about, not
be overfond of wine, not pushy but gentle, not thin-skinned, not
money hungry. He must handle his own affairs well, attentive to his own
children and having their respect. For if someone is unable to handle his own affairs, how
can he take care of God's church? He must not be a new believer, lest
the position go to his head and the Devil trip him up. Outsiders must think well of him, or
else the Devil will figure out a way to lure him into his trap.

The same goes for those who want to be servants in the church:
serious, not deceitful, not too free with the bottle, not in it for what they can
get out of it. They must be reverent before the mystery of the faith, not
using their position to try to run things. Let them prove themselves first.
If they show they can do it, take them on.

1 Timothy 3:1-10

To gain the tools for this new leadership journey, we recommend each new Leadership Board member be provided a copy of this book with an expectation of reading it before attending their training. In November, early December, or very early in January, each new leader should attend an equipping workshop led by a SAS Certified Coach. This workshop is typically five or six hours providing a deep-dive and understanding of the SAS model. *This equipping is critically important.* Without the proper training, the leader will come to the table on January 1 to serve without the proper tools and understanding to serve. We are setting leaders up to fail to ask them to serve without pouring into them with the proper training first. Each year the new members rolling onto the team should also have the same expectations. Additionally, if there is time, it is also helpful for the SAS Coach to lead a time with the new Leadership Board to get to know one another and to create their leadership covenant together prior to January 1, but after they have been trained. This would apply only to the first Leadership Board, but not subsequent years. This work will instead be completed at the fall strategic ministry planning retreat *(see Chapter I-12)*.

Investment in the equipping and discernment seasons early in the process will help out tremendously later and not just the emotional reactions to a change in leadership structure. You can't simply rely on an organizational chart to take care of your leadership challenges. Setting expectations through leadership covenants, guiding principles, and regular equipping creates a culture of leadership including leadership expectations, accountability, and valuing leadership by investing in leaders. At one church early in my ministry, I (Blake) thought I had embedded a fresh purpose and set of systems, but it was only after I left that I discovered that it was only embedded in the small team, not the larger body – a regret I still carry to this day. Earlier in this book, we shared about congregational leaders who inherited a "sports car of a structure," but only the initial Leadership Board and the pastor (or perhaps the last pastor before she was moved) understood the intricacies of the system. So, it fell apart, and simplified, accountable structure was deemed a "failure."

To enculture the changes, a host of new practices and commitments needs to take the place of the "way things are done around here." Building in written tools will help your Leadership Board become a covenanted group with clear roles, expectations, and boundaries.

During the first year of a simplified, accountable structure, your Leadership Board will need to set new patterns, behaviors, expectations, rhythms, and methods of "doing business." We must hold ourselves accountable to one another to *actually* do a new thing with this new structure. Otherwise, it will be the same old business in just a different configuration. Too often I (Kay) find congregations that simply conduct business as usual with fewer people or slip back into the old ruts too soon without some intentionality of something new. Here are a few tips to consider for your first year in the new simplified, accountable structure:

- Practice accountability from the beginning.

- Do not be afraid to ask questions. Often others have the same questions, but do not ask them either.

- Come with a sense of curiosity and grace.

- Have team members sit at the table and observers sit in chairs along the room's parameters to clearly define those with voice and voting rights.

- After practicing for a couple of months, invite your coach to attend the Leadership Board meeting, observe your meeting, and help you course correct as needed. It is difficult to stay on track with a new thing when you have not yet experienced it. It is a process into which you must live. Repeat the process with your coach in a few more months.

- Configure your space to have meaningful conversation and provide eye contact with all members of the Leadership Board.

- The pandemic of 2020 has made many of us experts in online meetings. Your Leadership Board will need to carefully consider how many regular meetings can use this technology without negatively affecting the teamwork of the group.

- There are times when your board will need to take votes. Consensus is a fine enough goal, and it is great when the board is all in agreement. But consensus cannot be a requirement for your church to move forward. We have seen churches who utilize a unanimous consent requirement become immobilized by a minority of members who control the church's future. Remember, alignment and responsibility to the mission and vision is the ultimate filter and outcome required.

- Remember that guiding principles are a living, breathing document that are open to edits and additions as needed to provide permission-giving ministry within healthy boundaries. The traditional church council model was often the bottle-neck in the decision-making process. The guiding principles are intended to empower ministries, not cause them to come to a screeching halt!

- As you live into this new structure, your team may find edits or additions to the leadership covenant are in order. Each year, the Leadership Board is composed of about a third new people. For that reason and for the on-going growth of leadership, review the covenant each year and edit as the Leadership Board and Spirit leads.

In this chapter, we will explore the best practices of getting off the ground in the most effective and healthy way possible. Being intentional about the work ahead and focusing on the right stuff is absolutely critical. But before we begin the work in the new simplified, accountable structure, we must first clearly understand our roles and how we function as a healthy, effective team with a new approach. We have also provided the primary roles of the pastor and the ministry team leaders/staff, too, so we are sure to stay out of their lanes.

Know Your Role

Leadership Board's Role in Accountable Leadership

- ❏ Accountable to Jesus Christ for the Great Commission
- ❏ Fiduciary responsibility
- ❏ Generative work
- ❏ Strategic work
- ❏ Church Governance - not management!
- ❏ Hold Senior Pastor Accountable to vision and goals in partnership with the DS
- ❏ Create & update policies, procedures, and Guiding Principles
- ❏ Align resources to the mission, vision, goals, & strategies
- ❏ Examples of mature spiritual leaders
- ❏ Adhere to the Leadership Covenant
- ❏ Annual Strategic Planning Retreat
- ❏ Understand shift in role & responsibility from congregant to leader
- ❏ Bless the vision cast with the pastor
- ❏ Work with the district superintendent to hold the pastor accountable
- ❏ Communicate with the Congregation

Pastor's Role in Accountable Leadership

- ❏ Spiritual Leader / Shepherd
- ❏ Keeper of Mission
- ❏ Caster of Congregationally Discerned Vision
- ❏ Example of Evangelist
- ❏ Chief Fundraiser
- ❏ Main Recruiter
- ❏ Develop New Leaders
- ❏ Hire, supervise, assess (and if needed, terminate) both paid and unpaid staff as outlined in the Guiding Principles
- ❏ Hold staff (paid and unpaid) accountable for leading their ministry areas and fulfilling the mission and vision of the church through goals and strategies
- ❏ Monitor the accomplishment of church goals and make adjustments in associated strategies and staff as required to ensure achievement of those goals

Staff/Ministry Teams' Role in Accountable Leadership

- In coordination with the pastor, create strategies to fulfill the Leadership Team's Goals
- Connect congregation to the church's discipleship pathway through all ministries and help them take their next step
- Identify, recruit, equip, and deploy ministry team members
- Coordinate ministry
- Create & update ministry team members job descriptions
- Follow Guiding Principles
- Hold ministry team members accountable
- Help ministry team members connect their ministry to the strategies, goals, vision, mission, and core values
- Evaluate all ministries (i.e. purpose, outcome, missional effectiveness & alignment, resource consumption)

Create a Leadership Covenant

Each year with a few members rolling off the Leadership Board and a few new ones coming on, a new leadership covenant is created for their work ahead. The covenant is completed at the fall strategic ministry planning retreat if all new members who will be coming onto the Leadership Board are present. If all are not present, the leadership covenant will need to be completed at the first meeting of the new Leadership Board at the beginning of the year.

A covenant is a sacred agreement with God and other Leadership Board members. This covenant is a written agreement of the expectations of leaders and a code of conduct for which each board member agrees upon. It speaks to how we will work together, collaborate with one another as a "team," and treat each other. Without a covenant, there will most likely be ambiguity.

A healthy team covenants together and expectations are known and agreed upon before the work begins. In Kay's consulting, she always suggests the covenant starts from scratch each year. The previous Leadership Board would not want to impose last year's covenant on the current board. Of course, it can be used as a template, but copying last year's over to this year takes away from its sacredness, the opportunity for new leaders to weigh in on its content, and the exercise of a fresh start and perspective each year. Once the covenant is agreed upon and put into writing, have each board member sign the covenant. This is a sacred time and practice, so approach it as such.

I (Kay) am often asked for a copy or a sample of a leadership covenant. I hesitate to offer one, as I see too many times that churches will not journey through the important process of discernment to create one their leaders "own" and articulate in their own words. This is important so that the Leadership Board does not feel the covenant has been imposed upon them. However, in the spirit of collaboration and connection, the following is a resource to get you started. Please *consider* the following as possible inclusions of your leadership covenant:

Sample Leadership Board Covenant

- Leadership Board members are role models for the congregation. Therefore, members will model mature Christian discipleship by being present in worship at least three times per month, tithing or moving toward a tithe, have an active prayer life, serve in mission three times per year, be active on a ministry team, be in a discipleship development group, and openly share their faith with others in the secular world.

- Leadership Board members are encouraged to invest in board conversations and decisions with vigor and passion. However, once the board has come to a decision, each Leadership Board member will openly and publicly support the decision of the Leadership Board whether the individual member personally agrees with the decision. We are a Leadership Board with a unified voice.

- Board members are expected to be present at all board meetings unless ill or out of town. (For members who might travel for their job, the Leadership Board may decide if they want to offer virtual call-ins and whether those are okay on a routine basis.) If members miss more than three meetings, the Board Chair will converse with the Leadership Board member to see if her/his seat needs to be vacated and filled by someone who can be more active.

- Leadership Board members will thoroughly review the meeting packet prior to meetings coming fully prepared and ready to participate. Packets will be sent to the members no later than five days prior to the meeting.

- Leadership Board members will be on time for meetings, silence cell phones, and fully immerse themselves in the meeting without distractions in respect for their fellow Leadership Board members' time and commitment.

- Leadership Board members will encourage and support our pastor, staff, and fellow Leadership Board members privately and publicly.

- Leadership Board members will hold ourselves, the pastor, and other Leadership Board members accountable for their leadership roles and responsibilities. This includes allowing others to hold the Leadership Board members collectively and individually accountable to this covenant, our work as the church body leading the church in its purpose of making disciples, and to Jesus Christ.

- Leadership Board members understand that conflict and disagreements are natural in any community, including the church. As a Leadership Board, we will approach matters of disagreement with transparency and maintain our missional focus as a Board. When approached by a person or group concerning a matter of disagreement or conflict, we will follow the path laid out by Jesus in Matthew 18 by encouraging the concerned party to go directly to the individual, to volunteer to go with the concerned party as a witness, or to invite the concerned party to address the full leadership or an assigned work team to address the issue. In accordance with the UM *Discipline*, the senior pastor will be present in all meetings unless the senior pastor is voluntarily absent. At no time will we support secret meetings that undermine the integrity or authority of the pastor or Leadership Board. This is of particular importance in relationship to staff remembering that staff report directly to the pastor and not to the Leadership Board. The Leadership Board will not triangulate themselves with the pastor and staff member.

- Appropriate confidentiality will be maintained. The Leadership Board, in its role and responsibility as the staff-parish relations committee, is held to a high standard of confidentiality in personnel and clergy appointment matters. Similarly, the Leadership Board, serving as the congregation's trustees, is required to hold certain legal information confidential. The Leadership Board may, therefore, move into executive session for some agenda items.

- The Leadership Board will conclude regular meetings with a discussion of a communications plan of decisions to encourage transparency and congregational sharing.

- Leadership Board members are representatives of the church and the Leadership Board at all times during their leadership terms. Leadership Board members have a fiduciary duty to the Board and the church to uphold the highest standards of integrity of relationships and to support the mission, vision, and values of the congregation including publicly supporting other congregational leaders, staff, and clergy of the congregation.

Feel free to add other covenantal elements that define the roles and authority of each Leadership Board member individually and collectively, such as boundaries about making demands upon staff and staff time without consulting the pastor (or at all), matters of conflicts of interest, and the limits of personal authority as a Leadership Board member.

Create Guiding Principles

Guiding principles are a set of policies and procedures which allow the ministry of the church to function on a day-to-day basis within healthy boundaries. Guiding principles keep the Leadership Board from managing and the pastor and/or staff from micro-managing. These principles are permission-giving strategies that protect the overall health and well-being of the church. Guiding principles allow for more effective decision-making by making macro decisions once rather than micro decisions continuously. Guiding principles free up the "decision bottleneck" that the old church council structure ultimately created and empowers the pastor, staff, and ministry team leaders with authority to match their responsibilities and accountability.

Most churches start with a blank piece of paper in creating their guiding principles. While all of us have our United Methodist Church's *Book of Discipline (BOD)* to guide and direct us, there is certainly a need for local policies and procedures. Guiding principles compliment the *BOD...not replace the BOD*. They might also further clarify the *BOD* in the local context.

Think of the guiding principles as a living, breathing document. Because our environment (people, ministries, community, etc.) changes constantly, guiding principles will need to grow and adapt as needed. Some churches might have some existing policies or procedures that might be adopted or adapted for the guiding principles. A church might also refer to policies and procedures (i.e., employee manual, facility usage) in the guiding principles as a reference to their acceptance or knowledge or make them a separate section of the guiding principles. Some church leaders have appreciated having all of these "policies and procedures" in one place or document. Because of the organic nature of guiding principles, we highly recommend they be offered digitally as an open resource which are easily accessed by staff and ministry team leaders.

Allow us to offer a filter for your Leadership Board's consideration. Every time a decision is made by the Leadership Board, ask yourself if there could be a guiding principle established or modified that would have allowed the decision to be made earlier, by the pastor, staff, or ministry team leader, and/or without the Leadership Board's intervention. We are not suggesting that there needs to be a guiding principle for everything. Yet, many times, we could allow for a more natural and timely flow of ministry and day-to-day operations if the Leadership Board could grant more permission within guidelines through a guiding principle. Creating a permission-giving culture for staff and ministry team leaders is a healthier environment for people to engage in their ministries when coupled with accountability throughout.

Here are some topics to consider as you write your guiding principles. Keep in mind that this is not an exhaustive list, but rather one to help you begin considering what guiding principles are needed for your church.

Potential Topics for Guiding Principle Consideration

- Mission, vision, core values of the church

- Identification of the Leadership Board's role, powers, responsibilities, and authority, in regard to the *Book of Discipline*

- Clear distinction for the role of governance for the Leadership Board - not management

- The Leadership Board will ensure there is a current organizational chart reflective of the current decision-making process and chain of command at all times. The chart will be included in the guiding principles.

- The Leadership Board is to provide transparent and routine communication to keep the congregation informed of missional effectiveness and resource alignment including quarterly town hall meetings providing the opportunity for two-way communication.

- Financial policies for staff/ministry team leaders, the pastor, and the building maintenance team including spending limits, bid requirements, credit cards, reimbursements, etc.

- Hiring, terminating, supervising, and evaluating authority of the pastor and other paid staff

- References or inclusion to church wide policies:

  - Building and equipment usage policies (for example, facility rental policies for members, internal ministry groups, outside non-profit groups or for-profit businesses)

  - Safe sanctuary policies for child protection

  - Employee handbook

  - Building safety

  - Technology usage and safety

  - Offering counters' policies and procedures

- Parliamentary rules of order, such as the usage of Robert's Rules of Order, the consensus method, or other variations.

- Include how to edit or add a guiding principle

- Official record keeping practices and access to records of meetings and executive session minutes

- Role and function of the building maintenance team

- Authority and responsibility of the treasurer

- Relationship of Nominations and Lay Leadership Development to the Leadership Board

- Boundaries stating how individual Leadership Board members may not make demands on staff time outside formal board requests

- How daycare and/or preschool relate to the church, pastor, and Leadership Board in terms of supervision of personnel and accountability (There is a huge legal and governance difference between childcare ministries that operate under a church's ministry and childcare ministries that exist as a separate but related 501(c)(3). These differences will impact how you write your guiding principle defining the relationship. See E-5 for more details.)

- Defining public meetings vs executive sessions (such as personnel matters when the Leadership Board is operating as the congregation's S/PPRC or legal matters when operating under trustee responsibilities)

Just like with the leadership covenant, I (Kay) am often asked for a sample of guiding principles. Again, I hesitate to offer a sample because so many will just adopt the sample and be done. If this were done, the whole spirit and purpose of the exercise is missed. Each church operates uniquely and therefore, a cut and paste approach will likely not be thorough or contextual for your specific church. It also does not address the intention of this being a fluid document that easily and frequently shifts as needed. However, once again in the spirit of collaboration and connection for resources, we offer the following as samples of some possible guiding principles.

Note that some of these items conflict with one another. This is intentional to provide a sampling of different approaches and decisions for the same topic. It is up to the Leadership Board to discern how you wish to balance the responsibilities and authority of the Leadership Board, pastor, and staff/ministry team leaders. You will also find additional guiding principle examples in the **Resource** section on pages 262-263.

Sample Guiding Principles

All references to the Church Council, Board of Trustees, Staff/Pastor Parish Relations Committee, Endowment Committee, and Finance Committee, in all congregational policies as of _____, and in all references in the Book of *Discipline* of the United Methodist Church, shall be understood to refer to the Leadership Board beginning _____.

- Once the budget is approved, those responsible (i.e., staff and team leaders) for the various ministry areas have the authority to spend their budget to align with the objectives for their ministry area approved by the pastor. No further approval is needed to access the budget in their area of responsibility. *

- The pastor is responsible for reviewing line items within ministry areas with the appropriate staff or team leaders for accountability from the staff and to the board.

- Any member of the Building Maintenance Team has the authority to purchase supplies for building maintenance and improvement up to $____ without approval. The Building Maintenance Team leader can authorize purchases for building maintenance and improvement up to $____. Purchases up to $____ can be approved by the pastor (executive pastor or business manager). Any purchases over $____ need Leadership Board approval unless the expenditure is already approved in a capital expenditure line item in the approved budget. *

- Any expenditure over $____ will require three bids. Preference will be given to hire local companies offering competitive bids within __% of other bids. If the expenditure is already approved in the budget and meets the previous criteria, there is no further approval needed. The ministry team leader or staff member responsible for the purchase will provide documentation of the bids to the Leadership Board for purposes of a paper trail only. *

- *The treasurer must be consulted concerning any single purchase or expenditure over $____ for purposes of cash flow. The treasurer does not approve or deny purchases but rather confirms large purchases will not create cash flow issues.

- The pastor has the authority to hire and release employees using the church's employee policies and procedures in the ___ UMC Employee Handbook. When terminating an employee, the pastor will invite a board member to sit in on the exiting conversation for purposes of liability protection. The pastor has the responsibility to supervise, discipline, and evaluate staff performance as outlined in the ___ UMC Employee Handbook.

  OR

- The authority to hire and terminate employees of the church shall be vested in the Leadership Board. The pastor shall have the authority to interview and recommend candidates to fill open staff positions. The Board shall have the sole authority to determine the number of staff positions, approve job descriptions for each staff member and set the salary paid to each staff member. The Leadership Board delegates to the pastor the authority to supervise, discipline, and manage paid staff.

- The pastor will review all paid staff annually using the approval evaluation process in the employee manual dated _____. Paid staff will review unpaid staff/team and leaders annually using the same evaluation process.

- The Weekday Child Care Advisory Board (BOD ¶ 256.2.c) is fully amenable and accountable to the Leadership Board and shall submit an annual budget and recommended policy changes to the Leadership Board. The director of weekday ministries is supervised by the pastor.

- The board recognizes and approves the Building Usage Policies dated _____.

- The board recognizes and approves the Building Security and Key Policies dated _____.

- The board recognizes and approves the Financial Controls Policies dated _____.

- The board recognizes and approves the _____ UMC Personnel Policies dated _____.

- All meetings of the Leadership Board shall be open to the public, with the exception of any meeting or portion of a meeting in which a personnel matter or a matter of legal negotiations is considered. In those cases, the Board will transition into executive session. Minutes of executive session agenda items concerning personnel matters will be kept separately as part of the "S/PPRC" files.

- Leadership Board members are nominated by a separate and independent Committee on Nominations and Leadership Development, chaired by the pastor, and elected by the Charge Conference as described in the BOD. The Nominations Committee will be responsible for developing new leaders and equipping them for future Leadership Board positions.

- Due to Leadership Board's serving as the congregation's Staff-Parish Relations Committee, no immediate family member of the pastor or other paid staff person may serve as a member of the board. Due to serving as the congregation's Board of Trustees, only Leadership Board members over the age 18 will have voting privileges in matters of property, incorporation, legal matters, contracts, insurance, investments, or other matters described in the BOD ¶ 2525-2551.

- The pastor will review all paid staff annually using the approval evaluation process in the employee manual dated _____. Paid staff will review unpaid staff/team and leaders annually using the same evaluation process.

- The Weekday Child Care Advisory Board (BOD ¶ 256.2.c) is fully amenable and accountable to the Leadership Board and shall submit an annual budget and recommended policy changes to the Leadership Board. The director of weekday ministries is supervised by the pastor.

- The Leadership Board recognizes and approves the Building Usage Policies dated _____.

- The Leadership Board recognizes and approves the Building Security and Key Policies dated _____.

- The Leadership Board recognizes and approves the Financial Controls Policies dated _____.

- All meetings of the Leadership Board shall be open to the public, with the exception of any meeting or portion of a meeting in which a personnel matter or a matter of legal negotiations is considered. In those cases, the Board will go into executive session. Minutes of executive session agenda items concerning personnel matters will be kept separately as part of the S/PPRC files.

- Leadership Board members are nominated by a separate and independent Nominating Committee, chaired by the pastor, and elected by the Charge Conference as described in the BOD. Due to Leadership Board's serving as the congregation's Staff-Parish Relations Committee, no immediate family member of the pastor or other paid staff person may serve as a member of the board. Due to serving as the congregation's Board of Trustees, only Leadership Board members over the age 18 will have voting privileges in matters of property, incorporation, legal matters, contracts, insurance, investments, or other matters described in the BOD ¶ 2525-2551.

At your first meeting of the Leadership Board Term:

- Create and join in a **Leadership Covenant**. A covenant is a sacred agreement with God and other board members. This covenant is a written agreement of the expectations and a code of conduct which should be agreed upon by the entire Leadership Board. Without a covenant, there will most likely be ambiguity.

- Explain and discuss your **model agenda** for healthy board meetings *(see Chapter E-11)*.

- Elect a **Chair of Trustees** (annual requirement in the *Book of Discipline* and many state rules for nonprofit corporations) from the Board's membership. We recommend that the Leadership Board Chair be elected by the Board to also serve as trustee chair.

- Spend quality time working on the **Guiding Principles**. It will pay dividends for years to come! Be sure to orient the Leadership Board on Guiding Principles every year.

- Call attention to the rhythm of the Leadership Board's areas of responsibility to remind members of the larger scope of work *(see Chapter I-12)*.

- Share and discuss the **Accountable Leadership Cycle** *(see Chapter E-8)*.

- Schedule the **monthly board meetings** for the year and set the date for the fall strategic ministry planning retreat.

CHAPTER E-8

Accountable Leadership Must Come First

Don't look for shortcuts to God. The market is flooded with surefire, easygoing formulas for a successful life that can be practiced in your spare time. Don't fall for that stuff, even though crowds of people do. The way to life – to God! – is vigorous and requires total attention. Be wary of false preachers who smile a lot, dripping with practiced sincerity. Chances are they are out to rip you off some way or other. Don't be impressed with charisma; look for character. Who preachers are is the main thing, not what they say. A genuine leader will never exploit your emotions or your pocketbook. These diseased trees with their bad apples are going to be chopped down and burned.

Knowing the correct password – saying 'Master, Master,' for instance – isn't going to get you anywhere with me. What is required is serious obedience – doing what my Father wills. I can see it now – at the Final Judgment thousands strutting up to me and saying, 'Master, we preached the Message, we bashed the demons, our God-sponsored projects had everyone talking.' And do you know what I am going to say? 'You missed the boat. All you did was use me to make yourselves important. You don't impress me one bit. You're out of here.' These words I speak to you are not incidental additions to your life, homeowner improvements to your standard of living. They are foundational words, words to build a life on. If you work these words into your life, you are like a smart carpenter who built his house on solid rock. Rain poured down, the river flooded, a tornado hit – but nothing moved that house. It was fixed to the rock.

But if you just use my words in Bible studies and don't work them into your life, you are like a stupid carpenter who built his house on the sandy beach. When a storm rolled in and the waves came up, it collapsed like a house of cards.

Matthew 7:13-27

I (Blake) remember the most disheartening planning meeting of my ministry. It was the first meeting of the team to set our plans for the year. A key leader would bring preliminary copies for everyone. What we received was disheartening. We each received a single sheet of paper (with the date of three years ago printed at the top) and a listing of events for January through December. For each item/event, the printed dates from three years ago were marked out and last year's date was handwritten beside each event. Additionally, last year's "preliminary" schedule was marked out and instead the current year was scribbled beside all the other years' updates. It was planning by photocopy!

In a church culture where we often do ministries *"just because..."* (i.e., *just because* it sounds charitable, or *just because* Mrs. Matriarch wants to, or *just because* we always have done it that way), accountable leadership feels radical. Rarely do we create ministries with the transformational impact in mind and work backwards from that goal. However, both of your authors are formed by Wesleyan Christianity and so accountability is part of our history. The early Methodist societies always kept count of members, money, and ministry. While we may think of Annual Conference as a business meeting, revival, or equipping event, its origins were as an annual accountability tool: how many new class meetings and bands (small groups) were formed, how many souls were reached for Christ, and how well were our traveling preachers leading the expansion of the Church into new territory for new people? We can recover that meaningful accountability today. That is if we are willing to start with our end in mind (impactful transformation) and then work backwards from our goal while creating systems of accountability under the stewardship of the new Leadership Board.

Accountable Leadership

I (Kay) always offer this caution in training on the simplified, accountable structure:

> **_Some_** churches can move to a simplified, accountable structure and be effective.
>
> **_All_** churches should practice accountable leadership.
>
> **_No_** church should move to a simplified structure without accountable leadership practices.

I (Kay) have found the book, *Winning on Purpose*, by John Edmund Kaiser to be an invaluable tool to apply to simplifying structure. In working with pastors and churches across the nation, it has become very apparent that most churches do not practice account-ability. In fact, some churches are quite resistant to enacting accountability practices. In my work with churches, if they are unwilling to adapt to accountability practices, I do not recommend simplification. If accountable leadership is not put into place along with simplification, it will simply not be conducive in being a healthy organization. In fact, it can quite possibly create the opposite. Accountability can be put into action with simplification, but simplification without accountability is bad news!

Accountability is marrying responsibility and authority. In other words, accountable leadership is when a person is given the responsibility and authority for a job, project, or ministry and his/her supervisor holds the person accountable for the intended and agreed upon outcome. Accountability often gets a bum rap because it is often confused with blaming or disciplinary actions. Yet blaming is really quite different than accountability. While accountability connects responsibility and authority, blaming usually occurs when someone has responsibility but no actual authority or capacity to fulfill the expectations. Accountability isn't about disciplinary action or punishment. Rather, accountability is about support, encouragement, identifying needed resources, uncovers stalls, and provides clarity in how to get back on track.

Accountable leadership in a church is quite simple in concept, but much less readily or eagerly practiced. Here are some other great reasons to consider for why you will want to consider implementing accountable leadership into the life of your church beginning with the Leadership Board:

1. Marries responsibility and authority with accountability

2. Promotes church unity

3. Functions on a high level of trust

4. Decisions are made very quickly

5. Mission/Vision fulfillment is the driving force...not management (or maintenance)

6. Goals and objectives of ministries can be adjusted as needed

7. Stumbling blocks are identified much more quickly and thus course correction occurs sooner

8. Clear expectations are set so there is much less confusion, wasted energy, and time

9. There is a basis for both pastoral and staff evaluations

10. People generally feel more encouraged and supported

Who Holds Who Accountable?

The first entity that a Leadership Board must hold accountable is themselves. As the governing board, it has both the responsibility and the authority to lead. The governing board is accountable to God to fulfill Christ's mission and to use its authority to hold the rest of the church accountable to Christ's mission as well. The Leadership Board is accountable to Christ (the owner of the church) for the church being faithful in fulfilling its mission of making disciples of Jesus Christ for the transformation of the world (the Great Commission).

If we only talk accountability, but are unable or unwilling to live it, it will never work! Accountability is simple! Here are the steps to holding one another accountable:

S = Set Expectations

I = Invite Commitment

M = Measure Progress

P = Provide Feedback

L = Link to Consequences

E = Evaluate Effectiveness

Accountable leadership is dependent on clarity of roles and expectations. One reason we advocate for simplified, accountable structure in congregations is that the complexity of offices and committees creates blurry authority and undermines accountability. Churches with no clarity around authority often argue so much about who "gets" to make a decision that often the decision is made too late or is undermined at the first chance. John Edmund Kaiser's *Winning on Purpose (pages 46 & 107)*, has deeply influenced our understanding of the roles for the various positions for accountable leadership:

- **Board/Council** = Role is **governance** (fiduciary, generative, and strategic work)

- **Pastor** = Role is **leading** the people into the mission field through communicating God's mission and vision

- **Staff** (paid & unpaid) = Role is **managing** the day-to-day ministry **as equippers and coordinators (not do-ers)**

- **Members** = Role is **ministering** to the church, the neighborhood, and the larger world

Understanding these roles is vitally important in moving into both simplification and accountability. Through a thorough understanding and the distinctions of these roles, all four areas (board, pastor, staff, and members) can stay in their respective lanes. This proper understanding is critical in the shift of becoming more effective, efficient and faithful as a church.

Most churches we work with have an understandably steep learning curve when it comes to understanding these roles. The biggest shift most churches need to make is the board/council moving from **managing to governing**. We often share with congregations we work with that if the board/council is not talking about and monitoring its effectiveness in its mission of making disciples, that I can assure them no one is monitoring it! What we pay attention to is what we deem important.

If all we are paying attention to are such things as the calendar, the building, and the money, we lose sight of the most important reason we exist – the mission. And, when we are not paying attention to our effectiveness in reaching the mission, we most assuredly drift away from the mission.

Accountable Leadership Cycle

In our book, *IMPACT! Reclaiming the Call of Lay Ministry*, (pages 112-113), we shared what accountable leadership looks like in a local church. Start with your missional purpose as a congregation and then doing the necessary discernment, planning, implementation, evaluation and reflective learning:

Assessment, evaluation, and reflection are critically important to a healthy governance model when practicing accountable leadership. We must become proficient with assessment at every level. The board is accountable to Christ for the church living its mission of making disciples. The pastor is accountable to the board for the church's annual goals and living into its vision of God's preferred future for how it uniquely makes disciples. The staff (paid and unpaid ministry leaders) are accountable to the pastor for the day-to-day ministry, with the pastor ensuring that the ministries are aligned with the church's annual goals. Constant and consistent evaluation at all levels is critical to enable the church to assess its fruitfulness and remain in alignment of its purpose/mission. Finally, the board needs to take time to reflect on ministries and their effectiveness. Accountability is not about blaming, but it's certainly about learning. An organization that never reflects on their work never learns or adapts. A word of warning: Evaluation and accountability are key, but please know that this is an incredibly difficult shift to live into because it will take persistence and patience, but it will be so worth the investment.

This chart offers a graphic representation of the accountable leadership cycle:

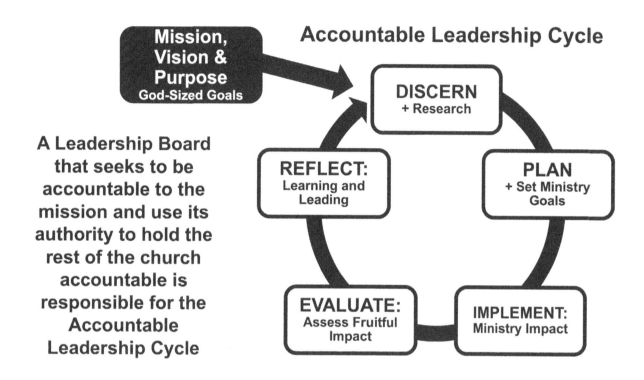

Accountable Leadership Cycle	
Mission, Vision, & Purpose (God-sized Goals)	Ministries should come out of your mission, vision, and goals. Accountability is ultimately rooted in following the mission that Christ has for the congregation.
Discern + Research	The first step of the cycle is to discern ministry needs, as rooted in the mission. That not only takes prayerful conversation, but also research such as demographic studies, neighborhood prayer walks, community stakeholder interviews, and an assessment of a congregation's spiritual gifts and passions.
Plan + Set Ministry Goals	The Ministry Team should plan and set goals for the proposed ministry. For example, a "bridge event" to connect to neighbors will need plans for event staff to greet and get to know guests, not just "run the event." Similarly, a goal for such an event would be for appropriate guest follow-up within 24 hours. Ministries without planned goals for transformational impact become random "feel good events." The MInistry Team should connect with assigned staff or the pastor to ensure that clear goals are created and the ministry plans are designed to fulfill the goals.
Implement: Ministry Impact	The responsible ministry team is now ready to execute the plan. Ultimately, every serving disciple on the team is accountable to the mission of not only the particular ministry but to the congregation's larger overall mission and vision. Impactful ministries seek to make disciples and transform the world.
Evaluate: Assess Fruitful Impact	The Ministry Team should collaborate with the pastor or assigned staff/ministry team leader to assess the ministry from proposal to event to follow-up to thank you notes. What worked well? What needed work? What surprised the team? Was there Kingdom impact? How did the ministry align with the stated goals? What did the team learn? Were there any Holy Spirit sightings during the ministry? This evaluation is a vital step in accountability.
Reflect: Learning and Leading	A solid evaluation allows the staff/ministry team leader and pastor to learn about the mission field and the congregation's ministry capacity. This reflection time is different from an evaluation. While an evaluation is about doing things right, reflection is about doing the right things. Reflection is a skill and an intentional practice that invites the congregation's leaders back into the season of prayerful discernment. The pastor will want to share their reflection learnings with the Leadership Board when it relates to the overall mission, vision, and church goals to identify any needed shifts required.

While a Leadership Board may not have a direct hand in every step of this process (for instance, ministry implementation and the first set of evaluations happen at a staff or ministry team level), the governing board should be engaged by ensuring that others are held to an appropriate level of accountability. While the Leadership Board will not be planning the ministry or the event themselves, they can, for example be very clear about the goals of particular ministries.

The Accountable Leadership Cycle can be used throughout the church to maintain alignment and accountability. For instance, a pastor can use it in supervisory or staff meetings. A children's ministry director can use it with the Vacation Bible School Ministry Team. Using the same accountability tool throughout the church keeps everyone focused on the larger mission and purpose of the church and provides ongoing evaluation and reflection. It also creates a culture of accountability that can grow missional fruitfulness. We disciples are not being called to just keep our churches sustainable. We are called to make disciples of Jesus and make a transformational Kingdom impact in individual lives, our communities, and the world. Why would we not want to consistently pursue trying to do this more effectively, efficiently, and frequently?

Setting goals (expected outcomes and results) for ministries not only creates a compelling purpose that will attract more congregational energy, it also reminds every one of our purpose for a specific ministry. For instance, if we know that a goal of a neighborhood carnival is to get names and do excellent follow-up, we will organize the ministry very differently than if we didn't include that evangelistic element. What might have been just a nice event for the neighborhood becomes a disciple-making bridge event to build relationships. Having a clear understanding of the expected outcome matters!

Strategies matter, too! Strategies are the activities and ministries that occur from day to day in the life of the congregation. Sometimes these activities are strategic, but most often they are "just what we do because that is what we have always done." What we do day to day in the life of our church must align to our mission of making disciples. Strategies are the reflection of our "doing ministry" in connection with our purpose - our mission. When the simplified, accountable structure (the Leadership Board) sets the annual goals of the church to help the church live into their mission and vision, the pastor then works with the staff (paid and unpaid ministry team leaders) to align the strategies (the day-to-day ministries) that will help the church live into the mission of making disciples specifically through the goals for the upcoming year. The goals are to be purposeful next steps for the vision becoming reality as we make disciples. The pastor holds the staff accountable, the Leadership Board holds the pastor accountable.

When I (Blake) coach congregations, one of the questions I ask to determine how committed the leadership is to accountability is: "Tell me about the last few ministries you intentionally shut down a ministry." Congregations often clutter up their calendars with busy work, not Kingdom work, thinking a full calendar is a sign of missional impact. Meanwhile, the abundance of ministries struggle to find enough folks to serve, soak up budget resources, exhaust staff, burn out volunteers, distract the congregation from larger goals, and leave no space for new endeavors that could actually capture people's missional imaginations. Until church leaders are willing to make the hard call and conduct funeral services for worn out or distracting ministries (well done, good and faithful ministry!), accountable leadership will always remain theoretical.

The governance responsibilities of the board are four-fold:

Stewardship: The board tends to the fiduciary responsibilities and alignment of God's people and resources. This could include things like ensuring the facility is properly insured and safe, that personnel policies are appropriately followed, and the church's finances are regularly audited to ensure that the treasurer is appropriately handling the congregation's money. Fiduciary responsibility speaks to the appropriate care and management of the church's assets such as real estate, cash, human resources, and investments.

Strategic: The strategic work of the Leadership Board ensures the assets are aligned and leveraged in the best way possible so that the mission, vision, and goals are accomplished within the boundaries of the core values. The Leadership Board is monitoring the progress of the goals and the strategic data (vital signs) and makes adjustments as required.

Generative: Conversations, dreaming, and thinking with a generative focus is one of the more difficult adaptive leadership shifts most Leadership Boards have to make. Generative work is framed around big-picture questions, as opposed to current stewardship or strategic priorities. This is the creative, adaptive, and innovative work of discerning God's future dreams for the congregation and discerning the faithful next steps in leading the congregation.

Accountable Leadership: Setting a culture of well-aligned, impact-focused ministry that fulfills the congregation's mission, vision, and God-sized goals. This is accomplished through leading with authority and taking responsibility for missional fulfillment.

Unpacking the Four Responsibilities

Since some of these concepts may be new or perhaps not currently a part of your church's leadership conversations. Therefore, it is perhaps difficult to imagine what types of conversations these areas of focus might include. Let's take a look at an example of each of these four key responsibilities to provide some clarity.

1. Stewardship

This is probably the responsibility that is most familiar to most of our church leaders. Typically most churches do a pretty good job of taking care of this key function and responsibility. Stewardship is ensuring the facilities (church building, parsonage, parking lot, etc.) are well-maintained and insured. It also includes oversight of the finances including the budget, investments, and cash flow. The legal entity responsibilities are also part of stewardship.

2. Strategic

This area of responsibility is keeping the congregation, pastor, and staff/ministry leaders focused on the mission through strategic planning and monitoring progress monthly. This is typically where the pastor reports back to the Leadership Board on goal progress at the monthly meeting. The Leadership Board also monitors trends in giving, professions of faith, number of new and existing people engaged in ministry and discipleship, and number of new leaders and makes adjustments as needed to align and leverage resources. Strategic work could be considered navigating the ministry that is before us now or in the near future.

3. Generative

Generative responsibility is likely a new area for Leadership Board members. In its very basic form, the Leadership Board is *generating* work to do. Most boards simply navigate the decisions that are placed before them. So, the very idea of generating work is counter-intuitive. In addition, generative work is typically focused outside the current congregation. It is future-focused work, discerning work, and cultural competency/intelligence that helps us stay relevant and compelling to our mission field. Generative work could be considered the futuring work needed to provide clarity and focus for our future faithful paths.

4. Accountability

This, too, is likely a new area of responsibility for most new Leadership Board members. Accountability was not the usual method of leadership or expectation for churches. Consequently, this will likely be a new way of how we think, expect, and implement our leadership. I (Kay) often offer my sense of ultimate accountability as a church leader in workshops as thinking about it in these terms - imagine getting to the pearly gates (hoping and still working to get there) and being asked the question, "How did you lead the church on your watch?" That's the ultimate question for accountable church leadership. Ultimately as members of the Leadership Board, we are given authority (by the congregation through the election) and have taken responsibility (by saying yes to serve and agreeing to the leadership covenant) to ensure the church is living its purpose as Jesus proclaimed in the Great Commission to go and make disciples and train them in His ways so that the world will be transformed. It is when we understand this ultimate accountability that we will lead the church with a new sense of direction in awe of the responsibility that has been placed in our laps. My hope is that this first causes you pause to consider, but then shifts to a sense of urgency and persistence. When Leadership Board members truly come to grips with this piece and become Kingdom focused rather than personally or congregationally focused, the church can then begin to truly live out its potential and more people will come to know Jesus Christ than we can ever imagine.

An Accountable Leadership Conversation

I (Kay) was once coaching a church living into their first year of simplified, accountable structure. It was one of those situations where both the new Leadership Board and the pastor were all-in and ready to embrace this new leadership style. We journeyed through the strategic ministry planning retreat setting goals and identifying core values. The pastor had worked with staff to create the strategies to ensure the goals were met. The budget to support the strategies was approved. The stage was set! A few months later I attended one of their Leadership Board meetings to hold them accountable for the process of living into simplified, accountable leadership.

Here is a sampling of some of the conversation that occurred that evening:

Board chair: Pastor, tell us how each of the church goals is progressing?

Pastor: Goal one - the bridge event had 400 people in attendance. We collected 240 names. The connection team was able to engage in the first step of the follow-up system with just under 100 of those attending.

Goal two - the worship design team has been assembled. They have had one training session. We will have another training session next month. The following month we will begin to work on the next six months of worship planning. I feel I am missing the perspective of a new believer on the team and will be praying on who might be a good fit for that team. Do you have any suggestions?

Goal three . . .

Board member: Pastor, things are really progressing well on the church goals. I believe you also had some personal goals that <u>you asked us</u> to hold you accountable for including taking sabbath time. Tell us how those are going for you.

This was simply an amazing blessing to witness. So many church leaders struggle with accountability as it is seen as a negative -- it often feels more like blaming than graceful and missional. Yet during this encounter that I was privileged to observe, it was the power of accountability leadership demonstrated at the church and personal level. All felt empowered. All felt they were part of this collaborative, supportive team that were collectively making a difference in the life of the church and in the life of the pastor. When accountable leadership is embraced and fully practiced, it is a powerfully positive force.

We created a video to demonstrate accountability conversations for a Leadership Board. The video includes some best practices and some not-so-great practices. Some leaders struggle with really understanding what accountable leadership is and how it looks and sounds in Leadership Board settings. We offer this video to you as a resource to view with your Leadership Board and perhaps even in training potential leaders in your leadership development process. The video can be found at kaykotan.com.

Coaching Questions as you Consider Accountable Leadership

How ready is your church to practice accountable leadership? Use these coaching questions to reflect on your readiness:

- How does your current board or church council hold ministries accountable to the mission and vision of the church? For instance, do you require evaluations, study metrics, or spend time assisting ministry leaders in reflecting upon the purpose of ministries?

- When was the last time your church intentionally shut down (or put on evaluative "hiatus") a ministry for being ineffective? Reflect on how it was done and how you might do it differently now.

- How do your committees and ministry teams utilize your church's mission, vision, and goals when you need to make decisions or prioritize items in your budget? If the mission statement is read at the start of the meeting before the prayer, but never brought up as your team discerns next steps or influences your spending decisions, then is it actually being used for guidance or is it just a marketing tagline?

- How effectively is your accountable leadership practiced currently at all levels (board, pastor, staff/ministry team leaders, teams)? If we do not routinely inquire about what is being accomplished and hold one another accountable for moving forward towards our goals, we may be encountering an accountability crisis.

- Take a look at the common SAS Gaps on Page 283 under the accountability section. Which of these gaps will your Leadership Board likely struggle with unless they are diligent about leaning heavily into accountable leadership? Why? How will you prevent this gap from developing?

CHAPTER E-9

Adaptive Leadership:
Changing the Conversation at the Table

As Pharaoh approached, the Israelites looked up and saw them – Egyptians! Coming at them! They were totally afraid. They cried out in terror to God. They told Moses, "Weren't the cemeteries large enough in Egypt so that you had to take us out here in the wilderness to die? What have you done to us, taking us out of Egypt? Back in Egypt didn't we tell you this would happen? Didn't we tell you, 'Leave us alone here in Egypt – we're better off as slaves in Egypt than as corpses in the wilderness.'" Moses spoke to the people: "Don't be afraid. Stand firm and watch God do his work of salvation for you today. Take a good look at the Egyptians today for you're never going to see them again. God will fight the battle for you. And you? You keep your mouths shut!"

Then Moses stretched out his hand over the sea and God, with a terrific east wind all night long, made the sea go back. He made the sea dry ground. The sea waters split. The Israelites walked through the sea on dry ground with the waters a wall to the right and to the left. The Egyptians came after them in full pursuit, every horse and chariot and driver of Pharaoh racing into the middle of the sea. It was now the morning watch. God looked down from the Pillar of Fire and Cloud on the Egyptian army and threw them into a panic. He clogged the wheels of their chariots; they were stuck in the mud. The Egyptians said, "Run from Israel! God is fighting on their side and against Egypt!"

Exodus 14:10-14, 21-25

You have your structure set. The initial set of guiding principles is complete. A leadership covenant has been created and signed. Now it's time to have a meeting, right? But wait! Don't fall into the trap of thinking a new structure will automatically create better conversations at the table. After all, even Moses had to deal with the "Back to Egypt Committee." More than technical fixes are needed to lead the congregation into fulfillment of Christ's vision. Now is the time to deeply consider how adaptive leadership changes the very nature of leadership.

The 2020-2021 COVID pandemic demonstrated the inadequacy of technical fixes and "change by copy/paste." In his 2021 book, *Strengthening Congregational Decision Making and Governance for the Expeditions (The Greatest Expedition series)*, Blake wrote:

> *In spring 2020, almost every church in America suddenly, with a few days' notice, had to adapt: from ministries designed to huddle together people in intimate settings to becoming online worshiping and discipling communities. I had to learn a new sentence: "Our primary worship service is online, but we are also offering several intimate, socially distant and safe in-person worship experiences throughout the week. Please bring your own mask." I did not learn that particular string of words in seminary. Very few of our preachers were trained to be televangelists, but adaptation was key, not only for institutional survival, but for missional fruitfulness. We all learned a powerful lesson – the inherited, multiple-months process of decision-making would no longer work. To be fruitful during a pandemic, adaptive leadership in churches meant that congregations would either succumb to unsustainable pastoral authoritarianism or create simpler systems of lay leadership decision-making. Rapid cultural change is not going away.*[4]

The strong executive leadership needed in the first couple of weeks of the crisis evolved into a few different patterns:

- Some congregations never moved out of crisis reaction mode, with clergy authoritarianism resulting in either an appreciative (but sidelined) membership or an angry membership who were exiled from decision making and congregational leadership. One pastor speaking to me (Blake) explained this binary by saying, "They were all behind me saying, 'We have your back,' then I looked back and suddenly they were all carrying knives."

- Some congregations figured out a way to limp through the crisis with their existing committees making decisions, but with little alignment and stunted creativity. Existing ministries stalled, creativity became sluggish at best, and the rich interconnectedness of the congregation deteriorated.

- Some congregations simply folded under their own weight and inertia. While they might not yet be closed, the difficult future that seemed five or ten years away was now on their doorstep.

4 Blake Bradford. *Strengthening Congregational Decision Making and Governance for the Expeditions.* Market Square Books Publishing, Knoxville.2021.

- And some congregations thrived. Lay and clergy leadership structures were simple enough and connected enough to seek out information, and make timely decisions that had group support. Other groups and ministry teams were held accountable to the continuing mission of the church and were given the freedom and flexibility to adapt or allow their resources to be shifted toward new ministries that enabled the Gospel to be shared and the community to be served.

While adaptive leadership may feel like a new term, leadership in a changing world is nothing new. It is part of our Bible-based DNA as Christians.

The biblical narrative of the Jerusalem Council in Acts 15 shows us an example of ancient adaptive leadership. The fledgling church had to consider a new way of being (the potential inclusion of Gentiles into the church) while staying connected to their traditions and identity (including the rite of circumcision). There was deep disagreement, and because the issue was important, the disagreement was deeply felt. The Book of Acts, Chapter 15, says that "The apostles and leaders called a special meeting to consider the matter. The arguments went on and on, back and forth, getting more and more heated." In seasons of change, when the established systems and expectations are failing us, leaders must figure out how to understand and interpret the new reality, adapt the organization (in this case, the Church) to respond to the new reality, and stay true to the foundational values and mission of the institution. It is not easy. If challenges were easy, we couldn't call them challenging. In Acts 15, the Apostle Peter attempted to re-frame the issue based on his experience of what Jesus Christ, through the Holy Spirit, was doing amongst the Gentile believers.

Then Peter took the floor: "Friends, you well know that from early on God made it quite plain that he wanted the pagans to hear the Message of this good news and embrace it – and not in any secondhand or roundabout way, but firsthand, straight from my mouth. And God, who can't be fooled by any pretense on our part but always knows a person's thoughts, gave them the Holy Spirit exactly as he gave him to us. He treated the outsiders exactly as he treated us, beginning at the very center of who they were and working from that center outward, cleaning up their lives as they trusted and believed him. So why are you now trying to out-god God, loading these new believers down with rules that crushed our ancestors and crushed us, too? Don't we believe that we are saved because the Master Jesus amazingly and out of sheer generosity moved to save us just as he did those from beyond our nation? So, what are we arguing about?" There was dead silence. No one said a word. With the room quiet, Barnabas and Paul reported matter-of-factly on the miracles and wonders God had done among the other nations through their ministry. The silence deepened; you could hear a pin drop.

Acts 15:7-13

The leaders looked at the "presenting issue" and at the mission of the church as defined in the Great Commission and the Great Commandment of Love and figured out a pathway into an unknown future. It took the Apostle James to "break the silence" and suggest a new set of guidelines that met the needs of the new reality while remaining consistent to the words of the prophets.

> *James broke the silence. "Friends, listen. Simeon has told us the story of how God at the very outset made sure that racial outsiders were included. This is in perfect agreement with the words of the prophets…. "God said it and now he's doing it. It's no afterthought; he's always known he would do this. So here is my decision: We're not going to unnecessarily burden non-Jewish people who turn to the Master. We'll write them a letter and tell them, 'Be careful to not get involved in activities connected with idols, to guard the morality of sex and marriage, to not serve food offensive to Jewish Christians – blood, for instance.' This is basic wisdom from Moses, preached and honored for centuries now in city after city as we have met and kept the Sabbath."*

Acts 15:13-15, 19-21

After a process of discernment and consensus-building (Acts 15:22 says that "everyone agreed: apostles, leaders, all the people"), the decision was then communicated to the larger church through representatives and an apostolic letter. This first Jerusalem Council shows us that adaptive leadership may be difficult. But creative, well-discerned, missional decisions at the meeting table can change the entire trajectory of the church and its ability to reach new disciples for Jesus Christ.

When teaching a course of study class on polity and administration, I (Blake) was assisting a new pastor in understanding the principles of the simplified structure model, and, of course, the concepts of accountable and adaptive leadership came up. His assignment: write up a process to manage the divergent paths that members wanted to take in leadership. As we dug deeper, the matter of Robert's Rules of Order came up again and again. Apparently, the congregation had learned along the way that correct parliamentary procedure was the answer to their problems. The difficulty now was that "doing business right" was unable to solve the complex problems the church was facing. The challenges that the congregation was facing today couldn't be fixed by a technical change of better parliamentary processes of motions and seconds. So we decided on a radical course of action: an entire season of talking about ministry – of discernment, of discovery, and of conversation… with no motions and no voting allowed. Instead of everything in good order, and each "side" trying to "win" by having enough votes, the board would focus on being prayerfully dedicated to Christ's mission and vision for the congregation, and it would experiment with different processes to come to decisions.

We are living in a complex culture very different from the one in which our churches were founded. The solutions that worked so well for us in the past are now anchors pulling us underwater. There is a popular saying in the business world "what got us here won't get us there." Technical changes are not enough to get us into Christ's God-sized dream for your congregation. The technical changes of restructure (simplification) and accountable leadership provide space and a place for adaptive leadership (missional creativity).

There have been many books written about adaptive leadership, both secular and church-related. Tod Bolsinger has gifted the church with an excellent metaphor of "canoeing the mountains" by comparing the adaptive leadership to the explorations of Lewis and Clark as they literally created the map of the west for the young U.S. government. They had expected to find a river that would flow all the way to the Pacific Ocean, but instead they had to figure a way to turn their canoeing skills into mountaineering skills when they ran into the Rockies (see Bolsinger's *Canoeing the Mountains: Christian Leadership in Uncharted Territory*).

As part of his consultation work with the Arkansas Conference, Alban Institute Consultant Gil Rendle used a story about taking one step at a time to help our entire conference re-imagine leadership and ministry for a new generation. Gil asked us to imagine a mother sending her son to lock up the barn doors at night. It was dark. The son couldn't see the barn, much less the doors. So his mother gives him a flashlight and sends him out again. The son comes back – the flashlight, while appreciated, still is too dim to help him find the barn. The mother sends him out a third time, saying, "You don't need to see the barn. You know the basic direction. Just keep walking to the end of the light." As the son walked forward the path was illuminated more with every step. Eventually, the barn was revealed. All he needed was the faith that the barn was in a certain direction, the flashlight as a tool to help him move forward, and a willingness to take each step (Gil, now retired from the Texas Methodist Foundation, later published this story in *Doing the Math of Mission: Fruits, Faithfulness, and Metrics*).

In rural Arkansas, this story had quite a resonance. Many of our lay and clergy annual conference members had grown up on or still lived on farms. They knew the darkness of night outside the city limits. These metaphors and stories helped us see that part of adaptive leadership meant that we needed some level of comfort with the unknown and the uncharted. We could set some proximate goals, be clear about our direction, and start heading toward making an impact for Christ. We didn't need to know and plan for every step. In fact, we couldn't know every step of the journey. Our world and the soul of every person are simply too complex. We would have to monitor and adjust. We would have to be willing to *adapt*.

The legacy forms of leadership and structure we have inherited are simply not built to adapt. These legacy forms of structure and the style of leadership they encourage are about fixing problems to get the church "back to business." Business, in this case, usually means back to focusing on membership (not Christ-centered disciple formation or evangelism) and making folks feel comfortable (rather than transforming the world). The multiple committees and "checks and balances" built into our inherited structures are all about maintaining the status quo. But the status ain't quo. The church is losing ground. Lives aren't being transformed. Disciples aren't being made. Your church needs to be able to adapt to uncharted territory and into a future we can't quite see – setting proximate goals, being brutally clear about the mission and vision you have discerned and holding one another accountable to making an impact for Christ. By placing these adaptive leadership responsibilities onto your Leadership Board, you are enabling your church to get out of a maintenance mode and into a transformation mode.

Those churches that truly live into a new simplified structure with accountable and adaptive leadership have experienced a positive change in the trajectory of their church. The changes do not occur overnight. The changes are not easy, nor do they come naturally. But for those churches that are truly committed to leading a church on its mission and are willing to make the shifts necessary to do so, the outcomes are remarkable. First, there is a renewed healthiness in the leaders. Second, there is a change in the nature and content of conversation around the leadership table. Third, there is a renewed hope within the life of the congregation. Fourth, there is a renewed commitment and understanding of the mission of making disciples. Fifth, there is renewed focus – someone is piloting the ship. All the passengers know the itinerary. All the passengers realize they are on a working ship (like an aircraft carrier on a mission and not a cruise ship being entertained) and know their assigned task as part of the team. Sixth, there is the opportunity to create shared, common language – first with the Leadership Board and continuing as the Leadership Board guides the larger congregation into uncharted waters.

Time for Adaptive Change

As the Leadership Board makes the technical changes of consolidating the four administrative teams, the opportunity for adaptive changes are now upon them. The technical change of having the people representing the collective functions of trustees, finance, council, and SPR in the room at the same time is something we could imagine. This was most likely one of the motivating factors to move into this simplified structure. Now is the time the adaptive changes will need to kick into gear. Remember, adaptive change is all about implementing changes we do not necessarily know how to implement. Be patient with yourself and one another but hold each other accountable for living into the adaptive changes.

The biggest shifts for adaptive change are the modifications of the agenda, conversation, and focus. The Leadership Board is to govern, not manage the day-to-day operations of the church. To adequately govern, the Leadership Board must take a balcony view. Most churches find it difficult to move from the typical ground view (management) to the balcony view (governance). They historically have just not functioned at that level. If the Leadership Board modified the agenda as recommended, it will allow for this adaptive shift to begin. If the new Leadership Board uses the old agenda, the Leadership Board will typically only make the technical change of having fewer people around the table, but not change the conversation at the table resulting in the needed adaptive changes. Adaptive changes take shifts in our values, beliefs, attitudes and/or behaviors. As you can imagine, these types of changes are much more difficult to implement than changing the number of people sitting at the table or the number of meetings scheduled!

Remember, technical changes are solving known problems with known solutions. Adaptive changes result from addressing unknown problems with unknown solutions. Adaptive change starts with adaptive thinking and adaptive learning. We must be willing to take on new thoughts, understandings, and behaviors in order to achieve adaptive changes. We can't expect adaptive change at the staff and ministry team levels if it is not modeled at the Leadership Board level.

Adaptive leadership means risk, both from external factors (experiments sometimes fail) and internal factors, particularly sabotage from members concerned about all the changes happening. The more your Leadership Board focuses your congregation on the disciple-making mission, the more others with peripheral concerns or feelings of lost power will criticize the direction. I (Blake) remember from Latin class that the word "decide" means "to cut off." As your Leadership Board makes decisions, folks will feel cut off or cut out. Gil Rendle writes about this experience in his book, *Next Steps in the Wilderness*[5] :

Adaptive work is not tidy. In his theory of change from a systems perspective that takes into consideration the insights of chaos theory, organizational consultant John Scherer notes that in order for change to be birthed, two "parents" must be present – pain and possibility. There must be a discomfort sufficiently strong to make the people want to be different and a possibility promising enough to support the people through change. Walter Brueggemann once commented that the central task of leadership is to manage the hopes and the fears of the people. Indeed, managing hopes and fears – pain and possibility – in a congregation, a

---

5 Gil Rendle. *Next Steps in the Wilderness*. Texas Methodist Foundation. Austin. p 8-9.

conference, or a corporation is a spiritual task of great faithfulness. Scherer demonstrates that if the leader can surface the appropriate pain, hold clearly the possibility of what can be, and help people let go of old assumptions, then the people will enter a stage of chaos – the truly creative environment where change happens.

It may be helpful to recall that the wilderness is required. In Mark's gospel, as soon as John baptized Jesus in the Jordan and the voice from heaven proclaimed Jesus as God's son, we are told that the Spirit immediately drove Jesus into the wilderness (Mark 1:12). Wilderness, chaos, change is neither tidy nor comfortable, which underscores the true difficulty of adaptive leadership in a system designed for the comfort of problem-solving management.

The wilderness is a difficult place. Like the explorations of Lewis and Clark, it is often uncharted, and like the story of the boy finding the barn, it can feel incredibly dark out there with your meager flashlight. Your Leadership Board's job is to keep pointing toward the Promised Land of God's dream for your congregation while carefully and prayerfully dealing with the inevitable push-back and sabotage inherent with adaptive leadership. Moses had to deal with the "Back to Egypt Committee" of murmurers (Exodus 16) who were more comfortable with slavery than the unknown. Your Leadership Board will need to help each other, and the larger congregation stay on track with the larger mission and vision that you have discerned. Keep casting the vision. Vision leaks!

A Word of Caution: Leading adaptive change is hard. Often adaptive change calls for cultural shifts in the church. It takes time, persistence, and perseverance. Too often when the new culture or approach is just about to break through, there is conflict, unrest, nervousness, or weariness that erupts. This is a time when some leaders or Leadership Boards throw in the towel and retreat (head back to Egypt). Yet, this is often the time when one last push will get the adaptive change over the last hump or hurdle. It just takes that last little burst of persistence for the adaptive change to take hold. Pay attention! If steady progress has been made, don't give up just before you cross the finish line because there is some negative tension. Leaders who are working on adaptive changes should expect some push-back. Don't ignore the opportunities of further equipping, communication, and reinforcement along the way either. On the other hand, remember that sometimes the biggest obstacles (hurdles) occur right before the finish line comes into full view. Keep your eye on the finish line and don't give up!

Staying on Track

Part of adaptive change is holding your fellow Board members accountable to not only the Leadership Covenant, but also to the role of governance. If one of your fellow Leadership Board members ventures out into what I refer to as the "tall grass" of management, it is your responsibility to call the member into accountability of their governess role and lane. Of course, we do this with love and grace! But we must do it. If we do not, we will soon find ourselves returning to our natural management tendencies where once again no one is steering the missional ship! Keep in mind this is not the sole responsibility of the chair or the pastor. It is the responsibility of every member of the Leadership Board.

Some churches I have worked with have had some real fun with helping everyone stay in the governing mode. Some have developed some pretty creative strategies, too. Some use vocal reminders such as "tall grass," "time out," or "management warning" to reign back in the conversation. Other churches have developed hand signals such as a time-out symbol or putting their hand up in the well-known stop signal. Others have placed an object in the middle of the table to be picked up when the conversation has veered off track. Use a method that fits your Leadership Board's personality and context. The method might even change from time to time. The important part is to have some sort of method to help a person recognize their lane drifting and get things back on track quickly, efficiently, and without debilitating the team.

Take a look at page 283. Identified in this chart are common gaps that develop in Leadership Boards using the SAS model. Specifically review the adaptive changes and leadership columns (accountability was evaluated in Chapter E-8). To stay on track, your Leadership Board will want to be attentive in staying away from these common gaps. Ask your SAS Coach if s/he sees any of these gaps developing and how to overcome them. Monitor this list so gaps can be identified sooner rather than later so the gaps do not progress into canyons!

God-sized Goals

In Chapter E-8, we shared how setting goals and measuring fruitfulness is the basis of accountable leadership. Adaptive leadership is about making sure that the goals we set are actually creative and compelling God-sized goals and not merely quick fixes. We must also be sure that goals set are not just for the sake of setting goals but are the next intentional steps in living into God's preferred future - the discerned vision. Alignment to the mission (making disciples) and the vision (God's preferred future for the unique way your church makes disciples) is essential. Without setting God-sized goals for making the vision a reality, the vision is merely a statement that we print on bulletin and post on our websites. Goals provide the intentional catalyst for the reality of the vision.

Alignment

It is the responsibility of the Leadership Board, pastor and staff to ensure alignment at all levels. There are three key areas of alignment: budget, calendar, and people (mainly staff and ministry team leaders).

It is the responsibility of the Leadership Board to ensure the budget aligns with the mission, vision, goals and core values. For example, we would be kidding ourselves to say that we value children if we have no children's ministry budget, or this is the first place we cut funding. Too many times the budget drives the church. Allow the mission to drive the budget. The budget should be a result of the needs identified to create the objectives to accomplish the goals that make the vision become reality as we uniquely live out our purpose – the mission of making disciples.

The calendar indicates what we value and how we use our time and energy. The calendar is a result of the objectives derived from the goals, vision, mission and core values. The objectives translate into the activities, events, and ministries that hold space on our calendar (time commitment) and expend energy. The calendar should reflect ministries and activities that align to our stated goals. If we simply copy our calendar over from one year to the next, we are a calendar-driven rather than a mission-driven church. The pastor is accountable for the calendar alignment with the staff and ministry team leaders.

Paid staffing (clergy and laity) should typically represent about 50 percent of a stable church's budget. For a growing church, the percentage might be as high as 60 percent. Typically, when the paid staff budget is out of whack, we see congregations hiring staff to do the ministry rather than equipping the congregation to do the ministry. Staff (whether it is paid staff or serving disciples who are like unpaid staff) need to be aligned with the goals and specifically the resulting objectives of their ministry area. We must ensure our staff is spending their time, energy, and budget on the areas the Leadership Board has deemed the focus (mission, vision, goals).

Strategic Ministry Planning and a Simplified, Accountable Leadership Board

Strategic planning is a part of what it takes to serve as accountable and adaptive leaders. It is about claiming that balcony space with the balcony view. We recommend that, in addition to regular checks on progress on your God-sized goals and impact in your congregation and mission field, that your Leadership Board take a strategic ministry planning retreat annually so that you can spend adequate time together discerning and intentionally mapping your congregation's future. We share more about the annual retreat in Chapter I-12, which also outlines an entire year in leadership.

In Kay's book, *Gear Up: Nine Essential Processes for the Optimized Church,* she goes into detail on strategic ministry planning (one of her favorite topics). Also, you can refer to her book co-authored with Ken Willard, *Strategy Matters: Your Roadmap for an Effective Ministry Planning Retreat.* This resource is a how-to guide on how to plan, conduct, and provide follow up for strategic ministry planning retreats. Allow us to provide a quick overview of the five parts of strategic ministry planning:

1. Mission: The purpose for the church – why you exist. Every church exists to make disciples of Jesus Christ for the transformation of the world as Matthew 28:19-20 indicates. It also happens to be the mission statement of the United Methodist Church as indicated in ¶120 of the BOD:

> ¶ **120.** *The Mission – The mission of the Church is to make disciples of Jesus Christ for the transformation of the world. Local churches and extension ministries of the Church provide the most significant arenas through which disciple-making occurs.*

Please do not waste any more time trying to figure out the mission of your church. It has been clearly laid out for us. Embrace it! The Leadership Board is accountable to Jesus Christ for the church being faithful in making disciples for the transformation of the world.

2. Vision: A church's vision connects its purpose, its identity, and its narrative. This is the unique method that your church makes disciples in your local context. Every church has the same mission, but its unique method and future is articulated in the vision. Vision is God's preferred future for your church. Vision emerges from the sweet spot of the gifts of your congregation, the passions of your leaders, and the needs of your community. In today's quick paced culture, vision usually needs to be re-cast every couple of years. The pastor is accountable for articulating the congregation's vision. Lovett Weems, the retired director of the Lewis Center for Church Leadership at Wesley Theological Seminary, shared in his book *Church Leadership* that a key question for leaders is "Are you willing to wear the vision the same way that people wear clothes?"[6] Vision provides the energy, momentum, and enthusiasm for church vitality.

3. Core Values: Values exist in your church whether you have named them or not. Think of it as your DNA or your church culture. It is who you are. It is the personality of your congregation. They guide your decisions. Core values are usually fairly static unless there is intentionality in moving towards aspirational values. Even if there is intentionality in

6   Lovett Weems. *Church Leadership.* Abingdon Press, Nashville. 2010. p 96.

moving towards aspirational values, this shift is normally slow. If you have not identified your core values, now is the time to do it. There is a worksheet to get you started in *Strategy Matters* mentioned above.

4. God-sized Goals: These are the action steps to be taken in the upcoming year that will enable the church to live into your vision and mission. Usually there are three to five big overall God-sized goals named each year to focus your congregation's resources. One of your goals may be implemented over multiple years (planning and building a new facility) that need updating based on your experience of the last year. The Leadership Board holds the pastor accountable for goals and casting/articulating the vision.

5. Objectives: This is where the rubber hits the road. Objectives are where the goals grow hands and feet. The staff (paid and unpaid – aka ministry team leaders) are responsible for the creating and implementing the objectives to make an impact in fulfilling the congregational goals. In the accountable leadership model, the pastor holds the staff and/or ministry team leaders responsible for meeting the objectives.

CHECKLIST FOR ADAPTIVE LEADERSHIP

- Ensure there is alignment: calendar, resources, budget & people.

- Hold one another accountable to adaptive leadership and governance rather than technical changes and management.

- Conduct an annual strategic ministry planning retreat.

- Ensure regular accountability to the goals set at the strategic ministry planning retreat.

- Be willing to walk in the wilderness as you grow and live into your understanding and practice of adaptive leadership.

THE IMPLEMENTING PHASE

What is this phase?

The Implementing Phase is the third step in the process after the Equipping
Phase. This Phase is identified as the first year of actually leading the church
using the simplified, accountable structure. During this Phase the Leadership
Board is creating the initial guiding principles, leadership covenant, policies and
procedures (if not already completed), the first strategic ministry planning retreat,
and living into both the technical and adaptive leadership changes in this model.
The Leadership Board is also growing into leading with accountability. This also
includes the Nominations Committee as it journeys through its first season of
selecting three new leaders for the Leadership Board that will be rolling off after the
first year and creating an intentional leadership development plan.

Who is involved in this phase?

The Implementating Phase's primary players are the new Leadership Board
members and the pastor. The Nominations Committee members are also involved
but in a different capacity. The Certified SAS Coach continues to play a key role as a
resource provider, supporter, and accountability partner.

What is the timing of this phase?

The Implementating Phase is the first year of a new simplified, accountable structure
in the local church. However, most churches discover that it sometimes takes years
to fully live into a leadership culture of living into this model adaptively with
accountability. Additionally, there may be new clergy appointed to the church
without experience in this model. Clergy new to the model will need some additional
equipping, coaching, and guidance during their first year in this model.

CHAPTER I-10

Multiple Hats, One Board

You were all called to travel on the same road and in the same direction,
so stay together, both outwardly and inwardly. You have one Master,
one faith, one baptism, one God and Father of all, who rules over all,
works through all, and is present in all. Everything you are and
think and do is permeated with Oneness.

But that doesn't mean you should all look and speak and act the same. Out of the
generosity of Christ, each of us is given his own gift. The text for this is,

He climbed the high mountain,

He captured the enemy and seized the booty,

He handed it all out in gifts to the people.

It's true, is it not, that the One who climbed up also climbed down,
down to the valley of earth? And the One who climbed down is the One
who climbed back up, up to highest heaven. He handed out gifts above
and below, filled heaven with his gifts, filled earth with his gifts. He handed out gifts
of apostle, prophet, evangelist, and pastor-teacher to
train Christians in skilled servant work, working within Christ's body, the church,
until we're all moving rhythmically and easily with each other, efficient and graceful
in response to God's Son, fully mature adults,
fully developed within and without, fully alive like Christ.

Ephesians 4:4-13

Your Role as a Board Member

Church leadership can be incredibly difficult. Your church is your family. You walk alongside your fellow members through births, deaths, and challenging life moments. You disciple one another, encourage each other, gather to swing hammers at a Habitat for Humanity build, pray together, and kneel side-by-side to receive communion. Moving into church leadership can place enormous stress on these existing relationships. Chapter E-9 focused on accountable leadership. We (Kay and Blake) both believe strongly that mutual accountability is a Christian Discipling value that has been underused in the modern iteration of Jesus' Church. However, accountability is even more important for those who willingly take on the mantle of a church leader. Let's' remind ourselves of the distinctive roles for the Leadership Board, pastor, and staff/ministry team leaders:

Leadership Board's Role in Accountable Leadership

- ❑ Accountable to Jesus Christ for the Great Commission
- ❑ Fiduciary responsibility
- ❑ Generative work
- ❑ Strategic work
- ❑ Church Governance - not management!
- ❑ Hold Senior Pastor Accountable to vision and goals in partnership with the DS
- ❑ Create & update policies, procedures, and Guiding Principles
- ❑ Align resources to the mission, vision, goals, & strategies
- ❑ Examples of mature spiritual leaders
- ❑ Adhere to the Leadership Covenant
- ❑ Annual Strategic Planning Retreat
- ❑ Understand shift in role & responsibility from congregant to leader
- ❑ Bless the vision cast with the pastor
- ❑ Work with the district superintendent to hold the pastor accountable
- ❑ Communicate with the Congregation

Pastor's Role in Accountable Leadership

- ❑ Spiritual Leader / Shepherd
- ❑ Keeper of Mission
- ❑ Caster of Congregationally Discerned Vision
- ❑ Example of Evangelist

- ❏ Chief Fundraiser
- ❏ Main Recruiter
- ❏ Develop New Leaders
- ❏ Hire, supervise, assess (and if needed, terminate) both paid and unpaid staff as outlined in the Guiding Principles
- ❏ Hold staff (paid and unpaid) accountable for leading their ministry areas and fulfilling the mission and vision of the church through goals and strategies
- ❏ Monitor the accomplishment of church goals and make adjustments in associated strategies and staff as required to ensure achievement of those goals

Staff/Ministry Teams' Role in Accountable Leadership

- ❏ In coordination with the pastor, create strategies to fulfill the Leadership Team's Goals
- ❏ Connect congregation to the church's discipleship pathway through all ministries and help them take their next step
- ❏ Identify, recruit, equip, and deploy ministry team members
- ❏ Coordinate ministry
- ❏ Create & update ministry team members job descriptions
- ❏ Follow Guiding Principles
- ❏ Hold ministry team members accountable
- ❏ Help ministry team members connect their ministry to the strategies, goals, vision, mission, and core values
- ❏ Evaluate all ministries (i.e. purpose, outcome, missional effectiveness & alignment, resource consumption)

As a Leadership Board member, you are now responsible for holding the pastor accountable, and to help the pastor hold ministry team leaders and staff accountable. As a Leadership Board member, you are always "on duty" until your term of office ends. That may just change the nature of some of your relationships with your fellow disciples. Sometimes that means initiating difficult conversations with your fellow church members. It means holding certain information about staff and clergy confidential. It means fulfilling the fiduciary and legal responsibilities of a Trustee and member of the Board of Directors even when it might be socially difficult. Gone are the days when you could gossip about the church (which wasn't in alignment with scripture anyway) or enjoy "roast preacher for Sunday dinner" with friends.

While accountable leadership, as described in Chapter E-8, means following the Accountable Leadership Cycle, pushing leaders and the pastor to align ministries to goals, and expecting evaluations of ministries, accountable leadership is not only a list of things your board *does*. Accountable leadership also concerns the attitude and approach with which you and your fellow Leadership Board members address your leadership roles.

Similarly, adaptive leadership never comes with a downloadable plan or a bullet point list of things "to do" in order to be effective and fruitful in every situation. If we had that, we would not need adaptive leadership. Instead, adaptive leadership is about a willingness to journey, to create and innovate, and to experiment.

So, regularly review Chapters E-8 and E-9 in the Equipping Phase. Both chapters are as much about "being" as "doing." Both chapters will provide you with the foundation to live into your role as a member of the Leadership Board. As a district superintendent, I (Blake) found that most of the congregational conflicts I was called upon to address had their roots in a lack of clarity about roles, not in theological differences. Similarly, both of us (Kay and Blake) have seen countless opportunities to reach new disciples lost because the pastor, staff member, or ministry team leader was not given creative space to innovate because of unclear expectations about authority or accountability. This means when we apply the lessons of accountable and adaptive leadership, clarity matters. The first application of this clarity uses a metaphor of four hats.

Four "Hats"

For members of the simplified, accountable structure to function in a healthy, faithful method, it is extremely important for the members and pastors to clearly understand how this new model works. In the traditional model, there were four committees (finance, trustees, staff-parish relations, and the council/board). Each committee met and operated separately within their specific area of responsibility. In this new model, there are NOT four separate meetings and four separate areas of focus. Instead, the entire new Leadership Board is jointly and simultaneously responsible for all four areas of responsibility. The Leadership Board IS the finance committee, which IS the Staff-Parish Relations Committee, which IS the Trustees. This inclusive responsibility creates a holistic approach. It is a comprehensive approach for leadership and allows for true governess. For example, rather than looking at an issue or decision through only the lens of finance, the Leadership Board can widen the lens and approach the issue or decision through a holistic methodology considering the ramifications of finance, trustees, staff-parish, and the overall church.

Often in training for simplified, accountable structure, we ask attendees to imagine having four hats on the table in front of them. One hat is **finance**. The second is **trustee**.

The third is **staff-parish**. The fourth is **council**. When the topic of finance is on the agenda, everyone picks up and wears their finance hat. Then the finance hat comes off and the trustee hat comes on for a different part of the agenda pertaining to the facility. In other words, every person on the Leadership Board has all responsibilities in all areas. To take the metaphor one step further, think of it another way. In the simplified structure, there actually are no longer four separate hats. There is now just one hat that covers all four areas of responsibility and authority – the single finance, trustee, SPR, council hat.

Meeting Attendance and Executive Session

The *BOD* requires all board meetings to be open meetings. Not only are open meeting a polity requirement, but it is also just good practice to build transparency and trust. The only exception is when the Leadership Board goes into executive session. Some examples that would require a confidential executive session include:

- S/PPR issues, particularly clergy consultation matters, but inclusive to all staffing matters

- Legal negotiations, such as land purchases

- Financial giving records

Note: The appointed pastor cannot be excluded from a Leadership Board meeting in the United Methodist Church as outlined in the *Book of Discipline*. The only exception to that rule is that the Leadership Board, in its role as the S/PPRC, may meet with the district superintendent (and the pastor is to be notified immediately afterwards).

Since Leadership Board meetings are open, it will be important to set the room up to assist people in learning the model more effectively. A best practice is for Leadership Board members to gather around a table and other attendees to sit around the room perimeter. This clearly denotes who is eligible to vote and who is not. It also allows for better control of the agenda. Having the Leadership Board sit at a meeting table where eye contact can be made with the pastor and all of the other board members is also helpful for communication and relationship building.

Staff are eligible to attend but are not required. In fact, we suggest staff (including most associate pastors) not regularly attend Leadership Board meetings. Appointed clergy in United Methodist Churches need to have access to the Leadership Board in its SPRC role, but *access* is different than attending every aspect of every meeting. Remember, the pastor is accountable to the Leadership Board – not staff. The staff is accountable to the pastor. When staff is present at board meetings, they get sucked into conversations. Accountability is more difficult and management conversations are more likely to creep into the agenda. We suggest that key ministry staff occasionally be included on the agenda as guests of the Leadership Board when a relevant topic is being discussed, but not to make a standard practice of it.

In our experience, once the Leadership Board gets up and running, the attendance from church members other than the Leadership Board is rare. There seems to be an inverse relationship between trust in the leadership and attendance in the open sessions of the Leadership Board meeting. When accountable leadership is modeled, the trust of the congregation is built up and people are comfortable engaging in ministry teams (the most important work) rather than church administration. If several people are showing up to observe the Leadership Board meetings, you probably need to be rethinking your communications and transparency.

USING WORK TEAMS

As we stated in Chapter E-5, there will be times that work teams from the Leadership Board will be needed. Examples of the need for work teams might be to work on a preliminary budget or a personnel policy update to bring to the Leadership Board for discussion and approval. Another example might be for a work team to do in-depth study on a new second campus multi-site concept and bring it back to the entire board for discussion and consideration. A third example might be to assemble a work team partner with the pastor on a proposed stewardship campaign to bring back to the board for discussion and approval. Do you see the theme here? They are a small group of people coming together for a specific task or project for a short period of time. Work groups do leg work, detail work, or preliminary work on behalf of the Leadership Board. They work outside the larger Leadership Board on some in-depth projects and then bring it back to the board for discussion and potential approval.

Work teams do not have the authority to make decisions on their own. We (Kay and Blake) have both worked with congregations in which the three SPR specialists (not the recommended model) completed the pastor's evaluation and submitted it to the district office without the knowledge or approval of the full board. Obviously, this is an unacceptable procedure. Three people working on behalf of the Leadership Board do not have responsibility or authority to make these types of decisions. Unfortunately, we have both witnessed this type of organization result in some very unhealthy and unfortunate consequences.

Utilizing work teams provides the Leadership Board the fruitful opportunity to widen the circle of leaders, experience, expertise, and gifts. The Leadership Board is not constrained in using only Leadership Board members for work groups. People from the congregation with expertise or passion around certain topics or projects can be pulled into work groups. It is amazing the number of subject experts that are sometimes in congregations that are never tapped to use their gifts and experiences in the life of the church. You may also have folks from your congregation that would love to work on a short-term project but are not yet ready or able to be a leader, particularly if leadership demands a three-year term of office. Additionally, work teams provide a great opportunity for former Leadership Board members to offer their expertise and experience and for upcoming leaders to engage at the next level as part of a larger philosophy of equipping the next generation of leadership. And, as we suggested earlier, this is also a fantastic opportunity to pull in people from the community to speak into the work of the Leadership Board. This would be especially helpful when it comes to strategic and generative work in connecting the church with the community.

Work teams will have at least one person assigned from the Leadership Board. This provides continuity, alignment, and communication between the work team and the Leadership Board. We recommend that the rest of the work group consist of non-board people. This spreads the work out and allows more people to use their gifts and experience. Being a part of a work team does not require attending a Leadership Board meeting. The Leadership Board member(s) on the team can likely carry the message and work of the group to the Leadership Board. However, it is certainly fine for a work team member to join a board meeting if it would be helpful to the work that is being considered by the Leadership Board.

CHAPTER I-11

Board Meetings that Make a Difference

When they got to Jerusalem, Paul and Barnabas were graciously received by the whole church, including the apostles and leaders. They reported on their recent journey and how God had used them to open things up to the outsiders. Some Pharisees stood up to say their piece. They had become believers, but continued to hold to the hard party line of the Pharisees. "You have to circumcise the pagan converts," they said. "You must make them keep the Law of Moses."

The apostles and leaders called a special meeting to consider the matter. The arguments went on and on, back and forth, getting more and more heated. Then Peter took the floor: "Friends, you well know that from early on God made it quite plain that he wanted the pagans to hear the Message of this good news and embrace it – and not in any secondhand or roundabout way, but firsthand, straight from my mouth. And God, who can't be fooled by any pretense on our part but always knows a person's thoughts, gave them the Holy Spirit exactly as he gave him to us. He treated the outsiders exactly as he treated us, beginning at the very center of who they were and working from that center outward, cleaning up their lives as they trusted and believed him.

"So why are you now trying to out-god God, loading these new believers down with rules that crushed our ancestors and crushed us, too? Don't we believe that we are saved because the Master Jesus amazingly and out of sheer generosity moved to save us just as he did those from beyond our nation? So what are we arguing about?" There was dead silence. No one said a word. With the room quiet, Barnabas and Paul reported matter-of-factly on the miracles and wonders God had done among the other nations through their ministry. The silence deepened; you could hear a pin drop.

Acts 15:4-13

When I was serving as a local church pastor, I (Blake) had the joy of serving alongside so many excellent lay leaders in congregations. While we certainly took our mission seriously, we tried to carry our responsibility with a bit of fun. After a series of multiple back-to-back meetings, one of my mischievous lay leaders presented me with a blue "participation award" ribbon emblazoned with an image of a coffee mug and a statement of deep and abiding truth written in gold foil. The ribbon said, "I survived another meeting that should have been an email." When the purpose of a meeting is misunderstood, preparatory work is inadequate, or the agenda is disorganized, you and your fellow leaders will miss a leadership opportunity. Bad meetings create a lack of ownership in the group's process and actions, encourages apathy, and degrades your leadership capacity as a team.

Changing the number of people around the table is never enough. You also will need to change the conversation at the table. If you move toward a simplified, accountable leadership structure, but continue to use the legacy Robert's Rules of Order agenda (old business, then new business, and filled with endless oral reports), your new Leadership Board will never be able to operate much less lead in a new way. It is time to create an agenda that reflects your missional focus, uses time efficiently, and assumes personal accountability of Leadership Board members to come prepared to lead. As the Leadership Board Chair and pastor plan the meetings for the simplified structure board, great care will need to be taken that meetings are fruitful.

Foundational Principles for Fruitful Meetings

In the Greatest Expedition resource *Strengthening Decision Making and Governance for Supporting New Expeditions*, I (Blake) offered the metaphor of gardening to explain how to design and practice fruitful board meetings. Group conversation, discernment, and decision making is like tending a garden. Gardening takes great seeds, weeding, tending the soil with water and nutrients, and ensuring ample sunlight. Luke 8 shares Jesus' parable of the sower and how the Word of God can produce a hundredfold harvest in the right earth. Similarly, meetings require care and good gardening if you expect them to be fruitful.

The Seeds

Let's start with the seeds: as fans of resources provided by the Lewis Center for Church Leadership at Wesley Theological Seminary, we know well the admonition from Lovett Weems: "Leaders do not need answers. Leaders must have the right questions." While this will take one only so far (after all, answers are eventually needed), the statement does re-frame the work of

leadership. The pastor or the Leadership Board Chair shouldn't be expected to come to every meeting with a set of answers, ready to unload them at the meeting. Why would you need a Leadership Board then? Instead, by asking critical questions, the leader can sow seeds of innovation and discernment amongst the Leadership Board, with the Leadership Board then formulating the prayerful answers and decisions that can take your congregation toward fulfilling the church's mission.

The right questions are the seeds that build up the capacity of the entire congregation to lead. In a March 19, 2005, article in the *Harvard Business Review* titled "How to Design an Agenda for an Effective Meeting," Roger Schwarz offered an excellent tool for building meeting agendas based entirely on the concept of asking the right questions. The article offers several best practices, but here are a few critical suggestions:

- First, he recommends leaders collaborate early and ask the team to contribute items and questions that reflect their needs so that the team will actually be engaged in the meeting. I've attended too many meetings in which I was a superfluous attendee and not a participant because the agenda only reflected the leader's needs and not the needs of the entire group. Further, Schwarz suggests that if the chair doesn't include a requested item, the chair should show her accountability to the team member by explaining why it was excluded. It actually might be a teachable moment in that the requested topic is not yet ripe for discussion, maybe it doesn't fit the steering role of the group, perhaps permission already exists in guiding principles, or the topic is not relevant to the entire board and needs to be handled offline. By explaining why you exclude a request, you are not only showing respect for the board member, but helping equip the team for a higher functioning leadership.

- The next helpful practice that Roger Schwarz uses is to convert agenda topics into action-oriented questions and include a designation of whether the purpose of the agenda item is to simply update folks with information (which I would suggest belongs in a written report in the packet, if possible), seek the group's input for a leader to make a decision, or if the group is being asked to actually make a decision or approve an action itself. Here is the problem that Schwarz is trying to solve: imagine an agenda item that simply says, "Fall Festival." Just looking at the agenda, some people might be coming to the meeting to argue whether the church can afford it this year. Other board members may be wanting to do an evaluation. Yet others think a theme is being selected, another is already ordering the pumpkins, and some Leadership Board members come with suggestions about relocating it to a downtown park location and converting into an evangelism opportunity instead of an insider event. By writing the item as a question, such as "How can we ensure that the Fall Festival is designed to be a Community Bridge Event to connect with potential guests?" you are setting expectations for the agenda item. Creating the right question also lets Leadership Board members know what is expected of them in the meeting. Schwarz writes, "It's difficult for team members to participate effectively if they don't know whether to simply listen, give their input, or be part of the decision-making process. If people think they are involved in making a decision, but you simply want their input, everyone is likely to feel frustrated by the end of the conversation." When the chair and the pastor prepare agenda items as questions, you also are empowering the entire team to help keep the meeting succinct and on track. Leadership Board members can police each other by referring to the agenda question when the topic strays from the question at hand.

Both of these suggestions take an approach to leadership that is collaborative. We see this approach as lifting up the power of "the right questions." By starting with the seeds of excellent questions, even in your agenda creation, you are focusing the power of the gathered wisdom of the Leadership Board.

Weeding

One does not have to be an expert in agriculture to know about weeds. While the right seeds may be planted by a solid agenda, a group is always in danger of heading off into the weeds, either by going off topic or by wasting valuable time. Gardening is a constant battle with weeds that threaten to pull resources from the plants or even overwhelm them by crowding out and smothering what we are trying to grow. As we apply the gardening metaphor to meetings, I think of the weeding task as leading meetings in a way that creates optimal focus on the actual work of the Leadership Board's governance and decision-making work. Here are some recommendations as you do weeding for your meetings:

- **Practice mutual accountability from the beginning.** We are accountable first to Jesus Christ and God's mission for us as a church. If the Leadership Board isn't accountable, then no one will be.

- **Encourage leaders to come to meetings with a sense of curiosity and grace.** Members shouldn't be afraid to ask questions. Outside agendas need to be left at the door. These meetings are God's time.

- **Configure your space to have meaningful conversation.** Gather in a circle so you can see each other. Have Leadership Board members sit at the table and observers sit in chairs along the wall to clearly define those with voting rights. Perhaps light a candle in the center representing Jesus at the table. I (Blake) once attended an administrative council meeting at a church I was coaching where all the board members were seated up front in a row and the "audience" were in rows in front of them. It reminded me of a City Council or School Board meeting where constituents could go up to the microphone to argue their point to the board. Meanwhile, the board members couldn't even see each other. The space and configuration dictated an "us/them" approach to everything that the board did.

- **Use Guiding Principles to reduce the number of decisions the Leadership Board needs to make.** Every time a decision is made, ask if it needs to become a church policy or a new Guiding Principle. A sample of topics to create your own Guiding Principles is in the **Resource** section on page 262. After you build your initial set, remember that Guiding Principles are a living, breathing document that is open to edits and additions as needed to provide permission-giving ministry within healthy boundaries.

- **Create a time docket for your meetings.** One of the recommendations in Roger Schwarz's *HBR* article, "How to Design an Agenda for an Effective Meeting," is to post a time window for every agenda item. This practice of allocating time to each item requires the chair to be realistic with the time available and to calculate how much time can be given to each item. With a nine-person Leadership Board plus the pastor, if everyone is expected to speak for a minute to share their opinion, there is ten minutes used up on an item. If you give an item five minutes, you are expecting no comments. Schwarz shares that when you have an agenda with printed times, board members can then adjust their comments to fit the time allotted. They can suggest that the item be picked up in a future called meeting or maybe a small offline team (aka work group) needs to work up a proposal for the entire board to act upon. I have used a time docket for years and I have found it helps the Leadership Board Chair create expectations for the Leadership Board. Of course, the group can always adjust as needed, but without any printed time allocation, team members can quickly get frustrated or feel like the Leadership Board Chair is railroading the meeting. Notice that in both the matter of the time docket and the use of printed agenda questions with action designations, I am attempting to harness the entire Leadership Board in being gardening partners in the weeding. By setting up clear expectations, the Leadership Board Chair can actually rely on the Leadership Board to self-regulate.

- **Creating clear processes for addressing agenda items.** There are times when your Leadership Board will need to take votes. Consensus is a fine enough goal. It is lovely when the board is all in agreement, but consensus cannot be a requirement for your church to move forward. I (Blake) still remember a classroom exercise during a leadership course at seminary. My classmates and I were all given roles to play and told our hypothetical church would be given a large financial gift. Then, we were set free to figure out what to do with the large bequest. It was a mess! Some wanted to vote, the assigned chairperson wanted unanimous consensus to move forward (a process she declared without input). Even with a bunch of seminarians playing with monopoly money, we all spent over an hour with nothing to show of it but bruised feelings. Since that time, I have seen churches who utilize a unanimous consent requirement become immobilized by a minority of members who held the church's future hostage. In the *HBR* article by Schwarz, he recommends:

Propose a process for addressing each agenda item… Agreeing on a process significantly increases meeting effectiveness, yet leaders rarely do it. Unless the team has agreed on a process, members will, in good faith, participate based on their own process. You've probably seen this in action: some team members are trying to define the problem, other team members are wondering why the topic is on the agenda, and still other members are already identifying and evaluating solutions. When you reach that item during the meeting, explain the process and seek agreement: "I suggest we use the following process. First, let's take about 10 minutes to get all the relevant information on the table. Second, let's take another 10 minutes to identify and agree on any assumptions we need to make. Third, we'll take another 10 minutes to identify and agree on the interests that should be met for any solution. Finally, we'll use about 15 minutes to craft a solution that ideally takes into account all the interests, and is consistent with our relevant information and assumptions. Any suggestions for improving this process?"[7]

Notice in his recommendation that the chair isn't expected to have a single decision-making process and stick to it rigidly for every item and topic. Instead, the process can be customized as needed depending on the matter at hand. For instance, I (Blake) was trained early in my ministry on the "Six Thinking Hats System" created by business consultant Edward de Bono, and I continue to dust it off for brainstorming and innovation work. However, there are plenty of situations where other techniques are more useful. Blake has a whole other toolbox for conflict transformation that involves listening sessions. In his particularly tense times as a judicatory officer, he pulls out Robert's Rules of Order because the congregation simply doesn't have the creative bandwidth for anything else. The point of this recommendation, though, is not to use a particular system, but to be clear about the system the group will be using and have buy-in <u>before</u> getting to the question at hand.

All these recommendations are about tending to the garden that is the Leadership Board members' relationships and emotions during the meeting, so that the decision-making work of the board can be appropriately addressed without getting "stuck in the weeds."

---

7 Roger Schwarz. "How to Design an Agenda for an Effective Meeting." *Harvard Business Review.* March 19, 2005.

Tending the Soil

For church Leadership Boards, tending the soil has to do with adding the healthy nutrients a team needs, such as spiritual formation and leadership equipping. You will notice that our standard agenda includes set aside times for spiritual formation and leadership equipping.

I (Blake) worked with a church that never thought they needed these components and it showed. One leader told me, "We already did church today. Just say a prayer, preacher, and let's move on." NO! If we lose Jesus Christ as foundation of our being and his Great Commission as our mission, I believe that we will cease to be the disciples God is calling us to be. If we simply plow through our agenda without connecting to the Holy Spirit, our leaders will start putting our own wants, desires, and opinions ahead of our Christian mission. Our meetings need some watering from the Wellspring of Life that is Jesus. I went back several years later after a new pastor had encouraged the spiritual life of the congregation's leadership. It was an amazing difference. The meeting started with scripture and spiritually formational sharing, with "business" only discussed once the soul of the team was ready to proceed. Every minute of the meeting that followed was imbued with the Holy Spirit!

And as for leadership equipping, we don't care how "successful" a congregation has been in its past; there is no way past effectiveness guarantees future fruitfulness. The world is moving too quickly for those assumptions, so we must always be a learning community of leaders. Additionally, we expect that new disciples are being added into the Leadership Board every year. Their fresh eyes are part of the new soil that the Leadership Board needs, and they will need equipping on congregational leadership.

Sunlight

One of the challenges of a simplified, accountable leadership structure is that it greatly reduces the number of leaders in positions to know what is going on in a congregation. If the church had five administrative committees and those responsibilities became condensed into a single Leadership Board, you need to communicate five times as much just to maintain your current level of communication. There is also a team-building process that grows with a Leadership Board that can become isolating. All the spiritual formation work and leadership development that the pastor and Leadership

Board do together at the meeting table can easily distance the Leadership Board from the conversations congregants are having. Unless carefully tended, the Leadership Board begins to operate within its own reality.

Supreme Court Justice Louis Brandeis wrote that "sunlight is said to be the best of disinfectants" in a 1913 *Harper's Weekly* article, entitled "What Publicity Can Do." The work of the Leadership Board needs sunlight, for our own accountability to God's mission and to maintain the integrity and trust that is required of spiritual leaders. We believe that every board meeting should be considered an open meeting except for very defined situations, such as staffing matters and legal negotiations (such as the sale of property). By being relentlessly transparent in matters of church leadership in the majority of matters, the congregation will come to respect your Leadership Board in matters that must be confidential.

In the next two chapters, we will encourage you to use additional gatherings outside regular meetings to encourage and model transparency. But transparency is not needed only for occasional meetings. A culture of sunlight and transparency should permeate your Leadership Board's work. We strongly recommend that every board meeting agenda conclude with a communications conversation. The questions that should end every meeting is "What decisions were made? What needs to be communicated to who about those decisions? What is the shared message about the decision? Who is responsible for delivering the message? How will the message be delivered?" Maybe a decision needs to be shared in an email blast written by the Leadership Board Chair, or included in an upcoming congregation-wide meeting, or a video of the pastor on social media. By closing each meeting with a communications agenda item, you are ensuring that the work of the Leadership Board gets sunshine, and that the work of the Leadership Board doesn't become detached from the life of the congregation.

"Consent Calendar Items" and The Board Packet

We have attended too many meetings that require attendees to pick up a dozen handouts before taking their seat at the meeting. Then as we move from one agenda item to another, we are all fumbling with all sorts of new information and budget numbers that we haven't had time to process. That makes for meetings that are inefficient and actually undermining to the leadership of the board members. By sending a Leadership Board packet ahead of time and including some content on a "consent calendar," the Leadership Board Chair and pastor are planting seeds and preparing the Leadership Board members to actually govern and lead.

To plant the right seeds for an effective meeting, a digital packet should be emailed to each Leadership Board member for review a week or so prior to the meeting. This prepares the leaders for what Robert's Rules of Order calls the *consent calendar* section of the agenda.

Sending the packet out ahead of time keeps the Leadership Board from having to take time in the meeting to read reports or listen to long (and often unprepared) oral reports. This also allows plenty of time to fully review the information and be prepared with questions, comments, or concerns as well as the ability to fully participate in conversations and decisions. For instance, the minutes of the previous meeting need only to be edited or approved since the leadership covets to review the minutes before arrival. The financial report needs no approval unless there are changes to the budget that was previously approved or a cash flow question is raised. A single covering motion can take care of any "approval" items in the packet including the minutes. If something needs to be removed from the consent items, you can do that and shift the item later in the agenda.

Preferably, the packet will be prepared by a person in a church administrative position (i.e. operations manager, church secretary) and reviewed by the Leadership Board Chair and pastor before it is distributed. Likely, the administrative person will need to send out reminders to people contributing to the packet. The pastor will hold the administrative person accountable for its timeliness, accuracy, and thoroughness.

The packet's purpose and its contents is to provide information for Leadership Board members to keep them abreast of the current status of the church as well as receive information ahead of the meeting giving each member the time to review. The packet is provided as both a resource for communication and a tool of preparation. Members of the Leadership Board should have read the packet and come prepared to either vote for approval of the items or to move the items toward the discussion phase of the agenda.

Below is a list of the recommended contents for the board meeting packet:

☑ **Agenda**

See the agenda section in this chapter for more information.

☑ **Covenant**

The signed Leadership Covenant is an ongoing reminder.

☑ **Vital Signs**

Vital signs provide a dashboard of the latest information, metrics and trends that are extremely important for leaders to know and understand. Vital signs include: worship attendance, professions of faith, small group participation, service participation and financial giving. The church is already tracking this information and submitting it to the general church for tracking and statistics. To start, the Leadership Board may need to see the past five or ten years' trends if this is new information to the members. Subsequently, the year's trends and how they compare to the previous year is probably adequate. All this information can be obtained from your conference dashboard or your district office.

> Note: We are also seeing a movement away from worship attendance as the go-to vitality gauge to other barometers such engagement (i.e.number of people engaged in ministry beyond worship) and/or development and deployment of leaders and disciples. It isn't so much about which signs of vitality to use, but rather pick two or three vitality signs and monitor them closely to observe.

☑ Describe-ables

Not all fruits of ministry will show up in the metrics of the vital signs mentioned above. Those fruits are what we refer to as the describe-ables or the stories of vital ministries. What lives are being touched by the ministries of the church? How are people growing in their faith? How is the church impacting the community in the name of Christ? The pastor will provide any pertinent describe-ables in the packet for the Leadership Board.

☑ Guests

This may be new information to capture. Record the number of first-time guests the church hosts each week. Also, record the number of second-time guests each week. These are important numbers to know and track. While numbers do not tell us the whole story, they are indeed early indicators. These two particular numbers help us catch a glimpse of how effectively three of our systems are working: evangelism, hospitality, and connection. *(see IMPACT! for more information on these systems.)* If we are not having first-time guests, we know the church is struggling with evangelism. If the church is having first-time guests, but not returning guests, we know we likely have either a hospitality and/or connection issue which needs to be addressed.

☑ Minutes

Minutes of the previous board meeting as submitted by the acting recording secretary.

☑ Financials

These reports should include a budget vs actual report for each category or ministry area (not each line item) and a comprehensive balance sheet. There may be a note attached from the treasurer if there is something out of the ordinary or noteworthy for the Leadership Board to know or understand. For example, some Leadership Board members might panic at the summer slump in generosity numbers. The treasurer might include an income statement from the previous year showing the trend is to be expected and the church is on track to match or exceed last year's giving numbers.

☑ Goals

The pastor will provide a written update on goal progress. While the written report provides the leadership board with a more thorough and perhaps more time efficient glimpse of progression of the goals, this is also a time for questions and statements of accountability, support, encouragement, and celebration. This is often where there is a deep shift for Leadership Board members to have this type of conversation with their pastor. Therefore, accountability is sometimes not practiced. This is an extremely important part of the accountable leadership responsibility of the Leadership Board. Don't step over your responsibility!

☑ Reports

While we do not suggest or recommend requiring the inclusion of reports, there may be a group that just feels strongly compelled to share information with the Leadership Board. A group can write a report to include in the packet with the permission of the Leadership Board Chair. If a church must have reports, one suggestion is to have a standard report form with some simple questions that clearly asks at the beginning if the special report is an update or if some sort of Leadership Board action is required/requested. This may keep reporting ministry teams on mission and clear about why they are reporting. It might also help them identify that their request does not even need to go to the Leadership Board. In one church I served, I (Blake) created a simple standardized reporting form that was available online. One of the first questions, after the contact information, required the reporting individual or group to click a box indicating whether the report required action on the part of the church council or if it was "for information only." It also required submitters of proposals to describe any financial implications. See a sample reporting form in the **Resource** section on Page 268.

☑ Special Reports

From time to time, there may be special reports, information, bids, etc. which need to be shared with the Leadership Board. For example, there may be roof bids included for a planned capital expenditure. If the Leadership Board or a work group is working on a new policy, a Leadership Board member might include some preliminary work towards the project as a springboard for the work of the entire Leadership Board. For the pastor's annual evaluation there may be information inserted into the packet.

The Agenda

The agenda is a guide for the most effective and efficient use of time and resources of the Leadership Board members. It is a plan of action. Working the plan allows us to be good stewards of our time and resources. Agendas are crucial and a necessary tool for effective, efficient leadership. Without an agenda, conversations will drift off topic and we might not tend to the top priorities.

In the beginning, the Leadership Board may not be as efficient as they will become over time as they practice the model. You will likely come to a point where the Leadership Board can finish their meeting in about 90 minutes. Of course, there will be times when longer meetings are needed, but most will be able to work within the 90-minute format. The agenda consists of three major portions that could be chunked into about thirty-minute segments. Spend one-third of your time in spiritual and leadership development. Spend one-third of your time on goal and people evaluation. Spend the remaining one third of your time on problem solving and generative work.

As noted above, we suggest creating a "docket" format that includes a running time for each agenda item, so that the Leadership Board members can appropriately budget their discussion time. Estimating a realistic amount of time for each item requires some preparation work. If you have a dozen members on your Leadership Board, but only schedule five minutes for the discussion of an item, then you are expecting everyone to have well under 30 seconds to speak. That does not include the time taken to vote or come to consensus on an issue.

In preparing the agenda, the Leadership Board Chair can send a notice out to Leadership Board members asking if there are any items that might need to be discussed. We say "might" because not every item requested needs to be on a Leadership Board agenda. Some matters need to be held off-line or by a work team or other group before it is ripe for inclusion in the Leadership Board's agenda. Some items are simply not the work of the Leadership Board. If the matter is properly before the Leadership Board, then the Leadership Board Chair should do some organizational preparation: first, get clarity of the purpose of an item (is it about making a decision, answering a question, or simply sharing information?), second, estimate the time required, and third, prepare a proposed process for addressing the matter (such as taking a few minutes a discussion followed by a vote or suggesting a new guiding principle to handle similar matters in the future). Be sure to make the agenda preparation a collaborative effort of the pastor and the Leadership Board Chair. Neither of these two people should ever be surprised by a topic at a meeting!

You will want to meet monthly in the beginning. In a year or two, you may be able to move to bi-monthly meetings. Kay even has worked with churches that have used the simplified, accountable structure for years and have quarterly meetings. But in the beginning while setting up policies, procedures, guiding principles, and setting the stage for a culture of accountability and adaptive leadership, the Leadership Board will likely need to meet monthly. Note that even if your Leadership Board has created a tradition of less frequent meetings, when you receive a new pastor, the Leadership Board will need to switch back to monthly (or even more frequent) meetings for several months to a year.

On each and every agenda for the Leadership Board (including all other church agendas), print the mission (making disciples…), vision, and core values of the church. This is a great reminder of the basis and focus of our conversations and decisions. One church I (Kay) worked with had large posters printed with their mission, vision, and core values and posted them in the room where the Leadership Board normally met. Not only was this a great reminder for the Leadership Board members, but every person who used that same room was also reminded.

In this chapter you will find a sample agenda and an annotated explanation of each agenda item. This basic format can be used for each meeting, with the understanding that some meetings, such as the annual pastoral assessment, may require adjustments in the schedule and flow of the agenda. Notice the order of the agenda. It might appear as though the agenda is reversed and familiar items are missing from your typical board agenda. This is very intentional. The items of most importance are at the top. If the first few items were placed as additions to the bottom of the agenda, we would never have time for those items!

Also, notice there are no oral reports from committees on this agenda. This is certainly intentional and not an oversight. The purpose of the Leadership Board is not to hear reports. The purpose of the board is to govern, guide, and set policies by being the congregation's lead body for stewardship, strategic, generative, and accountability. The day-to-day ministries which make up the activities of the church should always reflect the congregational goals articulated by the Leadership Board. Those objectives established by staff to relate to the goals all roll up into the goal (accountability) report from the pastor. If the Leadership Board spends time hearing about each and every ministry, they are in management mode on the dance floor. The job of the Leadership Board is to be in the balcony with a missional focus, overseeing the entire "dance floor" of vital ministry and the congregation's relationship with the community.

When I (Blake) served as an executive pastor in a large multi-staff congregation, I would often attempt to explain staff responsibilities in comparison to a naval ship's executive officer: I, as the executive pastor, was in charge of the ship… the senior pastor was the captain responsible for the ocean. Adapting this staffing metaphor to the leadership of a governing board, the simplified, accountable Leadership Board is responsible for the ocean – the direction and mission of the "ship" of the church and its impact on individual lives, neighborhoods and communities, and the larger world. Your agenda needs to reflect this larger role and tremendous responsibility.

Sample Agenda for Simplified, Accountable Leadership

Following, you will find a sample agenda for your review. A sample agenda can also be found in the **Resource** section on Page 267. After the sample agenda, you will find an explanation of each agenda item.

First United Methodist Church
Leadership Team Meeting
Date _____

Our Mission: To make new disciples of Jesus Christ for the transformation of the world.

Our Vision: Each of us at FUMC is on a journey to grow closer to God, to be more like Jesus, and to be filled with the Holy Spirit. No matter where you are in your walk with Christ, you are invited to journey and grow with us, through the power of the Holy Spirit, so that we can fulfill God's commission.

Core Values: Excellence, Evangelism, Engagement, Equipping, Expansion and Encouragement.

6:00pm	Opening Prayer	Jennifer Jackson, Chair
6:00pm	Spiritual Formation	David Dent
6:15pm	Leadership Equipping	Carol Clark
6:30pm	Review of New People	Pastor Taylor
6:35pm	Goal Review and Accountability Conversation	Pastor Taylor
6:50pm	Packet and Consent Calendar Items	
6:55pm	Generative and Strategic Work	Jennifer Jackson
	6:55: Item #1	
	7:05: Item #2	
	7:15: Item #3	
7:25	Communication	
7:30	Closing Prayer	Maria Martínez

Next Meeting is (date) _____

Explanation and Responsibility of Agenda Items

Prayer

Each person on the Leadership Board takes turns giving the opening prayer. As servant leaders and disciples, we need to become comfortable praying in a group. This may also be a time to ask for personal prayer requests from fellow Leadership Board members.

Spiritual Formation

Again, take turns allowing each member to share. Relate the devotion to the leadership equipping topic or something on the agenda if possible. Another option is a time of spiritual development related specifically to spiritual leadership. This might be a time to challenge leaders to share where they are seeing God at work in their own lives this past week. This helps prepare them to share their faith in their day-to-day life. (see *Get Their Name* by Farr, Kotan, & Anderson for more information on sharing your faith in small groups.) This is a time to dive deep and help our leaders mature in their faith and grow in their knowledge. Do not glaze over this important time in the faith development of the Leadership Board collectively and each member's individual spiritual journey. Bring topics that challenge the members and promote dialogue. Refer back to the list of topics created as suggestions for this time completed at the previous fall retreat. Allow about 15 minutes.

Leadership Equipping

Yep, you guessed it. The responsibility for leadership development is shared. Rather than choosing a random subject, be intentional in brainstorming leadership equipping and development topics and resources identified at the strategic ministry planning retreat. Leadership Board members can then choose a topic from the list the group collectively decided to dive into that the person leading the teaching time is passionate about. This approach provides ample preparation time, too. Make this an interactive time for the Leadership Board. Do not shy away from challenging subjects or diving deep into subjects or materials. Remember, this time is to develop and grow our leaders who are modeling leadership for the congregation. Allow about 15 minutes.

New People

Take a look at the report on the number of first and second-time guests. What is noticed?

Are there improvements to celebrate? Are their gaps to be addressed? Questions of accountability will be directed to the pastor.

Goal Review and Accountability Conversation

Remember those annual goals set at the strategic ministry planning retreat? The pastor will provide an update on the progress of each goal. Friends, this is really where the rubber hits the road! This is where accountability most likely will need to kick in through adaptive change. Board members are not likely experienced in the practice of holding their pastor accountable. If progress is lacking, ask about it. Talk about it! How can we be encouraging? What support is needed? Are there gaps in training or resources from either the pastor or staff? Is the pastor having trouble holding staff and leaders accountable? If the goal progress is not on track, what progress is expected by the next meeting? Be specific in setting up expectations. Be sure to also acknowledge and celebrate progress and accomplishments!

Packet

This is the time of the meeting where items are reviewed and/or discussed from the (electronic) packet that was sent out the week prior to the meeting. Questions or observations about vital signs would be discussed or reviewed at this time if needed. The usual method of working through most of the leadership packet is a Consent Calendar. A Consent Calendar methodology should include all the agenda items that a Leadership Board needs to receive for archival reasons or to vote on for legal or *Book of Discipline* purposes. The minutes of the last meeting are an example of a calendar consent item. Other items could include the signing of a contract that has already been approved or regular shifting of funds between accounts. The Leadership Board Chair will ask if there are any corrections to the consent calendar agenda, if anything needs to be removed from what is presented in the packet, for corrections or further discussion under *Generative and Strategic Work*, a future meeting, or by common agreement to adjust the agenda. If not, a covering motion for approval will be called for and seconded for all items that remain on the consent calendar. A vote to approve will then be taken. This is more a formality than anything. Yet, it is important to have an accurate historical document of the governing decisions of the Leadership Board. For some items, especially financial matters and statistical data, a short oral description may prove very helpful. This also addresses the complexity of learning and processing styles among Leadership Board members. The focus of any oral report should be to frame a fruitful and effective discussion. Beware, though – it is easy to get off track and start long discussions of items in the consent calendar, which voids its purpose and distracts the Leadership Board from the more difficult – and more meaningful – generative and strategic work of the board.

Generative and Strategic Work

While the previous two sections involved accountability to goals and understanding the church's health and missional fruitfulness, this agenda time may be used to reflect on the value of the goals themselves. What goals may need to be added, adapted or changed to meet the changing ministry landscape and the needs of the mission field? What strategic work is required to keep us in alignment to our mission and vision? For our generative work, what is changing in our culture that we need to adapt with in order to remain relevant to the people in our community we are trying to reach?

Chapter I-12 offers a January through December flow of work for boards. Many of the items of focus in this annual calendar fit into this agenda item, including the annual pastor's assessment, budget preparation, the stewardship campaign, and organizing the strategic ministry planning retreat. This type of work allows us to be proactive rather than reactive. This is the generative and strategic work of the accountable leadership that may likely be new or at least not formally identified as the rhythm of the church to become or stay contextually relevant for vital ministry to occur. This is also likely the work that did not previously have the needed attention or was off the radar of the former church council in the traditional model.

Additionally, reports or items pulled from the Consent Calendar may need to be discussed. There also could be an issue that brings about the need to establish a new guiding principle to allow ministry to flow without the Leadership Board's approval or intervention. It might be that a new policy or manual is being created and needs to be reviewed and approved by the Leadership Board. It might be an issue that could be handled by a guiding principle, but the principle has not yet been created and needs to be created. It could be a decision which fell just outside a guiding principle and needs to be handled as an exception.

This portion of the agenda provides space and time for the Leadership Board to address any places the Leadership Board is stuck and needs to work through and when individual team members may have questions, comments, concerns that need to be addressed for the overall good of the congregation as it pertains to church governance. This is also a time for Leadership Board members to ask for help from other board members if they are stuck in individual or work groups assignments from the Leadership Board such as the annual budget.

Beware that this time in the agenda does not become a catch-all for miscellaneous discussion with no structure or plan. Take time to get feedback from the Leadership Board members so issues or questions can be placed on the agenda before your meeting so that the Leadership Board's time can be used efficiently.

Communication

While a few items, such as personnel issues, require that the Leadership Board go into executive session and the minutes preserved as confidential, the overwhelming majority of your Leadership Board's business is designed to be shared. However, Leadership Boards get so wrapped up in their discussion that they forget to take the important step of communicating their actions and strategic work to the larger congregation. So, every meeting should end with a time to discuss your communication plan:

- What decisions were made tonight? This ensures everyone is on the same page and is well documented in the minutes.

- Who needs to hear those decisions? What needs to be shared from this meeting?

- Who is responsible to communicate the decisions and when? How will the responsible person know about their responsibility to communicate if they are not at the Leadership Board table? What will be the methods used (email, newsletters, etc.)?

- How can the board support the ministry of the pastors, staff and ministry teams by keeping the congregation abreast of the board's strategic priorities and work toward the church's mission?

Clarity about what should be communicated keeps the Leadership Board on task, places the work of the Leadership Board during the meeting in context and connects the Leadership Board to the larger congregation. See Chapter I-13 on Communicating for a larger perspective on connecting the work of the Leadership Board to the larger church and community.

Prayer

Everyone takes turns providing the closing prayer. This is a great time to check-in with prayer partners, too (for information about Leadership Board prayer partners, see the section on leadership retreats in Chapter I-12).

CHAPTER I-12

A Year in Leadership

[Jesus said,] "Is there anyone here who, planning to build a new house, doesn't first sit down and figure the cost so you'll know if you can complete it? If you only get the foundation laid and then run out of money, you're going to look pretty foolish. Everyone passing by will poke fun at you: 'He started something he couldn't finish.' Or can you imagine a king going into battle against another king without first deciding whether it is possible with his ten thousand troops to face the twenty thousand troops of the other? And if he decides he can't, won't he send an emissary and work out a truce? Simply put, if you're not willing to take what is dearest to you, whether plans or people, and kiss it good-bye, you can't be my disciple."

Luke 14:28-33

Before you know it, it is the end of the year AGAIN. It just slips up on you. We all have the best of intentions of making this upcoming year our best ever. Sometimes we even put some initial steps in place. Other times we have great intentions, but we just never quite instigate the plan to make it happen. Time and time again, we see councils/boards set some really great goals for the year. They are worded just so. Then they are packed away ... until the end of the year. Then someone mentions them and we pull them back out to review. Upon review, we find we missed accomplishing our well-intentioned goals for the year. We simply did not keep them on the front burner directing our focus, time, resources, and energy. We wanted them to happen, but we missed the intentionality in guiding our church towards the accomplishment of our goals. So, we encourage you to plan your year in leadership, keeping your goals in front of you the entire year, and being intentional on how you use your meeting time.

Leadership Rhythm

There is a natural rhythm to sound leadership. When a natural rhythm is discovered and practiced by the Leadership Board, pastors, lay leaders and the congregation are usually much more comfortable with a simplified, accountable leadership structure. A natural rhythm provides much desired transparency and missional clarification. Sound rhythm helps manage healthy expectations, establish good communication methods, and sets a clear congregational direction. Rhythm promotes growth in leadership and spiritual maturity – vitally important since a congregational Leadership Board partners with the pastor as spiritual leaders of the church.

The stewardship, strategic, generative, and accountability functions of board governance is itself a rhythm. As you look at the monthly flow of meeting topics in this chapter, notice how these four beats show up month after month as the Leadership Board focuses on stewardship work (care and management of resources), planning and alignment (strategic work), creatively assessing its work toward fulfilling God's vision (generative work), and taking responsibility for leading the congregation in its mission of making disciples (accountability). For reminders on these four key functions, refer back to Chapter E-8.

There is also a natural rhythm of the regular "church stuff" (i.e. pastoral review, budget preparation) we tend to year after year at specific times of the year. A new natural rhythm develops when we are able to artfully combine the new work of the simplified, accountable leadership (stewardship, strategic, generative, and accountability) with the regular business of congregational life.

Has your church found its rhythm? Please allow us to offer some insights on the rhythm of accountable leadership in the life of a church. We have found this rhythm to work with most churches, but feel free to adapt it to meet your needs and context. For instance, since your Leadership Board probably includes the duties and responsibilities of the staff-parish relations committee, your annual conference may have specific due dates for assessment and consultation paperwork. Once the Leadership Board has found its rhythm, worship planning and ministry objectives will more likely be able to find their rhythm to sync with the Leadership Board.

January

Start the year with an intentional and well-organized orientation and formational time for new Leadership Board members. This will also help the continuing Leadership Board members "reset" and be reminded about the congregation's vision, the principles of accountable leadership, and the mutual expectations of Leadership Board members. There is a lot of organizational work to complete at this first meeting:

- This is a time of reviewing the expectations of leadership and practices of the board for new people. Finalize and have each Leadership Board member sign the leadership covenant (if this was not completed at the strategic ministry planning retreat).

- Set the board's calendar of meetings, town hall meetings, and annual strategic ministry planning retreat for the year if you haven't done this already.

- This is the first time newly elected board members are joining you at a regularly scheduled meeting. Make sure they feel welcome, and they have received the appropriate training and resources.

- At the first gathering of the new Leadership Board and each subsequent year, the board will need to elect the "chair of trustees" as required by the *Book of Discipline*. It is recommended the Leadership Board Chair serve as the "chair of the trustees" for legal purposes and disciplinary requirements. (In most states, the Board of Trustees are considered the Board of Directors for purposes of incorporation with your secretary of state.)

- A person (recording secretary) will need to be named or a rotation will need to be set up for taking minutes at each meeting.

- Each Leadership Board member could be assigned a month to communicate to the congregation through newsletters, social media, and/or worship. Use the opportunity to share about the general work of the Leadership Board, offer spiritual equipping from a lay leader's perspective, and keep the Leadership Board connected relationally and emotionally to the larger congregation.

- This is also a great time to assign responsibility for spiritual and leadership development times in the upcoming months of Leadership Board meetings.

As you begin your new year, be sure to have a commissioning of service for the Leadership Board in congregational worship if it was not done in December. The congregation needs to be able to see their leaders, and this commissioning also serves as an opportunity to teach the congregation about the responsibilities of spiritual leadership. Remember to also acknowledge and thank the Leadership Board members and Nominating Committee members who have just rolled off.

February

Easter is coming! This would be a perfect time to ask accountability questions of your pastor around expectations of first-time guests and returning guests for the upcoming Lenten season. You also need to be sure to support the spiritual health of your Leadership Board members. It is easy to focus on the business of doing church while forgetting that our real business is Jesus Christ. So, perhaps plan a spiritual retreat for the pastor and Leadership Board to kick off the Lenten season. The spiritual retreat is a time for fasting, prayer, relationship building, and spiritual discernment.

At the end of January, your congregation submitted statistical end-of-year information on membership, ministry, and financial health. Your February meeting is a great opportunity to compare trend lines over multiple years. Your district or conference office can get you charts that track annual statistics back over a decade. What is growing? What is shrinking? Where are the gaps?

If you run a January-December financial year, you should have closed your books by the February meeting. Take the opportunity to look at the rhythm of giving and expenses over the year and be sure to fulfill your fiduciary responsibilities concerning church finances, taxes, audits, etc.

In order to get ahead of work schedules, midwinter is usually the best time to begin preparing for any needed facility improvements that may likely be completed during the spring or summer months.

March

It is a good idea to have three or four gatherings (i.e., town hall meetings) with the congregation to keep lines of communication open and demonstrate transparent accountable leadership. March might be a good time to schedule a congregational Town Hall, perhaps connected to your Lenten theme. Leadership Board members should share about the state of the church, pray together for the church's neighborhood mission field, celebrate wins, and provide a progress report on the church goals. Take some time for feedback, which could include intentional "table talk" (imagine several round tables with a different Leadership Board member at each table, asking a set group of questions and doing intentional listening) or other methods that have proved fruitful in your context. The purpose of these town halls is to inform, encourage, receive feedback, and build trust.

April

With first quarter financial numbers now in, your Leadership Board should assess the congregation's finances in greater detail. Is the church on stable footing as you begin to head into the summer months when giving is traditionally lower? What will the stewardship or generosity campaign be for this fall? Who will lead the campaign? What preparations need to be made? Is a temporary work group needed to help prepare with the pastor?

Consider a time for the Leadership Board to serve together in the community as an action of missional leadership and team building.

May

Review policies and procedures. Are all job descriptions complete? Do any need to be updated or revised? Are there any updates needed in the employee manual? Are guiding principles in place (see chapter E-7)? Do any of these need to be revised or updated? Are the building usage policies updated? Are there any missing policies or procedures that would make everyday church life work more efficiently or effectively?

June

We are now halfway through the year. A more in-depth review of goals might be helpful. Are we on track to meet all goals? Where are the gaps? What shifts need to be made? Are more resources needed? Do we have the right personnel in the right place to accomplish the goals? How can the Leadership Board be encouraging and supportive while practicing accountability?

July

July is the usual time that new pastoral appointments often begin in the United Methodist Church. In our book *IMPACT! Reclaiming the Call of Lay Ministry,* we devote an entire chapter to the huge evangelism opportunity of receiving a new pastor, and offer some tips for leadership teams to be "co-owners" of the pastor transition process alongside a new pastor. If you are receiving a new pastor, the June meeting will probably be about supervising the work of various teams assigned particular tasks:

- Prepare a welcome celebration for the new pastor and her family, if applicable

- Share a pastoral transition with the wider community and local media as an evangelism opportunity.

- Organize a process of intentional relationship building and orientation through cottage meetings or listening sessions with congregation members for July, August, and September.

- Schedule a series of appointments and make introductions for the new pastor to meet with community leaders and strategic church members.

- Work with the current and incoming pastor to share information, congregational metrics, and community demographics.

As the Nominations Committee begins to meet, what gifts would be helpful for the Leadership Board members to have in the next season of the church's life? Notify the

Committee of requests the Leadership Board might have. What would a potential new Leadership Board member need to know about the commitment and expectations of being a Leadership Board member before accepting the nomination?

This is a great time to ask accountability questions of the lead pastor around plans on reaching new people during the Back-to-School and Advent seasons.

This might be the time for another Town Hall meeting. While not usually a "high attendance" month in many churches, July could provide a time for your Leadership Board to engage with your deeply engaged members and leaders.

Use this time to gather information, such as community opportunities to reach new people, ideas to launch or grow ministries, and gauge what areas might bring excitement or passion. Use the information you get in your fall strategic ministry planning retreat to set your upcoming goals and priorities.

If you have received a new pastor, use the July meeting to help the pastor understand how your church is using the simplified, accountable leadership structure. It is one thing to see the simplified structure on a piece of paper, it is quite another to experience it in practice. The enculturation of a new pastor to the church's mission and vision, the congregation's guiding principles, the concepts of accountable leadership, and the board's template agenda is all squarely the responsibility of the governing board in its capacity as both the church council and the staff-parish relations committee. If the new pastor has no prior experience in SAS, seriously consider a SAS certified coach to work with the pastor and Leadership Board Chair to ensure a healthy and thorough introduction and implementation.

August

This is a very important month! The Leadership Board will be making final preparations for the strategic ministry planning retreat and conducting the retreat in August or early September. Are staff evaluations complete and any compensation change requests received from the pastor for budgetary considerations?

If you have received a new pastor, the listening sessions or cottage meetings should be in full swing. What has your new pastor learned about the congregation? Also, district superintendents will often check in with the Leadership Board Chair (if it is also the SPRC contact as recommended) to inquire how the first few weeks of the new appointment are going. How is the Leadership Board helping your new pastor connect to the congregation, to community leaders, and to the larger mission field?

September

The strategic ministry planning retreat will be conducted. (Note: budget accordingly.) We recommend that the retreat is led by a neutral third party so that the chair and pastor as well as other Leadership Board members can fully participate in the retreat and the Leadership Board will not be swayed by the retreat leader. There will be a time of review and analysis of the current year as well as planning for the upcoming year. The end of this chapter outlines more about the retreat and its objectives, but please note that the "work-product" of a strategic ministry planning retreat is about so much more than just getting plans on paper. The retreat is a time for team building. It is also a time of play and fun. Do not forget to begin work on the new leadership covenant for the upcoming year as well as your leadership development and spiritual formation topics. Your Leadership Board has learned a lot over the past several months about how to be healthy, accountable leaders of your faith community. Use some time to make sure your learnings are incorporated into the leadership covenant and identify how best to invest in the leadership.

For a comprehensive resource on planning, implementing, and following up for a strategic ministry planning retreat, be sure to check out *Strategy Matters* by Kotan and Willard. You will find it to be an invaluable resource in tying accountable leadership, the leadership rhythm offered in this resource, and details on creating a strategic ministry planning retreat that leaders actually want to attend.

In many annual conferences, early fall is when you begin work on your charge conference documents. Work teams may need to be deployed to work on different aspects of the report. That means you may assign a Leadership Board member to pull together a work team to get assistance from church members or staff with expertise outside the Leadership Board to complete different portions of the report such as the facilities and finance reports. Eventually, your entire Leadership Board will need to approve and recommend the charge conference packet to the charge conference.

The Leadership Board will also need to coordinate with the independent Committee on Nominations and Leadership Development on preparing the slate of new Leadership Board members for approval at the charge conference. Chapter E-6 offers some tips to assist your Nominating Committee in fulfilling this important task. The current Leadership Board will want to offer a copy of the current leadership covenant to the Nominations Committee so potential new leaders will have an idea of the leadership expectations. Also be sure to provide the date of the strategic ministry planning retreat so the incoming leaders can also participate. If the Leadership Board is bumping up against some deeply ingrained leadership culture of the past, the Leadership Board Chair may want to share this with the Nominations Committee so that this could be covered in the interview process and hopefully eliminate future issues.

October

Depending on your annual conference calendar, this may be the time of year for the pastor's evaluation by the Leadership Board to be submitted to the district superintendent. Since the goal evaluation was completed the month prior at the strategic ministry planning retreat, the Leadership Board is now fully prepared for the evaluation. The Leadership Board has evaluative information rather than personal preferences and experiences for the basis of the evaluation.

After the upcoming year's God-sized goals are set at the Leadership Board's strategic ministry planning retreat, the pastor will be working on the objectives with the staff and ministry teams. This is most likely in an off-site staff retreat. (Note: Budget accordingly.) Once the objectives are set, budget requests can be made available to the Leadership Board for consideration via the pastor.

The second Sunday in October is Clergy Appreciation Day. How will the Leadership Board acknowledge and celebrate their clergy? How are the staff, ministry leaders, and other servant leaders celebrated?

November

The upcoming year's budget needs to be in its final revisions based on the stewardship campaign and the staff/ministry team leaders' budgetary requests. How is your budget aligning with the mission, vision, and strategic goals of the church? If you are not funding your God-sized goals, then it will be very hard to hold your pastor accountable to the results.

This might be the charge conference month if you have not already had one in October.

For the newly elected Leadership Board members, make sure you are providing thorough training to get them off to a solid start. This includes supplying them with the latest copy of *Mission Possible* and attendance at an equipping workshop on SAS. Make sure this is not merely a one-hour overview workshop. Get your leaders to the deep dive workshop that is usually three to five hours. If your district or conference is not providing this training, reach out to us at kay@kaykotan.com and we will be sure to find training options for your leaders.

December

In early December, it is a great time to hold a "state of the church" gathering with the congregation. This is a time to review the year and share goals for the upcoming year. Celebrate the fruitful ministries and accomplishments of the year!

In December or January, your Leadership Board will probably need to complete consultation documents for the bishop and cabinet in consideration of the pastor's appointment. This work is both sacred and confidential. Only elected Leadership Board members (identified as staff/pastor-parish relations committee (S/PPRC) members) should be present in discussions and the eventual vote recommending that your pastor return or move.

The Annual Strategic Planning Retreat

There are those that might cringe (maybe you did just now) at the thought of a leadership retreat. But allow us to challenge you a bit. In our experience, this can be one of the most transformational times in the life of the Leadership Board and thus the congregation. The focused time away evaluating the current year and seeking discernment on direction and its leadership of the upcoming year is absolutely critical. Without this crucial gathering time, we find Leadership Boards have more difficulty with focused leadership. Those Leadership Boards that have gotten into the rhythm of annual strategic ministry planning retreats have not only begun to look forward to them, but they are great fun that builds excitement for the entire church.

As best practices, we offer a couple of thoughts for your consideration in planning your annual strategic ministry planning retreat.

- First, make sure the date goes on your Leadership Board members' calendar early. Stress the importance of each and every member attending. Don't forget about the newly elected board members. All voices and thoughts matter!

- Second, we highly recommend taking the Leadership Board away from the church and out of town for the retreat. Make it an overnight experience if possible. Ideally, we find a 24-hour experience from Friday night through Saturday to work best for most. Incorporate some team building exercises and playing together into the agenda. I (Kay) also like to assign prayer partners leading up to and during the retreat. Plan times for prayer partners to pray with and for one another at the retreat, too.

- Third, we recommend having an outsider lead your retreat if at all possible. Someone leading the group from outside allows everyone (including the pastor and all Leadership Board members) to be able to participate more fully without having to lead. This allows more of an immersion opportunity for everyone. The core of your time at the retreat is strategic ministry planning, which is outlined in Chapter E-9.

The annual strategic ministry planning retreat of our Leadership Board is the time for deep evaluation and strategic planning. In Kay's book, *Gear Up: Nine Essential Processes for the Optimized Church*, she goes into detail on strategic ministry planning (one of her favorite topics). Also, refer to the book she co-authored with Ken Willard, *Strategy Matters*. In Chapter E-9, you will find a list of the five primary components of strategic ministry planning that will guide your work:

- Mission   — To make disciples etc.
- Vision
- Core Values - 5 core values.
- God-sized Goals
- Objectives/Strategies.

Retreat Objectives

At the strategic planning retreat, evaluate the church's impact in reaching the mission. How many new people are coming to know Jesus Christ through the life of the congregation? How are people growing in their faith? Take some time at the retreat for spiritual discernment amongst the Leadership Board members. How is the Leadership Board discerning God's will and direction for the church? How is each member individually and collectively spending time with God throughout the year in this discernment? Are any needed shifts needed in leadership direction because of the team discernment?

Next, review the vision statement. The vision statement should be a guiding focus for the congregation. It should provide energy and momentum. Is the vision statement now a reality? Is it time for a new vision statement? What led you to that conclusion? It is often helpful to review the life cycle of your church to evaluate the vision's effectiveness in driving the church. Vision is needed for a growing church. If vision is not driving your church, it will soon be in decline or further decline. We recommend familiarizing yourself with the Bullard Lifecycle of the Church and using it for a vision evaluation.

Now review the current year's goals. God-sized goals are evaluated monthly with the pastor at the Leadership Board meetings, but this is a time to dive deeper. A great deal of the time at the retreat will be spent on setting goals for the upcoming year. What steps need to be taken to live into the vision of the church and being more faithful in its mission? Typically, there are three to five overall church goals identified each year.

Consider what training might be needed. What gaps were identified in meetings on topics discussed by the Leadership Board in the previous year? What topics are missing completely? Are the new members coming onto the Leadership Board familiar with the structure, policies, responsibilities, etc.? Bring in outside information or trainers, if needed and budget accordingly, to make sure everyone is up to speed on what they need to know and so that every Leadership Board member is equipped to be the best possible leader for the church.

Allow us to offer a friendly reminder. Creating strategies/objectives are not the work of the Leadership Board. This is the work of the staff and ministry team leaders. If you are talking about specific ministries or dates, you are managing and not governing. Stay out of the weeds of management! Stay in your governing lane. Remember, if you aren't driving in the governing lane, then no one is! Your job as the Leadership Board is to discern the congregation's purposeful *why* and define *where* the church needs to head to be faithful. *What* and *how* is the responsibility of the staff and ministry team leaders.

Spiritual and Prayer Time at the Retreat

Spend some in-depth time in spiritual development with the Leadership Board at the retreat. This might include a time unpacking the difference of being a secular leader versus being a church leader. Consider what scripture might be helpful in diving deep into these distinctions. Have the Leadership Board share where they are in their spiritual journey. Ask them to suggest spiritual development and formation topics they would like to spend time on in the spiritual development times when the Leadership Board meets monthly. Ask each Leadership Board member to commit to an area of spiritual growth in the upcoming year. This whole process may be uncomfortable for some leaders. This may be the first time these types of questions and conversations have taken place. Be patient and grace-filled around this conversation. However, do not shy away from it. Again, these are your spiritual leaders of the church and it is important to help them grow and mature in their faith and model it for others.

Prayer is an essential part of the retreat experience. Pair people up as prayer partners leading into the retreat and during the retreat. Some Leadership Boards even maintain their prayer partner for the upcoming year. This is also an opportunity to have an accountability partner. Spend time in the retreat all praying aloud, praying in silence, and sharing prayers for one another. If possible, have the Leadership Board go on a prayer walk. You might ask them to spend time seeking God's direction for the church in the upcoming year. Ask them to consider seeking God's will for their own spiritual leadership in the upcoming year. I have even asked leaders to find something in nature that reflects the future of the church and bring it (or a picture of it) back to share with the rest of the Leadership Board. If you have leaders who are a bit uncomfortable with prayer, you might even include a teaching time on the different types of prayers. Be creative with this time, but do not overlook the importance of bathing the entire retreat in prayer. You might even consider launching a prayer initiative with the Leadership Board that will be used for the entire congregation in the upcoming year. For example, check out Sue Nilson-Kibbey's book from The Greatest Expedition series, *Open Road,* and her breakthrough prayer initiatives.

At the retreat, spend some time developing the leadership capabilities and understanding of your Leadership Board. Also, take some time to identify gaps in leadership knowledge or practices that the Leadership Board would like to learn about in the coming year. Make a list of topics and resources. These lists will be used to design the leadership development time for the monthly board meetings. Assign topics and times for each month to the Leadership Board members.

Planning Your Leadership Retreat	
Month	**Action Step**
August	Inform new leaders of retreat dates
August	Assign/select prayer partners for retreat
September	Strategic ministry planning retreat led by third party
September/October	Staff retreat led by pastor
October/November	Budget requests to Board from staff via pastor based on goals
December	Meeting and strategic planning retreat dates set for next year
January	Reservations at retreat center for September retreat
February	Recruit third party leader to lead retreat
March-August	Board chair and pastor work with the retreat leader to assure effective and efficient retreat experience including team building, missional evaluations, setting spiritual and leadership formation for upcoming year, SMARTER goals for upcoming year, and other relevant deeper strategic and generative work.
Use *Strategy Matters* as a strategic ministry planning retreat resource and comprehensive guide.	

Checklist for Planning your Leadership Rhythm

- Establish your leadership rhythm and tweak it as necessary

- Always plan at least one season ahead (bonus points for planning a year ahead!)

- Conduct at least one strategic ministry planning leadership retreat annually

- Consider a spiritual retreat and times for the Leadership Board to serve together

- Evaluate mission, vision and progress on goals monthly

Annual Rhythm Reference Chart for the Leadership Board

Month	Focus
January	Elect "trustee" chair, covenant, roles/responsibilities, commissioning service for out-going and in-coming Leadership Board members during worship
February	Easter plans, statistical trends, facility improvement plans
March	Town hall meetings with feedback
April	Deep financial dive, stewardship campaign planning, serve together
May	Ensure policies, procedures, and guiding principles are up to date
June	Deep dive into goals to identify any needed shifts
July	Possible new pastor arrival, Town Hall
August	Final retreat preparations, staff evaluations completed by pastor, feedback from cottage meetings if a new pastor has been appointed
September	Strategic ministry planning retreat conducted, nominations working on discerning new leadership for upcoming year
October	Clergy evaluation, staff retreat, staff budget requests, clergy appreciation
November	Finalize budget, charge conference, new leader training
December	State of the church town hall, clergy consultation

CHAPTER I-13

Communicating

My good friend Tychicus will tell you all about me. He's a trusted minister and
companion in the service of the Master. I've sent him to you so that you would know
how things are with us, and so he could encourage you in your faith. And I've sent
Onesimus with him. Onesimus is one of you and has become such a trusted and dear
brother! Together they'll bring you up to date on everything that has been going on
here. Aristarchus, who is in jail here with me, sends greetings; also, Mark, cousin of
Barnabas (you received a letter regarding him; if he shows up, welcome him); and
also Jesus, the one they call Justus. These are the only ones left from the old crowd
who have stuck with me in working for God's kingdom. Don't think they haven't
been a big help! Epaphras, who is one of you, says hello. What a trooper he has been!
He's been tireless in his prayers for you, praying that you'll stand firm, mature and
confident in everything God wants you to do. I've watched him closely and can report
on how hard he has worked for you and for those in Laodicea and Hierapolis. Luke,
good friend and physician, and Demas both send greetings. Say hello to our friends
in Laodicea; also, to Nympha and the church that meets in her house. After this
letter has been read to you, make sure it gets read also in Laodicea. And get the letter
that went to Laodicea and have it read to you. And, oh, yes, tell Archippus, "Do your
best in the job you received from the Master. Do your very best." I'm signing off in my
own handwriting – Paul. Remember to pray for me in this jail. Grace be with you.

Colossians 4:7-18

Our church needs better communication! Have you ever heard this? It is rare to do any
sort of consulting work in a church without hearing this from at least a few. Some may roll
their eyes when they hear this. Their perception is that people do not pay attention to what
is said or what is printed. Yes, it is true that communication is a two-way street. Yet, the
burden of providing clear, distinct, and timely communication is on the church (Leadership

Board, pastor, staff/ministry team leaders). Effective communication builds trust and a sense of transparency. Trust and transparency are key in transitioning to simplified structure and modeling accountable leadership.

Communication must come from several different levels of the organization: all Leadership Board members, pastor, staff, and ministry areas. We believe part of the common communication concerns come when the burden of communication is placed at only one or two levels. Certainly, there needs to be a communication hub (perhaps a communication coordinator or office administrator), but information needs to come in and go out at all levels.

If we can all agree that congregations need to do more to communicate, contemplate the communication effect of four or five committee's worth of members being consolidated into one board. Your church may have been depending on those committee members to share the "business of the church" through casual conversations. Now that much fewer people are in the "room where it happens," you will need to quadruple your communications just to stay even with your previous level; that is, the level you think is already inadequate.

Because this resource is intended for Leadership Boards moving to simplified, accountable leadership, we will concentrate on communication responsibilities of the Leadership Board. There are five communication strategies we ask you to consider: congregational conversations, newsletter articles, digital communications, and commissioning of leadership.

Board Reporting

In our sample agenda for every Leadership Board meeting, the last agenda item we suggest is communication. A simplified structure immediately becomes less accountable when others inside the congregation perceive the Leadership Board to be a secret group of insiders or the "pastor's buddies." As stated in Chapter I-11, every meeting of the Leadership Board needs to include a time of discussing what Leadership Board actions or discussions need to be shared with the larger congregation, and how best this message needs to be shared.

First, you may wish to make the leadership packet and minutes public for every member to read (except for executive session items, such as personnel matters). But beyond sharing minutes, how might the Leadership Board help to shape the congregation's Christ-centered purpose, its identity as an impactful faith community, and the congregation's ongoing narrative of faithfulness and fruitfulness before God? This chapter includes several suggestions, but we first recommend that Leadership Boards follow the slogan from the recovery community: "Take the cotton out of your ears and put it in your mouth." In other words, take time to listen – listen to God, listen to your fellow congregation members that we believe God is working through, and listen to the needs of the community.

Congregational Conversations

Sometimes we refer to congregational conversations as a "Town Hall Meeting," "Quarterly Conference," or a "State of the Church Address." Choose a name that is appropriate and appealing in your context. The important thing here is not in the title of the gathering, but in its practice. It is suggested to hold these quarterly as you transition into the simplified, accountable structure. As time goes by and the congregation becomes more comfortable with the model, the conversation frequency may need to be only a couple of times per year. The gathering is led by the Leadership Board Chair and/or other designee(s) from the Leadership Board. The pastor is in attendance but does not lead the conversation. The purpose of the conversation is to build trust, continuously cast the vision, offer information to the congregation, receive feedback, and answer questions. Most of the other communication strategies are one-way. Town halls and other congregational feedback opportunities offer the possibility for two-way conversations.

The format for this gathering is based on the governing focus of the Leadership Board. This means the Leadership Board would be presenting information on mission, vision, goals, and core values. The Leadership Board might offer information on the alignment of the church around these. The Leadership Board may also present the budget or perhaps a financial overview of the church.

As you consider the rhythm of your town hall gatherings, here are some suggested areas of topics that relate to the seasons of the life of the congregation.

- At the beginning of the year, you could offer a town hall gathering to present the newly elected Leadership Board and then the outgoing members of the Leadership Board. This would also be the time to present the new budget and goals for the new year.

- During the second quarter of the year, you might provide an update on the progress made of the goals and the year-to-date financial report (overview, not details).

- During the third quarter, you would have the opportunity to not only update the congregation on the goal progress and financial reports, but you would gain information from the congregation to help the Leadership Board discern the church goals for the upcoming year.

- During the fourth quarter, the opportunity is presented to celebrate the ministries, servants, and progress made through the goals to live into the vision.

Use your knowledge of your congregation's annual flow and expectations to build a schedule that works for your context. Chapter 12, "A Year in Leadership," offers some other examples as well.

These congregational gatherings are not meant to be a place for people to come and air their frustrations or dirty laundry. Therefore, create a controlled environment by having an agenda and a stated time limit. When opening the meeting for questions, ask for questions around the specific topic in hand. For example, "What questions might you have about the goals set for this upcoming year?" If someone tries to hijack the meeting, goes off-topic, or is not speaking with respect, politely tell the person you will have a private conversation with them immediately following the meeting. You can also use tools, such as table talks where Leadership Board members each facilitate a table discussion, to increase two-way communication while reducing the chance of one member attempting to "hijack" the conversation of the whole group.

Newsletter Articles

We often leave the newsletter creation up to one person. It is often the sole responsibility of a single human being to write articles, lay out the newsletter, add graphics, and distribute. One central person being responsible for the layout and distribution makes great sense. Yet, it is important for the newsletter to reflect multiple thoughts, perspectives, ideas, and information from various areas and voices of the church.

This is a great place for the Leadership Board to participate in the overall communication and transparency of the church. Assign various members of the Leadership Board to contribute articles or information to the newsletter each month. Share what the Leadership Board is working on and the progress made. Share general financial information. Share the celebrations of the church. Please do not depend only on the pastor for this leadership perspective or only the Leadership Board Chair. The Leadership Board's missional focus and responsibility can be communicated using the newsletter.

Digital Communication

In today's world, we must offer multiple engagement with social media and other digital communication. This might include text, videos on YouTube, Zoom, podcasts, Facebook, email, Instagram, Twitter, etc. Find ways to engage the congregation through social media that matches the context of both your congregation as well as the new people you are trying to reach. Sometimes we limit our communication means to the preferences of only our members, when we are quite likely missing the opportunity to communicate in more modern methods with new people.

Again, do not limit this responsibility to only one person. The Leadership Board must utilize new and creative ways to use digital communication to engage with the congregation. This might include newsy information, but it is also a chance to share a quote from a spiritual or leadership development time at the Leadership Board meeting. You could add an occasional "leadership update" special episode to the pastor's weekly "Behind the Sermon" podcast or host Zoom Q&A and brainstorming sessions with the congregation. If you have a daily devotional and shared scripture distributed on email and social media, intentionally include the Leadership Board members in the devotional-writing rotation. Using digital communication might also be as simple as a short Tweet about the record-breaking attendance at the Christmas Eve service(s) that everyone could celebrate. Be creative! Engage with your congregation!

Commissioning of Leadership

Lay leadership, especially lay governance, needs to be celebrated and lifted up as a valid form of ministry. In addition to all the informational sharing we recommend, another means to communicate with the congregation is through a service of commissioning during a Sunday morning worship. This could be right before or right after the new Leadership Board is seated each year. Bringing the new Leadership Board forward during worship allows the congregation to know the leaders of the church. It also gives the opportunity to offer a blessing and demonstrate gratitude for their service. This could be a time to sincerely thank those rolling off the Leadership Board, too. The service is short, but clearly demonstrates the responsibility given and expected of the Leadership Board. Don't forget about the Nominations Committee. Include them, too!

Individual Conversations

As a member of the church's Leadership Board, you represent the church when having conversations with fellow congregants. You also represent the church in your community. Make sure you are upholding a missional focus and the unified voice of the whole Leadership Board. You have an important role of being both a church and a Christian ambassador. People look to you to be a role model for the church. This does mean that you will need to set aside some of your personal agendas. During your term of service, you will need to represent not only the choir you sing in, the Sunday School class you lead, or your teenager's youth group. You are one of the representatives of the entire church, both inwardly to other congregation members and outwardly to the community. Conversations about church need to keep Christ's mission and vision for the congregation in the forefront.

Checklist for Communicating

- Use various forms of continuous communication

- Congregational town halls

- Newsletter contributions

- Social Media and other digital communications

- Commission the Leadership Board each year

- Individual conversations

SAS FOR DISTRICT SUPERINTENDENTS
Presiding Elders, and Other Judicatory Officers

This section has been compiled especially for judicatory leaders namely district superintendents, developers, directors of connectional ministries, and cabinets. We have found it to be of extreme importance to find alignment in terminology, procedures, and expectations when it comes to SAS. It is therefore in the spirit of collaboration that we offer these resources.

In this special section you will find:

- SAS and Annual Conference Alignment

- The Role of the DS in the Local Church SAS

- The Role of the DS in the SAS Discernment Phase

- A Question for DS Discernment: Is the Congregation Actually Too Small for SAS?

  - The Role of the DS in SAS Approval

  - DS Expectations for Presiding at the Church Conference

  - DS Expectations for the first SAS Nominations Report at the Annual Charge Conference

  - Partners in Discernment, Equipping, and Implementation: the DS and the SAS Coach

  - Walking alongside a SAS Board

- SAS at the District Level

- Next Horizon: SAS at the Conference Level

- Judicatory Accountability

- An Invitation to Our Judicatory Partners

CHAPTER J-14

SAS Introduction for Judicatory Leaders

Billionaire Clay Mathile, a former executive at Campbells Soup and co-founder of the Iams Company (a favorite of Blake's cat), offers a great quote in his training program for small business owners: "The only difference between a rut and a groove is how long you've been in it." The ruts of our current structure lost their "groovy-ness" a long time ago, and we know that structure changes can be a bit disconcerting to judicatory officials. I (Blake) am a big believer in appropriate checks and balances in structures, and I know that my district superintendent (DS) colleagues have had some bad experiences when leadership went off the rails and into the ditch. The ruts of our legacy committee structures feel "safe" because we think they will take us where we want to go, and we don't have to concern ourselves with ditches, going off road, or driving off a cliff. We have two answers to these concerns.

First, the ruts are not leading us where we want to go. God-sized dreams are going unfulfilled. Christ-centered impact is not happening. Disciples of Jesus are not being made and lives are not being transformed. We have plenty of "safe" systems and structures that are heading us straight towards irrelevance and missional death. Structural changes won't fix the church or our congregations, but we (Kay and Blake) believe that simplified, accountable structure will give congregations a fighting chance to unleash lay leadership, refocus priorities, and provide the adaptive leadership that congregations will need to face the future unafraid. "Safe" isn't really safe, it is just comfortable. Disciples of the Risen Christ were never called to be safe or comfortable – we were called to be bold witnesses to the Gospel.

Second, I (Blake) know that some of my DS colleagues with clergy supervision responsibilities worry that the "single board model" really is a power grab, with vague Disciplinary authority, that could result in overwhelmed committees and autocratic leadership (particularly on the clergy's part). Kay and I, however, never suggest the "single board model" – we refer to it as a simplified, accountable structure (SAS) for a reason. When properly organized and led, *accountability* runs throughout the system – lay ministry teams and groups, staff, pastors, Nominations Committee, and Leadership Board. That is why we never recommend only simplifying structure without first building in accountable leadership and significant time in churchwide discernment.

I (Blake) also understand the worry about not having a separate and independent Pastor-Parish Relations Committee with whom the DS connects. In fact I'll be honest in saying that this was a deep concern for me when I began my work on the appointive cabinet. One part of my concern was the sheer amount of conference-required "business" that we expected the PPRC/SPRC to accomplish. How could a Leadership Board with so many responsibilities complete all of that stuff? The answer is, in our case, literally "simple." In our conference, we simplified our assessment and consultation forms and instead offered tools to equip congregational leaders in their supervisory ministry. Second, I discovered that I would rather speak with a Leadership Board than a PPRC. PPRCs and SPRCs often see everything through only the lens of clergy appointments and staffing. Because their scope of work and options is limited and siloed, every problem had a staffing solution. Failing that, it is probably the pastor's fault!

I (Kay) am often confused by the push-back and concerns with a Leadership Board and a DS preference for instead a traditional separate S/PPRC. Often the push-back is specifically the concern of adherence to the confidentiality requirement of a S/PPRC that seemingly offers a DS a sense of comfort and protection. Both the Leadership Board in a SAS model and the S/PPRC in the traditional model are bound by the same BOD polity, expectations, and authority of S/PPRC. If breaches of confidentiality were to be encountered, it is just as likely to happen regardless of the type of structure the churches is using. These concerns and/or actual breaches are not caused or grounded in a particular structure. They are caused because there is a lack of training and the setting of expectations with accountability. SAS offers a much more of an emphasis in accountable leadership and expectations of a leadership covenant which provides (among many others) a much higher probability of confidentiality adherence than the traditional structure.

Another reason we ***strongly advocate and recommend*** SAS without a separate S/PPRC specifically (or any separate administrative committees in general) is the likelihood and often practice of triangulation. In our experience, having a separate PPRC promotes triangulation of the pastor, staff, and PPRC. Triangulation is not uncommon and is an unhealthy practice for the sake of the pastor, the staff, and ultimately the congregation and culture. One couldn't imagine a customer of a business having direct influence, conversation, supervision, or authority over the employee of said business. Of course not! The owner or manager of the business is the person who supervises, evaluates, and hires/fires employees. Yet, this is exactly how we are setting our systems up to fail in the church.

We have seen this story play out many times: The pastor has no authority to fire a staff member who is consistently under-performing, being insubordinate with the pastor, and/or sabotaging the pastor by feeding the staff rumor mill with lies and mis-truths because the S/PPRC won't approve disciplinary action or termination. A S/PPRC member was assigned to be the "liaison" to this particular long term staff member (who is also a friend of the staff member's mother) who now takes on the role of advocate and confidant for the particular staff member. This is done without having any first-hand knowledge or experience of the staff member's day-to-day job performance, interactions with other staff, or interactions with the pastor. It's now the pastor's word against the staff member's word, and the staff member now has a S/PPRC advocate. Of course, this is an extreme example (although very real in repeated contexts). In SAS, the staff reports to the pastor who supervises, evaluates, hires, fires, and holds staff accountable under the guiding principles set by the Leadership Board. This provides a much healthier system with very clear lines of authority, responsibility, and accountability that are simply not in place nor practiced in the traditional S/PPRC.

A Leadership Board brings a wider perspective, bringing together the whole of ministry, strategy, leadership, disciple and staff deployment, facility and resource use, finances, and stewardship. As a DS, I (Blake) am thrilled when a team with which I am consulting can bring such a holistic approach to the governance and strategy of the church. Yes, sometimes a DS will get concerned, and in those cases a coach or the DS will need to help the Leadership Board get back on mission just like we have to do sometimes in the traditional structure. But if a SAS Leadership Board is practicing appropriate accountability, the DS should be able to sleep at night knowing that the expectations for committees in the *Discipline* are being followed (as appropriately modified) and that, more importantly, the congregation is striving toward the mission Jesus Christ has given it.

SAS and Annual Conference Alignment

We (Kay and Blake) experienced the arrival of simplified structure differently in our ministry settings. As a layperson and consultant, I (Kay) was an early adopter and creator who brought a wealth of experiences from the secular world into the creation and implementation of the Healthy Church Initiative. Simplified, accountable structure was one of a host of prescriptions (recommendations) and existed as a part of this larger system of transformation in the conference. Over time the Healthy Church Initiative migrated across the country, being adapted for different contexts and conferences. But SAS's integration into a larger system with training and coaching made for a pretty orderly launch of SAS with a shared terminology. Yet, even with this broad approach, SAS still has many iterations. I (Blake), as a church developer and later a district superintendent, came upon SAS in a different way. My conference didn't have a single outlined process, so pastors and congregations grabbed hold of the ideas from friends serving in different conferences. We didn't have a shared vocabulary or guidelines in the conference, so many different permutations bloomed (along with some kudzu!). Since those early days, my conference has brought some order, expectations, and more of a shared vocabulary to the situation. Still, differences have been inherited, and I have had to work with various congregational leaders to shift their structures to be more in alignment with the *Discipline*, manage conflicts of interest, or encourage the healthy shift towards accountability.

It is with these different experiences that we both highly recommend that conferences have a shared, consistent approach towards simplified, accountable structure. Create some basic expectations and a common vocabulary. Blake has over 100 congregations in his district. While we appreciate contextualization, there is no reason to have 100 different structures! In addition, it is extremely helpful for conferences (especially cabinets) to have a commonly understood practice and implementation of SAS. Otherwise, district superintendents come and go, and the SAS rules and expectations change with each district superintendent appointment. When pastors are moved from district to district, without a conference-wide approach to SAS, the pastor has to learn new SAS "rules" in a new district. Also, laity from different congregations across the connection share stories and best practices. So, when there is not a consistent understanding, vocabulary, and implementation through the conference, there is confusion and lack of understanding and alignment.

Here are some best practices to encourage and enculturate a conference-wide approach to SAS:

Creating a Conference-wide Approach to Simplified, Accountable Structure

1. Start with accountable leadership at all levels: conference staff, SAS coaches, congregations, pastors, district superintendents.

2. Create conference-wide consistency, Disciplinary interpretation, and common SAS language (preferably through SAS Coach Certification).

   a. SAS Certified Coaches have on-going access to learning and best practices.

   b. SAS Certified Coaches is a national group sharing, supporting, and equipping specifically for SAS.

   c. Having Certified SAS Coaches ensures your conference has the most updated information, resources, and think-tank for simplified, accountable structure.

   d. Having Certified SAS Coaches provides a partner for district superintendents to assist in discernment, equipping and implementing phases with consistency and the latest best practices.

   e. Having Certified SAS Coaches will provide a team of equipped coaches to walk alongside churches in their discerning, equipping, implementing phases initially and on-going which ensures the best chance of a healthy transition and outcome.

3. Maintain clear expectations for congregations seeking to utilize SAS.

   a. Ensure adherence to BOD (term limits, qualifications, conflicts of interest, membership).

   b. Ensure existence of separate and independent Nominations Committees that relate to the charge conference.

c. Emphasize that all the Disciplinary expectations and authorities of the included committees are invested in the new Leadership Board. No one should ever say, "we got rid of all committees."

d. Recommend Leadership Board Chair also serve as the liaison to the DS.

e. Expectation for equipping ALL SAS Churches' New Leaders - this means SAS equipping would need to be offered annually by a Certified SAS Coach with the most current resources.

4. Create clear expectations for district superintendents to maintain alignment

a. District superintendents trained in the most current SAS recommendations (For instance, we no longer recommend SPRC or finance "representatives" as part of our board training). Take churches using the SAS model into consideration during the appointment process. If a pastor is not willing and/or able to lead and be held accountable and to hold staff accountable, extreme caution should be demonstrated. Consider another appointment or at the very least provide a Certified SAS Coach during the first year of the appointment for the purposes of equipping, supporting, encouraging, and accountability.

b. A willingness to tell churches "NO" regarding SAS as the best faithful step for a congregation when the church is not ready, it's not the right season to transition, has unresolved conflict, or unwilling to practice accountable leadership.

c. Create a conference-wide system for district superintendents to consider requests from congregations seeking to begin discernment and approval of SAS.

d. Deploy a conference-wide Charge Conference Nominations Form specifically for congregations that use SAS.

e. In assessment and consultation materials, support alignment of pastoral goals and congregational goals with conference strategic goals

5. Conference Cabinets and Developers should create and manage a SAS Coaching System

a. Encourage collaboration between the coaches and the district superintendents.

b. Coach Report should precede a coach payment for accountability.

c. Have a SS coach review SAS Nominations Form for accuracy and compliance.

d. Create a list of churches Implementing SAS well (confirmed by a SAS Certified Coach with on the ground confirmation) for others to talk to and "sit in" on their SAS Meetings (clergy & laity).

e. Have an evaluation process for SAS Coaches to ensure local congregations and leaders are being provided the resources needed and congregations are truly living into the SAS model.

These best practices will help your whole conference better live into the simplified, accountable structure approach to congregational leadership, cut down on needless conflict, and remove some of the fog that can envelope a process when multiple congregations and perhaps even DS's are trying to "go their own way" with little oversight. District superintendents, presiding elders, congregational developers, and congregational coaches have an opportunity to encourage healthier structures and greater alignment with the overall mission of the church.

CHAPTER J-15

Role of the DS in the SAS Discernment Phase

The district superintendent has three primary touch points when a congregation is seeking simplified, accountable leadership structure: **1. Exploration**, **2. Discernment**, **3. Approval and Church Conference**.

The first touch point is preliminary permission request for a congregation to begin discernment and open up the conversation:

> 2) Letter from Council Chair, Lay Leader, and Pastor to the DS seeking permission to explore the SAS model
>
> 3) Approval from DS to explore and assignment of SAS Coach
>
> Note: These items from the 12 Steps of SAS Discernment.

While the *United Methodist Book of Discipline* requires district superintendent approval, we added this additional step early in the process, as part of a larger understanding of accountability. As a DS, I (Blake) am usually frustrated when a big change comes as a fait accomplii with a request for me to preside at a charge or church conference in a fortnight. Involving the DS early means that the final result will meet the superintendent's interpretations of the *Discipline* and district or conference requirements. It will also enable your superintendent to involve conference resources, such as coaches, processes, checklists, and/ or consultants early in the process. Some conferences have a cadre of well-trained SAS certified coaches ready and able to walk alongside your congregations through all three phases of the process. We recommend this earlier step to congregational leaders to ensure alignment, starting with you as their DS who we hope has a partnership with a certified SAS coach. Therefore the congregation brings you into the conversation much earlier in the process and in earnest may save the congregational leadership from weeks of backtracking. This practice will also ensure the healthiest chance of discerning, equipping, and implementing.

In my district, I (Blake) require a letter from the Pastor, Lay Leader, and Church Council Chair so that I know the initial steps as outlined in Chapter D-1 have been followed and there is some buy-in from key lay leadership. While an official written request letter is required, here is the worksheet from Chapter D-1 (also found in the **Resource** section on Page 285) that I send to congregations seeking initial approval to begin a discernment process to move toward SAS. I ask congregations to use it as a tool to draft their letter.

Initial Consultation with Your District Superintendent

Share your motivations and reasons (your WHY) for a potential structure change.	
List the names and roles of lay officers involved in the discussion up to this point.	
Share which Disciplinary administrative committees you believe will be incorporated into the governing Leadership Board. While this may, of course, change as your church leadership wrestles with the possibilities and options, the DS may have particular recommendations or requirements so that your church's structure may be approved.	❑ Church Council/Administrative Board ❑ Council on Ministries ❑ Staff-Parish Relations Committee ❑ Board of Trustees ❑ Finance Committee ❑ Endowment Committee ❑ Other_____ ❑ Other_____ ❑ Other_____

Share your possible timeline for the structure change. Use the Discernment Steps.	Discernment Steps: _____
	Consultation with the DS: _____
	Contact SAS Certified Coach:
	Congregational Vote: _____
	Nominations Work: _____
	Charge Conference Elections: _____
	New Board Begins Service: _____

Potential Reasons to Say No

Of course, with any approval process, there is a possibility that the DS will need to deny the request. There are several reasons a DS might want to put on the brakes for a transition to SAS:

1. District superintendents may know that a change in clergy appointment in the church is upcoming and believe that the congregation might not have the bandwidth to simultaneously restructure and receive a new pastor. Perhaps the DS will want the new pastor to have a hand in restructuring.

2. The current pastor, while gifted and caring, may have a history of leading poor discernment processes. Visioning and structure are certainly not everyone's gifts.

3. The congregation may have a history of every pastor bringing their own structure and importing it into the congregation. The DS may direct more work on relationships and identity before approving a timeline for moving to SAS. SAS needs a commitment from laity leaders and the congregation as the preferred and recommended long term structure rather than the latest structure of the week brought by the latest appointment that is sure to change next appointment.

4. There may be lingering trust concerns, or a lack of accountability in the life of the congregation. Perhaps before a change to simplified, accountable structure, the congregational leaders will need to invest first in moving towards accountable leadership.

5. The Conference is about to launch a SAS program with a shared terminology and coaching system. Perhaps a delay of the discernment process for a few months will allow the congregation to be an early adopter or "pilot church" in the new initiative with a newly certified SAS coach.

6. There is a high level of conflict or mistrust in the congregation. Unfortunately, when this exists, sometimes simplified structure may be seen as the magic bullet. Or while some may want to move to SAS, others will only go along with this decision if there is a modification to the recommended SAS structure (i.e., separate trustee or finance committee). Rather than creating a structure that is not the recommended practice or forcing a new structure to be adopted that will not be trusted, it is a much more faithful step to pump the brakes on the SAS transition and work on the underlying issues of trust or conflict first. The current structure is working and obviously any structure won't be healthy until these other issues are addressed. Outside help with a coach or consultant specializing in conflict management or team development may be helpful to congregations in this situation.

For a DS, many of these concerns may be more about a delay of approval, rather than a denial. Perhaps the answer is not a "no" but instead a "not yet." Saying "no" or "not yet" can sometimes be the most faithful step for a superintendent. A bad start with simplified, accountable structure can ruin the opportunity for years, and create a false impression of the model for other congregations that would benefit greatly from SAS. Congregational memories of bad experiences can sometimes go on for a very long time. I (Kay) have worked with congregations that are still recovering a decade or two later from a "bad" experience. A strategic "not yet" may be a gift for a church that really needs to put their energy into answering some hard questions first.

A Question for DS Discernment: Is the Congregation Actually Too Small for SAS?

Since 247.2 was written for small churches, we don't think any church is too small for simplification. Of course, we do not recommend simplification without accountability. In extremely small micro-congregations, this often brings us to a dilemma: the board, the ministry team, and the worshiping congregation may be all the same people. There are some micro-churches that can't even come up with nine unrelated people to serve on a simplified structure!

Sure, a six-person Leadership Board may help when filling out Charge Conference paperwork, but let's be clear that this will always be just a technical change and not a true simplified, accountable structure leading to the needed adaptive changes. We often wonder if the discernment process of moving to SAS might be a delaying tactic for a deeper question of congregational sustainability: more small churches need to be asking themselves if they are actually still a church or are they perhaps a Wesleyan class meeting or a home church instead. Judicatory leaders, such as district superintendents need to help congregations start talking about these hospice or legacy options.

We also wonder about where we need to be investing our resources. If a micro-church moves to simplification out of desperation, but the congregation is unwilling to be accountable to the Great Commission, is this the best use of DS and coaching resources? So, as the district superintendent or Certified SAS Coach assists these congregations in their discernment, perhaps these larger questions can be asked. In the meantime, a similar structure will at least provide some clarity for the Superintendent's primary congregational contact. Maybe the real distinction here is if a micro-sized church moves to a simplified structure yet has the same people in board leadership and ministry leadership, can they at least separate out the Leadership Board fiduciary functions from ministry planning on their agenda, to help the board members remember which "hat" to wear? If not, they will likely never get to the point of asking the bigger, missional questions of sustainability or vitality.

Some further questions for consideration:

- Is the micro-church trying to do ministry beyond its capacity to do well? Could they offer fewer ministries done with excellence resulting in greater impact and fruitfulness?

- Without the focus on mission, churches almost always fall to management/ maintenance with resulting decline. How is the church reaching new people? If they aren't, how can they? If they spend time maintaining ministries that have not been reaching people, how will they ever reach new people if they aren't willing to focus on the mission?

- If the church isn't willing to focus on the mission, why do they remain open? Where is the accountability to Christ for the Great Commission?

- At some point is the simplification of structure a technical change designed to forestall closing because leaders are realizing that the micro-church is nearing death in its life cycle without any hope for the possibility of renewal.

- Is this where a district or conference comes in with *Small Church Checkup* (Kotan & Schroeder) or *Choosing the Faithful Path* (Crissmon) as a requirement for small churches moving to simplification without accountability?

- The district and conference have the ability (and duty) to ask difficult questions and there are processes in the *Book of Discipline* for such. Why aren't we intentionally implementing these strategies conference-wide when working with micro-churches?

- An Assessment of Local Church Potential ¶213

- A deliberate analysis in Transitional Communities ¶212

- Call of Ministry of All the Baptized ¶220

- Strategic Deployment of Clergy and Realignment of Pastoral Charges ¶419.9

- Financial Accountability Inquiry ¶604.8

- Membership (Making Disciples) Accountability Inquiry ¶604.9

The Role of the DS in SAS Approval

Towards the end of the Discernment Phase, the DS has a second touch point in the approval process: a formal request for approval of a modified structure according to ¶247.2. We suggest that the current Church Council, after completing all the listening work and getting a recommendation from a SAS Discernment Team, vote to request the DS consider the modified structure and also request for a called Church Conference for the plan to come to the congregation. It is our belief that having the whole church council vote to request formal approval to move to SAS is the healthiest way to approach the process. It makes it clear that this is the considered judgement of the congregation's lay leadership, not just the pastor or a few leaders.

7) Based on congregational feedback and leadership discernment, the Church Council votes to request adopting SAS. If a favorable vote results, the Pastor and Council Chair submit letter to DS to approve moving to (or not) SAS

8) DS reaches out to coach for feedback and makes decision

9) DS approval via letter (including church conference timing)

As a partner in the process, the DS has dispatched a Certified SAS Coach to walk alongside the pastor and leaders in their Discernment Phase offering resources, coaching, and accountability for the process. If/when the DS receives a request to move to SAS, the DS will want to have a conversation with the SAS Coach that was dispatched to the congregation. The DS will inquire about the Discernment Phase. Here are some recommended questions to guide the conversation to give the DS insights about the congregation and their readiness to move to SAS:

1. What is the *why* for the request to move to SAS? How widely understood and communicated is the *why*?

2. How was prayer incorporated into the discernment? How wide was the prayer participation?

3. How effective was the communication and conversation plan?

4. How many informational conversations were conducted? Who conducted them? What percentage of the congregation was involved in the conversations?

5. In your opinion (coach), is this congregation ready to move to SAS? Are they healthy enough? Do they fully understand what they are really voting to implement?

6. Is the pastor fully onboard and coachable?

7. Is there any underlying conflict or other issues that could cause issues with SAS implementation?

8. How ready is the congregation to do both the technical and adaptive work to fully embrace and live into SAS?

9. Has the leadership agreed to invest in coaching through the Equipping and Implementing Phases? Why or why not?

10. Would you recommend this congregation moving to SAS? Why or why not?

Inherent in this process is an expectation that the district superintendent will have the knowledge and understanding of the model to issue an appropriate approval. This is where conference-wide guidelines, DS training, and a shared terminology comes in particularly helpful. Knowing that, for instance, a separate Nominations Committee is required, or that all the strictest membership qualifications for all the included committees must be maintained, is absolutely necessary in order for the superintendent to properly consider the request. Obviously, the DS and the SAS coach need to be on the same page with how SAS will be implemented and practiced. Inconsistency between the DS and SAS Coach's approach and understanding of SAS will only lead to congregational confusion and frustration.

DS Expectations for Presiding at the Church Conference

After approving the modified structure with accountability, the district superintendent will then need to coordinate with the pastor and leadership to schedule a Church Conference. We recommend a ¶248 Church (as opposed to a "Charge") Conference to change leadership structures as an attempt to include all professing members of the church in the decision to reduce the number of elected leaders in governing roles. Of course, any calling of a Charge or Church Conference must be done in consultation between the district superintendent and the church leaders, but we highly recommend a churchwide vote to utilize this model to increase accountability and to ensure the new Leadership Board's legitimacy. One can only imagine the outcry of the members of the various administrative Disciplinary Committees if a church council, serving as the congregation's Charge Conference, voted by themselves to end everyone's terms and replace all the committees with the members of the council! And rightly so. Such a blunt approach would create the impression that the congregation's voices do not matter, and the goal was to reduce the numbers of people making decisions as a power grab. This will lead to mistrust of the structure from the onset making it almost impossible to launch well let alone shift to the accountability and adaptive changes required. Of course, the motivations behind SAS are far different, so district superintendents or Certified SAS Coaches should work with leaders to ensure that the change in structure is accomplished with transparency and congregational buy-in as intended in the Discernment Phase. Here are the steps in the checklist that relate to the Church Conference.

9) DS approval via letter (including church conference timing)

10) Church Conference to approve SAS model

I (Blake) never go into a Charge or Church Conference blind. As part of my expectations for congregations seeking to move into utilizing simplified, accountable structure, I ask for a draft of their resolution that will create the new Leadership Board. We highly recommend a two-step process:

1. A called Church Conference (all professing members vote) to transition to a modified governing structure, based upon ¶247.2 of the *Discipline*, and approval of instructions guiding the congregation's Nominations Committee to offer a slate of candidates for the Leadership Board, to be elected at an upcoming Charge Conference.

2. A Charge Conference (usually an annual Charge Conference held the fall) to elect the membership of the Leadership Board, along with other officers including the Nominations Committee, with terms of service to begin January 1. If the timing doesn't align with the annual Charge Conference to accomplish this task, a congregation can ask permission to hold a called Charge Conference to accomplish this task.

As the presiding officer, the district superintendent will need to coordinate with the congregation's leadership to determine how the voting will occur. Few congregations have a set of conference session rules (beyond Robert's Rules of Order), so a set of proposed Session Rules will need to be developed to oversee the work of the meeting. Include the preferred method of voting (voice, show hands, or ballot), number of speeches allowed, and any time limits on speeches.

We recommend that the resolution for the structure change be made available ahead of time for members to review. In fact, it should be published widely along with any FAQs (frequently asked questions). Here is a suggested text for a resolution (also found in D-4 and in the **Resource** section on Page 256.

Sample Resolution to Change Congregational Organizational Plan to Simplified, Accountable Governance Structure

WHEREAS, ¶247.2 of the 2016 *Book of Discipline* for the United Methodist Church allows alternative models of governance; and

WHEREAS, the simplified, accountable leadership structure is utilized as an alternative model throughout the denomination and fulfills the provisions of ¶ 243 of the 2016 *Book of Discipline* for the United Methodist Church; and

WHEREAS, the Church Council of_____ United Methodist Church prayerfully voted on (date) to explore the simplified, accountable structure for local church governance; and

WHEREAS, the congregation provided feedback concerning a potential change in governance structure on multiple occasions; and

WHEREAS, the congregation was motivated to convert for reasons of efficiency, alignment with our mission and vision, accountability, and missional focus; and

WHEREAS, the Church Council, Committee on Nominations and Leadership Development, [the task force on governance], and the pastor, after months of discernment, have crafted an alternative organizational for _____ United Methodist Church and offered this proposal to the district superintendent for approval; and

WHEREAS, the District Superintendent approved the alternative organizational plan on (date); and

NOW, THEREFORE, BE IT RESOLVED THAT:

1. On January 1, 20____, the Disciplinary authority and various responsibilities of the Church Council, Staff Parish Relations Committee (SPRC), Finance Committee, Endowment Committee, and Board of Trustees, will be combined into a single body called the Leadership Board. Existing elected leadership of all classes of all constituent committees that make up the new Leadership Board will conclude their terms of service on December 31, 20____, as the church transitions to the new organizational plan.

2. The Committee on Nominations and Leadership Development of _____ United Methodist Church is directed to submit a list of officers and members of a simplified, accountable structure known as the Leadership Board and a Committee on Nominations and Leadership Development, divided into appropriate three-year classes, as outlined in the *Discipline*, for election by the Charge Conference. All members of the Leadership Board and the Charge Conference will be professing members. The Chair of the Board of Trustees will be elected from among the voting Trustee members of the Leadership Board in the first board meeting of each year, in accordance with the *Discipline*, and s/he may be the Leadership Board Chair.

3. On January 1, 20____, the Charge Conference of _____ United Methodist Church will be composed of the members of the Leadership Board, appointed clergy (ex-officio), together with retired ordained ministers and retired diaconal ministers who elect to hold their membership in our charge conference, Lay Members of Annual Conference, the Lay Leader, Treasurer and Finance Secretary (if non-staff), and the elected membership of the Committee on Nominations and Leadership Development.

4. The Lay Member of Annual Conference and Lay Leader are ex officio members of the Leadership Board, if not already elected into a membership class of the Leadership Board.

5. All Disciplinary requirements and qualifications for each of the constituent committees (Church Council, SPRC, Finance Committee, and Board of Trustees) will continue with the combined Leadership Board, including Trustee age of majority qualifications and SPRC household membership limitations.

6. All references to the Church Council, Board of Trustees, SPRC, and Finance Committee, in all existing church policies, as of December 31, 20____, shall be understood to refer to the Leadership Board beginning January 1, 20____.

7. The Board of Trustees is directed immediately to make appropriate amendments to the congregation's bylaws to reflect the new plan for organization and submit an update to the Secretary of State's office in a manner defined by state law for nonprofit corporations.

8. In service to our common mission to make disciples of Jesus Christ for the transformation of the world, all existing ministry teams will be accountable to the Pastor and Leadership Board in administrative matters and in fulfillment of ¶243. The Weekday Child Care Ministry Advisory Board (¶ 256.2c) will be amenable to the Leadership Board in all matters, and is responsible for regular reporting to the Board. Alternative: If the Weekday Child Care Ministry is not a separate 501c3, this Advisory Board will be a ministry team and accountable directly to the Pastor.

9. The Leadership Board will abide with existing financial, child protection, building use, and personnel policies along with the inaugural Guiding Principles. The board will create a Leadership Board Covenant. The Leadership Board is empowered to amend these policies, principles, and covenant. The Leadership Board shall share updated Guiding Principles with the charge conference annually.

APPROVED, (date) .

_____   _____

Secretary, Charge Conference   Presiding Elder

As noted in Chapter E-5, we also recommend that any entities associated with the church that are not separately incorporated be brought into the new structure through the Resolution. For example, if the endowment is not a separate 501(c)(3) foundation, the endowment is now part of the responsibility of the new leadership structure. This allows the best alignment, flexibility, and focus. While advisory teams can always be created to assist in their leadership, this is the time to clean up these governance silos and align for accountability and missional focus.

DS Expectations for the first SAS Nominations Report at the Annual Charge Conference

Again, this is a two-step process, with a Church Conference approving a new structure and then a Charge Conference approving the people to fill the ranks of the new Leadership Board. To ensure buy-in and transparency, it would look like "the fix is in" if the same meeting approved both the restructure and a fully formed slate of officers and Leadership Board Members. After the Church Conference approves the new structure, the Nominations Committee is then assigned the task of creating a recommended slate of new Leadership Board members. Keep in mind there are also adaptive changes in how the Nominations Committee goes about their work of nominations and lay leadership development in a SAS model. The leaders should be divided into classes of terms of office. (Yes, we know that in the initial group, three people will only serve one year before rotating off!)

Rules for the election of officers and board members can be found in ¶249 of the *Book of Discipline*. The Charge Conference for nominations can occur as part of the regular annual rotation of conferences. The only exception might be if timing is such that the church would like to get terms started on (for instance) July 1 instead of waiting six extra months to move into the new system. Note: If a July 1 commencement date for new leadership occurs, we recommend the first class of leaders serve for 18 months.

If a member of the Leadership Board needs to be removed, the district superintendent can use ¶250 as guidance. The Leadership Board can, however, fill interim vacancies between sessions of the annual charge conference, in accordance with ¶252.4, a power to be used wisely in the event of an unexpected vacancy.

Partners in Discernment, Equipping, and Implementation: the DS and the SAS Coach

You have likely noticed the consistent mention of the Certified SAS Coach. This is very intentional as not only a reminder, but also as a helpful, sustainable, and effective approach to SAS in the local church. With the decreasing number of DS's across the nation resulting in larger districts and a growing number of congregations in each district, we believe having a Certified SAS Coach is not only an efficient and healthy partnership, but it will be a lifesaver to a DS. The amount of time, energy, and attention needed to help a church discern if SAS is the right structure, equip the leaders to lead in the SAS structure, and help them implement the SAS model and live into it fully and faithfully is enormous. Most DS's don't have the time and bandwidth to do this intensive work with congregations. Nor do DS's have the time to keep up on the latest best practices, resources, and teachings in SAS. It is therefore recommended that each DS have at least one Certified SAS Coach as a partner to be their go-to for congregations considering the model and equipping new and existing church leaders in the most updated model.

A couple of additional thoughts for your consideration in considering the value of a Certified SAS Coach:

- First, the pandemic brought the attention of even more congregations to the fact of the complexity, redundancy, and time-consuming nature of the traditional structure. Churches in the traditional structure struggled more to be flexible and nimble to make timely and efficient decisions. Therefore, we are seeing more of a demand for churches seeking to move to SAS. As more and more congregations move to SAS, more leaders are becoming more familiar and curious thus resulting in more interest.

- Second, it is often difficult for a DS to operate as a supervisor to the pastor and consultant to the congregation as well as do deep, transformational work that is part of SAS work and coaching. Separating the role of a coach and DS is often a healthier approach for both the congregation and the DS.

- Third, is a word of caution. We refer to coaching as "Certified" SAS Coaches. Yes, there is a training, certification, covenant, and on-going requirements to remain a "certified" SAS Coach. This is not a one-and-done approach. These coaches are a dedicated group of coaches committed to SAS, its on-going development, and to help churches move faithfully and fully into both the simplification of structure and accountable leadership. The caution here is that a leader who has attended some training at some point or who has led a local church through simplification is not necessarily a "Certified" SAS Coach. Too often someone with the best of intentions thinks they understand the model, but without being "certified," we are finding growing concerns in districts and conferences using these well-intentioned people without first being "certified."

Walking alongside a SAS Board

As a serving DS, I (Blake) quickly discovered the joys of working with a SAS board while wearing my district superintendent hat. I was now able to quickly jump from topic to topic – facility matters, pastoral supervision, and mission/vision strategy – with one cohesive group. The alignment meant that I was able to discern the overall vision of the church and not rely on only one lens (such as clergy appointments) in my conversations with leaders.

We know that this alignment can make some of my district superintendent colleagues nervous, however. Maybe it is concerns about confidentiality (which is covered by executive session), or just the newness of the concept (which has been operational well over a decade), Some DS's want a separate SPRC with which to relate. Some churches try to finesse this concern from their superintendent by creating a dual election SPRC and Board. While we show this system in our appendix, the reader will note that it is not the recommended model, and it creates its own challenges. Another method used to satisfy DS restrictions is to bring back the "specialist" or "representatives" from the original and now outdated simplification models. In that model, which is no longer recommended, two or three members of the board are listed as SPRC specialists. The problem with this system is that, instead of acting like a work group to pre-process some SPRC work for the Board to consider, the 2-3 specialists become a mini-SPRC and start acting independently from the Board, creating a governance gap. While sub-committees or specialists may sound efficient, these smaller teams are not as founded in the *Discipline* and can create alignment dysfunction. These sub-committees often acted as though they had the same authority as the full committee in the traditional committee model and often made decisions without the larger Leadership Board's voice or vote. In addition, the sub-committee or specialist format feels and looks too much like the traditional model and consequently structuring in this way blocks the adaptive changes needed to lead in a different way. Remember, the point of simplified, accountable structure is to change the conversation at the leadership table, not just reduce the number of people around the table (see the Work Team section in Chapter E-5).

In my (Kay's) experience, I often find one main underlying motivation for DS's to require a separate SPRC. When DS's require this, the DS has very often not been equipped in the SAS model (or updated model) or has a misunderstanding or lack of understanding of accountability. There is no more confidentiality in a SPRC than there is in SAS. There are more "checks and balances" through accountability in SAS than in most traditional model practices.

As a DS you would want to only meet with the entire SAS Leadership Board and not a sub-committee or a group of specialists (ideally the representatives or specialists would not even exist!). Even if you are sure to follow this protocol, there is still danger in these sub-committees or specialists even existing. The example I (Kay) share in my SAS training is a SPRC sub-committee in a church I was working with met without the knowledge of the Leadership Board or even the chair, completed the clergy consultation, signed it, and turned it into the DS. The sub-committee asked for the pastor to stay while the larger team wanted to consider asking the bishop for a move. It wasn't until much later in the appointment season that the larger board realized what had happened. This resulted in huge conflict and a late pastoral move. It was a mess! But, all of this could have been circumvented had the sub-committee not existed and the district superintendent met with the full Leadership Board.

CHAPTER J-16

Simplified, Accountable Structure at the District Level

When we began teaching simplified, accountable structure in workshops, often the district superintendent that hosted us would pull up a chair after the closing prayer and start asking us, "Do you think I could simplify my district committees, too? I've got all these committees, the work is redundant, and I'm having trouble seeing why we need all of this in my district." Well, yes! Your district leadership structure can also be simplified. Some of the metaphors and concepts need a bit of adjustment, but there is no reason that a district could not simplify their structures with accountability and still remain under the *Discipline*.

Judicatory structures are not just a variation on a local congregation. While the overall disciple-making mission of the Church is the same, the local congregation is the primary place of disciple-making while district, conference, diocesan, and presbytery structures provide support, resourcing, equipping, governance, connectional and shared ministries, and shared missional direction.

Just as the purposes are different between local congregations and judicators, leadership structures must also differ. District leadership structures need to match its purpose and match the unique conference and district context. For instance, some districts operate quite independently from the conference, and even have multiple congregational development and administrative staff, while other districts operate as regional "branch offices" of the conference. So, creating a district structure model that fits all these contextual and governance variations has proven challenging. In other words, start with the mission and vision for your district in your context and conference.

However, we have created a framework for districts to creatively address both the *Book of Discipline* concerns and provide some flexibility in your leadership. First off, like ¶ 247.2, the *2016 Book of Discipline* allows for some modifications to district structures:

¶ 661 Each district of an annual conference may organize to develop, administer, and evaluate the missional life, advocacy needs, and ministries of the Church in and through the district. It shall maintain connectional relationships, organize to develop and strengthen ethnic ministries, including ethnic local churches and concerns, and provide encouragement, coordination, and support for local churches in their ministries of nurture, outreach, and witness in accordance with the mission of the United Methodist Church.

This flexibility is a huge help because when we (Kay and Blake) started reading and graphing out all the district structure and committees on a giant spreadsheet, we found that the paragraphs outlining the structures and committees didn't offer too much clarity. There were a lot of "recommended" and "if" statements and even a contradiction or two. So, a huge challenge as you enter into this process is seeking clarity out of chaos.

In order to not add to the chaos, we highly recommend that, as you approach the matter of district simplification, part of the discernment should include the larger conference. We believe that all the districts in a conference enter into a SAS model simultaneously and use a common terminology and building blocks. This allows for better coordination with conference committees, agencies and staff, and it means that the district structures will be in alignment with one another. The conference and districts are therefore modeling alignment for local churches along with (we hope) simplification and accountability.

Structure should follow purpose, and the particular architecture of your district restructure will need to take certain contextual realities into consideration. So, with the flexibility of ¶661 in hand, the district superintendents and key district and conference stakeholders should answer some questions to provide more clarity for possible structural options:

1. What is the purpose of your District Boards? How do you currently utilize them? How do you need to utilize them for missional fruitfulness (mission/vision)?

- **Current use:**

- **Potential Use:**

2. Do your district entities have authority or governing responsibility, particularly in relationship to the Annual Conference?

3. What are the Annual Conference expectations or rules for district structures? Are there ex officio officers from conference-level committees that have a role or a seat on district structures?

4. What is the role, responsibility, and authority of the district lay leader?

5. How does the district superintendent, in the role of chief mission strategist, work alongside the conference and/or district developer to utilize district entities for strategic or church-planting work?

6. Is your district separately incorporated? ❑ Yes ❑ No

7. Does your district own property (office, parsonage, etc.)? ❑ Yes ❑ No

8. Does your district employ & pay staff? ❑ Yes ❑ No

9. How does your district handle its bookkeeping, financial decisions, and assets? What kind of financial and facility oversight is required? (Mark the box or boxes that apply to indicate who has responsibility for each category. Make a note when responsibility is shared.)

	RESPONSIBILITY		
	District Level	Conference Level	Other/ Outsourced
Bookkeeping			
Budgeting			
Check writing			
Endowment			
Restricted and Designated Funds			
District Parsonage Maintenance			
District Office Maintenance			
Vehicle for DS			

Your answers will impact the structural design choices you will need to make when considering your district's leadership. For instance, if most of the governing work of the district and its program need to live separately from church-planting or congregational development work, your new simplified structure may do well to keep these two universes as separate entities. A district that owns an office and a parsonage is different from a district that has a housing allowance and shares administrative help through a remote office with staff under conference supervision.

We will show you two options to consider as you rethink your district leadership through the lens of SAS. The first option has three district committees to whom the DS relates:

- A governing board (a simplified District Leadership Board),

- A strategy team for building and church planting matters (supercharging the District Board of Church Location and Building)

- A clergy credentialing body (the District Committee on Ordained Ministry

Here is a graphical representation of the three committees, along with the Disciplinary responsibility each particular committee will take on and additional some notes:

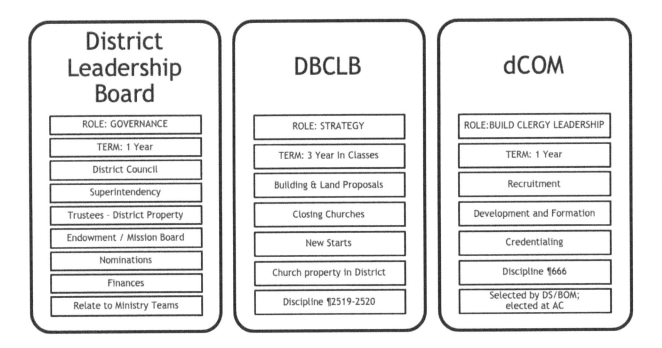

The District Leadership Board's role is focused squarely on GOVERNANCE. It offers a container for most of the governing committees found in the *Book of Discipline:* The District Council, the Committee on Superintendency and the District Board of Trustees. This SAS board also serves as the district's committees on finance and can manage assets of any district mission board or endowment committee. You will note that the District Leadership Board (DLB) can also serve as its own nominating committee. Unlike the restriction requiring a separate nominating committee at the local church level, no such requirement exists for the district structure. Here is the composition of your new District Leadership Board, which is compliant to *Discipline's* combined qualifications for the District Board of Trustees and the District Superintendency Committee.

- District Lay Leader

- 2 Lay Women (Trustees)

- 2 Lay Men (Trustees)

- 2 Clergy (Trustees)

- 2 At Large Members (We recommend a Finance Steward or Treasurer and a District Ministry Team Liaison)

- 2 Members selected by DS

- Any Non-Voting Advisory Members as needed (There may be ex officio officers that your conference requires, or that would prove helpful in your context such as disaster response coordinators.)

Membership on the District Leadership Board would be by single year renewable terms, except for the District Lay Leader, whose term is a four-year quadrennium. You will note above that the two lay women, the two laymen, and the two clergy on this Leadership Board roster have a "trustees" notation next to their name. These six persons will fulfill the legal role of the District Board of Trustees (¶2518) and the legal function of nonprofit corporation Board of Directors if the district is separately incorporated.

The second district committee is the **District Board of Church Location and Building**, which has a focus on STRATEGY. When I (Blake) first started serving on the district, I thought the Board of Trustees and the District Board of Church Location and Building were closely related. Well, they share a place in the 2000's paragraphs and both deal with property, but the similarities really end there. While the District Board of Trustees is responsible for the district assets, such as its office, equipment, and perhaps a parsonage for the DS, the focus of Trustees is internal. The District Board of Church Location and Building, however, has a mission field focus with expectations to consider requests for new buildings and remodels of church facilities, requests for churches to relocate, and where to start new churches. Many districts have separate "district strategy teams" to provide wisdom and guidance to district superintendents concerning opportunities in the district, but I (Blake) have found that this work again and again required the strategy team to meet up with the District Board of Church Location and Building, which has actual *Book of*

Discipline authority to back up its strategic work. Instead of having redundant meetings, we recommend that the district supercharge its District Board of Church Location and Building and utilize it for strategic conversations and analysis of district demographics, growth, church locations, and missional opportunities. Call it a strategy team if you want, but make sure that the district clergy and lay leadership knows that it is operating as the district's Board of Church Location and Building with all of its legal and *Discipline*-derived authority.

The third district committee is the **dCOM,** the District Committee on Ordained Ministry, which is focused on BUILDING CLERGY LEADERSHIP, particularly the credentialing work of interviewing and recommending candidates for ministry. The dCOM is amenable to the conference's Board of Ordained Ministry and its membership is elected at the conference and not the district level, so it is a bit of an outlier. In many ways it operates similar to a ministry team at the local church level, with a focused ministry and set of expectations and rules. We include it in our governance section in this chapter because dCOM work could require quite a bit of time and resources from the district superintendent and district staff.

These three groups together form the primary outlets for committee responsibility at the district level, and each connect to a different part of the district superintendent's ministry within the district: governance, strategy, and clergy credentialing. Some districts, depending on workload and conference support, can simplify even further with the District Leadership Board also encapsulating the District Board of Church Location and Building, and those six Trustees additionally serving as DBCLB members. Note that attention must be paid to the 3-year terms of DBCLB members and the ratio qualifications (lay women, laymen, and clergy) of both DBCLB and Trustee members. Here is a graphical representation of this further simplification:

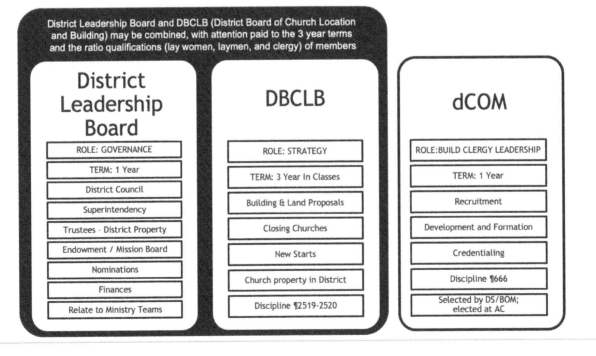

This very simplified option with only two committees is possible. A district superintendent will need to take care to help the committee "switch hats" when moving back and forth from fiduciary work to strategy work, but it is a definite possible district SAS option.

CHAPTER J-17

Next Horizon: Simplified, Accountable Structure at the Conference Level

Just like local churches and districts, conferences could likely benefit from a simplified, accountable structure or at least beginning a conversation about the possibility. The purpose of the annual conference is outlined in ¶601, "to make disciples of Jesus Christ for the transformation of the world by equipping its local churches for ministry and by providing a connection for ministry beyond the local church; all to the glory of God. In ¶610.1, it states the following regarding conference structure:

The annual conferences are permitted the flexibility to design
conference and district structures in ways that best support the mission
of making disciples of Jesus Christ in an increasingly diverse
global community and that place secondary any prescribed structure,
except for the mandated entities in ¶610.

The introduction of ¶610, it states:

The annual conference is responsible for structuring its
ministries and administrative procedures in order
to accomplish its purpose (¶601), with the exception of the
mandated provisions of ¶611, 635, 636, 637, 639, 640, 647, 648.

After thorough review of the BOD for conference structure requirements, we offer the following illustration for your consideration. Rather than a dozen or more teams, we believe it is possible to simplify to a total of only six to eight teams. Not only is this simplification, but it is much more efficient and effective. The BOD paragraphs in parentheses identify the area of responsibility and authority for each of the teams/committees.

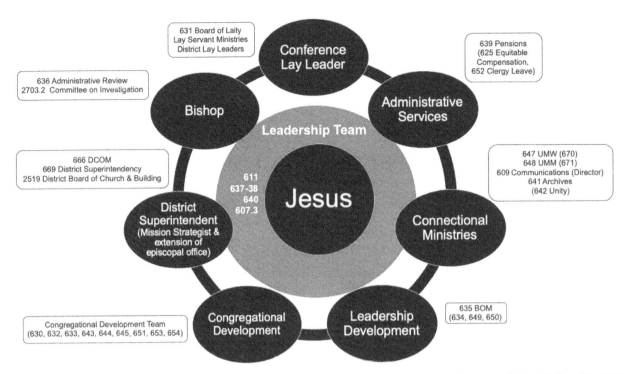

636 Administrative Review
2703.2 Committee on Investigation

631 Board of Laity
Lay Servant Ministries
District Lay Leaders

Conference
Lay Leader

639 Pensions
(625 Equitable
Compensation,
652 Clergy Leave)

Bishop

Administrative
Services

Leadership Team

666 DCOM
669 District Superintendency
2519 District Board of Church & Building

611
637-38
640
607.3

Jesus

647 UMW (670)
648 UMM (671)
609 Communications (Director)
641 Archives
(642 Unity)

District
Superintendent
(Mission Strategist &
extension of
episcopal office)

Connectional
Ministries

Congregational Development Team
(630, 632, 633, 643, 644, 645, 651, 653, 654)

Congregational
Development

Leadership
Development

635 BOM
(634, 649, 650)

All numerical references correspond to the 2016 Book of Discipline of the UMC

Conference Leadership Team:

- Chair: Conference Lay Leader (in collaboration with the Bishop)

- 12 people: 1/3 laywomen, 1/3 laymen, 1/3 clergy with 1/5 appointed by Bishop

  ¤ Include first lay and clergy delegates elected to General Conference

  ¤ Directors of Cong Development, Leadership Development, Connectional Ministries, and Administrative Services

  ¤ Chair of Board of Ordained Ministry,

  ¤ Chair of Cong Development Team

  ¤ Chair of Leadership Development Team

  ¤ Chair of Connectional Ministries Team

Note: Conference Staff Directors and Bishop are non-voting members.

While the option above demonstrates seven teams, the option below simplifies further into fewer teams by combining congregational development and leadership development and rolls them into an overarching connectional ministries team.

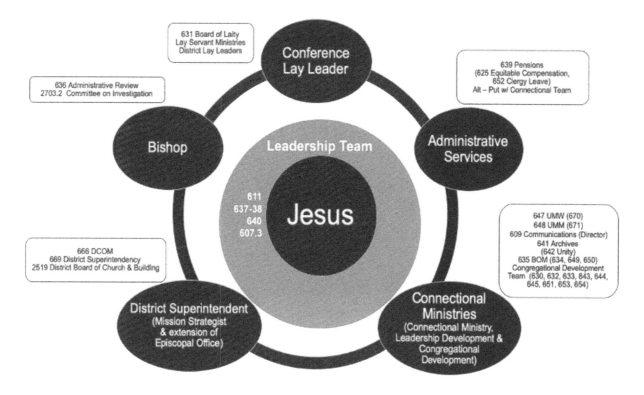

All numerical references correspond to the 2016 Book of Discipline of the UMC

Keep in mind, neither of these models have been tested. We are simply offering some starting points for conversation towards simplification for more conference-level efficiency, effectiveness, and accountability as well as modeling SAS for our local congregations.

CHAPTER J-18

J-18 Judicatory Accountability

I (Kay) have often felt and even occasionally admitted that while training leaders in SAS especially while serving as a judicatory leader it felt hypocritical to suggest local congregations practice accountable leadership when our districts and conferences were by and large not practicing accountable leadership. It is absolutely critical for us as judicatory leaders to model and practice accountable leadership if we desire and expect leaders in the local churches to do so. How are we being accountable to Christ as we lead our districts and conferences? If the local church is to make disciples, the district and conference is to equip congregations and leaders in their work to make disciples. If the churches aren't making disciples, aren't the districts and conferences (and their leaders) ultimately responsible for this? How are the leaders on the leadership teams at the district and conference levels holding judicatory leaders accountable? How are resources being aligned and leveraged for this purpose? Just like SAS (structure) is not the answer for church transformation, we do know that when structure is not supporting and aligning the mission and vision, the local church is in decline. The same can be said for districts and conferences. When the structure is not aligned with the mission and vision through aligned resources and accountable leadership, the districts and conferences are in decline. Ascertaining the structure is healthy and functioning with accountability, provides the local churches, districts, and conferences alike the best possible opportunity to be the most vital, effective, and efficient through missional focus.

CHAPTER J-19

An Invitation to Our Judicatory Partners

Please consider us as your SAS partners. If we can be helpful or of any assistance to you as a judicatory leader, please feel free to reach out to us. If your district or conference is considering moving to SAS, would you please share your journey with us? As more and more are considering this move, we would love to be able to connect them and continue to be a common gathering ground for the latest best practices and evolutions of the process. In addition, we have begun working with districts and conferences in their discerning, equipping, and implementing of SAS. If you would like some assistance, please reach out to Kay at Kay@KayKotan.com or Blake via his website at www.blakebradford.org. We also offer periodic calls with judicatory leaders for the purposes of information-sharing and equipping. If you would like to be included in those calls as a judicatory leader, please reach out to us so we are sure to include you on the invitation list.

Afterword

In the course of a few months, the church had been through a comprehensive consultation process, a lightning strike, an assault on a board member in the facility and a building flood. The consultation team offered some very adaptive recommendations dealing with worship, leadership development, and faith development among others. The lightning strike affected the alarm system, internet and some of the electronic equipment. The personal assault was horrific for the board member and set a whole new security process in motion with new equipment. The flood was only a few inches, but it created enough damage that the church had to relocate to another facility for a few months while repairs were made. You could say this church had a bad year of unfortunate circumstances to say the least!

Yet, in the midst of all of this, the pastor shared with me a silver lining. As part of the consultation, there was a recommendation for the church to move to a simplified structure with accountable leadership. With all of the happenings at the church, the pastor could not have imagined trying to maneuver through four different administrative teams in a timely manner to manage all the discussions, processes, decisions, and new policies needed. The numerous situations the church had to deal with certainly tested the new structure. The pastor emphatically believes the simplified, accountable structure allowed them to maneuver through the situations with greater ease, focus, timeliness, and clarity for decision-making based on a missional focus. If that weren't enough, he went on to share that the transition to the new structure was what he was most excited about. Not the new sound board. Not the new carpet. Not the renovated worship space. Not just the face of having fewer meetings. Not just the agility and flexibility of the new structure. What he was most excited about is that SAS had changed the whole trajectory of the church and provided more intention and focus on his own leadership.

This isn't the only story of churches realizing increased vitality or even church transformation as a result of moving to SAS. There is story after story after story. But, be reminded that this is not how all stories end for churches moving to SAS. What's the difference between SAS being the linchpin or not for better missional focus and fruitfulness? To sum it up in one word, it would be **commitment**. The churches who are truly committed to SAS because they had a clear understanding of why it was important and were fully informed and aware of what they were saying yes to, had the best outcomes. They were committed to the simplification. They were committed to the accountability required to successfully implement and work it consistently. They were committed to implementing both the technical and the adaptive changes that would be required to fully adopt the model. They were committed to leaning into it fully to be able to live into it fully. They were committed to the hard work the changes would require of them. They were committed to practice transparency and communicate thoroughly to build and maintain trust and credibility at all levels. In a word, it is about commitment - being "all in." And at the end of the day, it really came down to this bottom-line commitment– of being sold out to this commitment – the commitment to the Lord, Jesus Christ to lead the church in its mission to make disciple-making disciples to transform the world.

Remember the Why

Simplified, accountable structure is not the potential "magic bullet" some churches are searching for to suddenly create an avalanche of people coming in the doors. We hope this was not your expectation. Yet, in our experience, when we have a simplified means of being focused on our purpose, the mission is certainly possible. Simplified, accountable leadership is a means to refocus the church on its purpose in a modern, efficient, and effective manner. We circle back to your motivation – why does your church desire this change? If the change is the hope of a magic pill, you have come to the wrong place. If the change is being considered as a means to be more faithful at making disciples of Jesus Christ for the transformation of the world, we offer hope, prayers and resources for that journey.

Out of complexity, find simplicity.
Albert Einstein

We believe that Jesus called for the formation of "church" in his teachings. By church, we believe he meant a means through which people could learn about God, worship God, and hold one another responsible for their faith walk. In our efforts to do this, we believe we have unnecessarily complicated our churches practices. Now, please do not hear we are suggesting this from a theological perspective, doctrine, or conviction – quite the contrary. What we are suggesting is that in our efforts to "do church" we have perhaps created systems and processes that have complicated the church needlessly.

Simplification of the structure allows us to focus back on the basics, the roots, the purpose, they **why** – making disciples. Simplification does not mean easy, but it is a clear, distinct pathway. Simplification allows us to adjust and focus upon the basic essentials of church. SAS not only simplifies the structure, but also reconnects authority and responsibility. Laity are unleashed from the meeting room monotony to instead being released to an even greater cause of making an impact in the mission field of your community. With the adaptive changes of simplification and accountability, we will once again become better focused on our true purpose – our *why* of being church. When we have a laser focus on our purpose, we can most effectively align and leverage our resources to be the most faithful in living out our mission of making new disciples.

It is our prayer that your church is both challenged and excited about the potential outcomes of this journey. Be patient with one another. It will take time to embrace simplified, accountable leadership. But, oh the efforts are worth it! Be blessed in this time of moving closer to faithful effectiveness in reaching new people for Christ so your church can faithfully proclaim:

Mission Accomplished!

Resources

- R-1   12 Steps to SAS Discernment Transition
- R-2   FAQs for SAS
- R-3   Common Potholes
- R-4   Organizational Structure Charts
- R-5   Rules to Remember for Structuring and Nominations
- R-6   Nominations Interest/Recommendation Form (application)
- R-7   Nominations Interview Questions
- R-8   Sample Nominations Report
- R-9   Sample Church Conference Resolution for Structure Transition
- R-10   SAS Charge Conference for Nominations
- R-11   Sample Board Leadership Covenant
- R-12   Sample Guiding Principles
- R-13   Leadership Board meeting Agenda
- R-14   Online Request/Report for Governing Board
- R-15   Leadership's Annual Rhythm Checklist and Reference Chart
- R-16   Suggested Strategic Ministry Planning Steps and Timeline
- R-17   SAS FAQs for the DS
- R-18   Requirements for Initial DS Consultation
- R-19   A Recommendation for District Governance Simplification
- R-20   A Recommendation for Conference Governance Simplification
- R-21   Creating a Conference-wide Approach to Simplified, Accountable Structure
- R-22   SAS Shifts
- R-23   Common SAS Gaps
- R-24   Initial Consultation with your DS
- R-25   Formal Request to the DS
- R-26   Brief Overview of SAS

R-1: Steps in the SAS Discernment Phase

- Church Council votes to explore SAS after assessing the *why*

- Letter from Council Chair and Pastor to DS seeking permission to explore

- Approval from DS to explore and assignment of SAS Coach

- SAS Coach works with leaders to establish a SAS Prayer Team and SAS Discernment Team to lead in learning, organizing, and communicating the SAS discernment process.

- The SAS Discernment Team implements communication and information plan

- Based on congregational feedback and leadership discernment, the leaders submit letter to DS to approve moving to (or not) SAS

- DS reaches out to coach for feedback and makes decision

- DS approval via letter (church conference timing)

- Coach begins to work with Nominations and continues to work with leaders on communication strategies (see Equipping Phase)

- Church Conference to approve SAS model

- Nominations completes their work

- Church/Charge Conference to approve Nominated Leaders

Note: After completing the Discernment Phase, move into Phase Two: Equipping and then onto Phase Three: Implementation. We *highly recommend* partnering with a SAS certified coach through all three phases for the most effective and healthiest outcome!

R-2: Simplified, Accountable Structure (SAS)

Frequently Asked Questions

1. **Which positions can be combined for one person on the Board to hold?**

    Most all positions can be combined as long as the minimum number is elected. The Lay Leader, Lay Member to Annual Conference, S/PPR Chair and Trustee Chair must be designated but could all be the same person.

2. **Is there an absolute minimum number for the Board?**

    Nine is the standard and recommended minimum. Very small congregations may be able to have a Leadership Board of six, composed of two individuals in each three-year class at the discretion of their district superintendent.

3. **Does the pastor have a vote?**

    No. Because the Leadership Board's work switches roles quickly from Disciplinary committee to committee, we recommend that the pastor not vote, in order to preserve clarity and unity in the Board. If a matter comes up that depends on one vote of the pastor, that is probably a sign that more conversation and discernment is needed.

4. **Can family members serve together on the Board?**

    Per the Book of Discipline, family members cannot serve on the Board together. If it cannot be avoided, the family members may need to excuse themselves from the room or not vote on issues with potential conflict of interest. Staff and family of staff cannot serve on the Board.

5. **Should staff (paid and unpaid) serve on the Board**

    No

6. **Who should take notes at the meeting?**

    Someone can be assigned or elected to take notes who is not on the Board. That person could also be selected from the existing members of the Board, a person recruited outside the Board to take notes (needs to be excluded from S/PPR conversations) or a person who is an addition to the Board with the sole responsibility of taking notes.

7. **Are the Financial Secretary and Treasurer required to be on the Board?**

    No, but they can be. The recommendation and best practice is for them not to be on the Board.

Resource from *Mission Possible 3+*, by Kay Kotan and Blake Bradford. Market Square Publishing, 2021. Permission to copy for use with *Mission Possible 3+*.

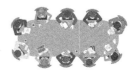

8. **Which position on the Board serves as the liaison to the district superintendent for Staff/Pastor Parish Relations Committee purposes?**

   It is recommended that the Board Chair serves as the S/PPRC liaison to the DS.

9. **Are there still three-year terms and classes?**

   Yes. One third of the Board will roll off each year.

10. **Is the Board self-nominating?**

    No. There is still a requirement that there be a separate Committee on Nominations and Leadership Development to nominate the Board Members to the Charge Conference each year.

11. **How long can a person serve on the Board?**

    Board members serve a three-year term. Since all members are serving as S/PPR, Trustees and Finance, it is recommended they roll off after each three-year term. After being off the Board for a year, the person can roll back onto the Board if elected.

12. **Are UMM, UMW, and UMYF representatives required to be on the Board**

    If the church has these chartered groups, a member of that group may serve if requested on the Board as a leader of the local congregation (not to report about their group).

13. **How many must be present to take an official vote? What requires an official vote?**

    A quorum is described as whoever is present (Note of exception: In rare matters that require the Trustees to function as a legal body, a majority of Leadership Board members who are Trustees must be present). Simple majority of Leadership Board members attending approves a motion.

14. **How is the Trustee Chair elected or appointed as required by the corporate resolution**

    At the first meeting at the beginning of each new year, the Board will elect a Trustee Chair to satisfy the corporate resolution requirement. It is recommended the Board Chair serve as the Trustee Chair. Please note that all members of the board who will serve in the role as a trustee must be of legal age (18+ in most states).

15. If a church moves to the simplified, accountable structure, how does ministry happen?

Even though the restructuring occurs, ministry teams are still needed and in place. Fewer people on the Board means more people are available to do ministry. Simplifying structure is the combining of the four administrative teams of the Council, Trustees, Finance and S/PPR Committees. The only change for ministry teams is that the Nominations Committee is no longer responsible for identifying and nomination leaders and members for ministry teams.

16. Do I need approval from my DS to move to the simplified structure?

Yes. A letter from the pastor and Council Chair requesting to move to simplified structure to the DS is the first step. In the letter, state the missional purpose for moving to this structure. Refer to the Discernment Phase for the steps towards moving to a simplified, accountable structure.

17. Where can I find information on simplified structure in the *Book of Discipline?*

¶ 247.2 in the 2016 edition

18. How should we pick Leadership Board members? Do we need to seek out people with different skills, such as financial, human resources, legal, and marketing? Should we try to create a team composed of people with personality test results?

By Discipline, all Leadership Board Members will need to be professing members of the church because some of the constituent committees require professing membership. The right team is composed of devoted disciples of Jesus who can think strategically about the church's mission, hold clergy, staff, and fellow members accountable to the mission, and partner with other Leadership Board members to guide the congregation into making a God-sized impact. The Leadership Board should be as diverse as possible so that the leadership table will have the different voices that God needs for the congregation to discern its future direction. Other skills can be added through work groups. While teams can be designed using a variety of tools, don't let these tools get in the way of the fact that Jesus' mission needs Jesus' disciples and that accountability must come before any other considerations.

19. What size church is too small or too large for SAS?

While 247.2 was written for small churches who had difficulty finding enough people to fill all the "slots" in a committee structure, it was some of our largest churches that first discovered the power of SAS. Churches with an average worship attendance under 50 may already be doing a de facto simplified structure, and it may or may not be using accountability. Large Churches that worship in the thousands have discovered the need for SAS as they seek to counteract ministry silos and mission drift. Mid-size congregations from 50-500 in worship will quickly discover the power of SAS in unleashing more laity for ministry and focusing the church on Christ's mission.

20. What are the *Discipline* requirements for Leadership Board composition?

The Leadership Board should be made up of professing members, with a Discipline-recommended minimum of 1/3 being laywomen and 1/3 being lay men.

21. Who can attend the meetings?

Congregation members are always invited to attend the meetings, but do not have voice or vote. When the Board needs to move to executive session to address S/PPRC matters or to consider legal negotiations (such as buying or selling property), these church members will need to be excused.

22. Should we assign Board Members to specialist roles for finance or personnel?

No! This defeats the purpose of the simplified structure and interrupts Leadership Board accountability. While the Board may assign a work group to work on a special project and report back, only the entire Leadership Board can act and make decisions.

R-3: Common SAS Potholes

- Leaders not holding one another accountable (including clergy)

- Pastor over or under leading

- Difficulty shifting out of maintenance to governance

- Not shifting to the new agenda (and thus new conversation)

- Congregational communication and transparency

- Incomplete or missing guiding principles

- Skipping Town Hall Meetings

- Staying out of ministry planning and conversations

- Difficulty or avoiding asking the hard questions

- Wrong and/or immature leaders at the table

- Not understanding how and when to use work teams

- Spiritual and leadership development adoption

- Not seeing the opportunity in communication on agenda

- Not getting packet out and/or wrong person preparing it

- Leaders not preparing for meetings

- Items placed on agenda that should not

- Employees or their relatives on leadership team

- Resistant to the new structure/mode of operation

- Incompatible room set up

Resource from *Mission Possible 3+*, by Kay Kotan and Blake Bradford. Market Square Publishing, 2021. Permission to copy for use with *Mission Possible 3+*.

R-4: Samples of Organizational Charts

EXAMPLE 1:

Organizational Chart of the RECOMMENDED simplified, accountable structure

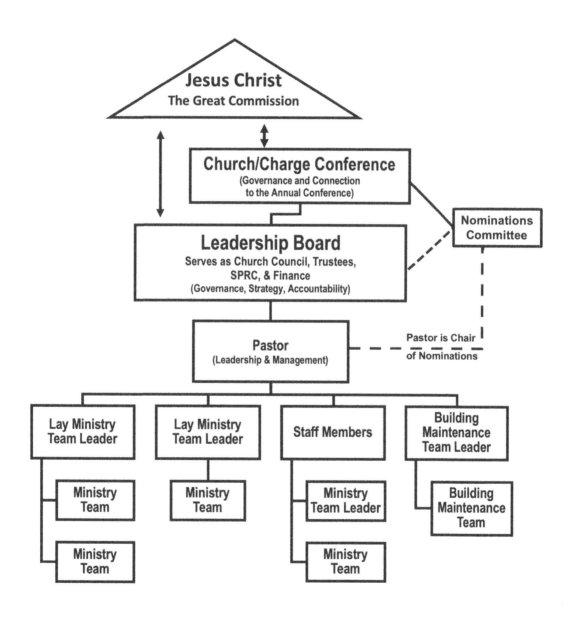

EXAMPLE 2a:

Organizational Chart of a simplified, accountable structure representing the relationship of additional delegated teams:

- Weekday Childcare Ministry (¶256.2c)

- Work Groups

- Chartered Ministries (such as United Methodist Women ¶256.5)

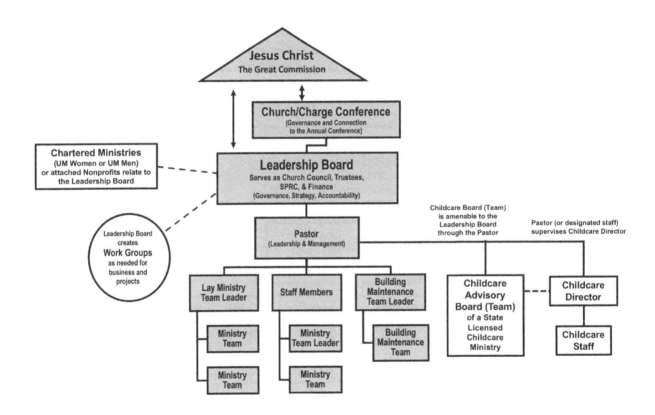

Resource from *Mission Possible 3+*, by Kay Kotan and Blake Bradford. Market Square Publishing, 2021. Permission to copy for use with *Mission Possible 3+*.

EXAMPLE 2b:

Organizational Chart of a simplified, accountable structure representing the relationship of a separately Incorporated Weekday Childcare Program:

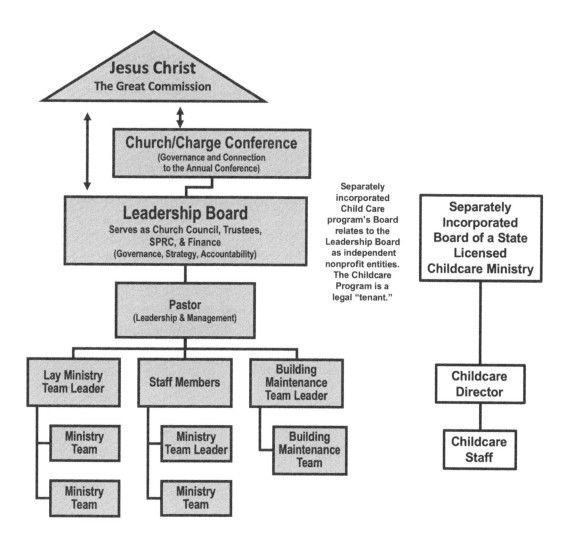

EXAMPLE 3:

Dual Election Model with a separate SPRC (Not Recommended)

- In this modification of the recommended model, the Leadership Board contains 3-4 members of SPRC, including Chair and Lay Leader who serve both on the SPRC and on the Leadership Board as Personnel Specialists. SPRC continues to report to the Leadership Board.

- This is an alternate modification of the "pure" simplified, accountable structure.

- While we do not recommend this model, we provide it in case your district superintendent or annual conference requires an independent SPRC.

- There are challenges to having a separate SPRC:

- The shared Board members/SPRC can create authority issues and operational vagueness

- Separate SPRC dilutes the efficiency and accountability of the Leadership Board

- Pastor can receive mixed messages about priorities

- So, instead of having a fully separate SPRC, having half of the separate SPRC's membership be "dually elected" to both the Leadership Board and the SPRC can attempt to protect alignment to the congregation's goals and mission.

- While we encouragedistrict superintendents and congregations to engage fully in the standard and recommended single SAS board, if the annual conference or district superintendent requires a SPRC to be elected, this model might provide a compromise that retains as much accountability as possible.

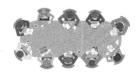

EXAMPLE 4:

A Two-Point Charge or Cooperative Parish utilizing the SAS Model

- Local Church simplified, accountable structure Leadership Boards select representatives to a Charge Leadership Board that also serves as a Parish-wide SPRC and Parish Council

- The Charge Leadership Board coordinates with the congregations to rotate Charge Conference election of Lay Members of Annual Conference

- Local Churches retains the responsibility and authority of the Boards of Trustees (as part of the SAS Leadership Board) because of legal responsibilities

- Local Churches continue to have independent Nominations Committees that select the congregation's Leadership Board and appoints representatives to the Charge Board

- Staff, supervised by the Pastor, may be amenable to the local church SAS or to the Charge Board, depending on the nature of the staff position. For instance, some churches, as part of a charge, support a single charge administrative assistant. Job descriptions will need to be clear which governing body staff are amenable.

- If one of the local churches on the charge is not ready to transition to the SAS model, the congregation can keep its legacy committee structure and appoint representatives.

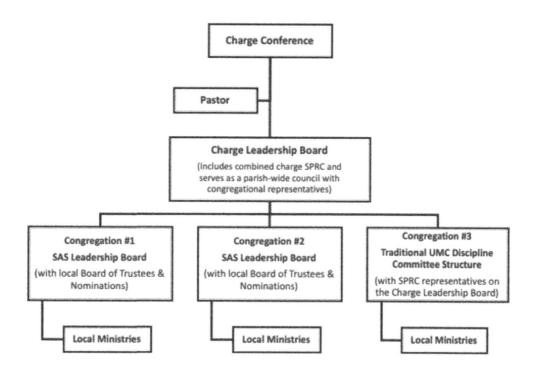

Resource from *Mission Possible 3+*, by Kay Kotan and Blake Bradford. Market Square Publishing, 2021. Permission to copy for use with *Mission Possible 3+*.

R-5: Rules to Remember for Structuring and Nominations

All the Disciplinary requirements and limitations of each of the new Leadership Board's constituent committees remains in effect. Rules to remember:

1. A separate **Nominations Committee**, chaired by the Pastor, is required because the Board cannot self-nominate.

2. You will need **nine** members. Board members serve a **three-year term**. The Lay Leader and Lay Delegate are exempt from the three-year term. After being off the Board for a year, the person can roll back onto the Board if elected. SPRC and Trustees have minimum and maximum limits on the number of members, so (depending on your Leadership Team's size and composition), a few members of the Leadership Team may be barred as voting members of some of the constituent committees. For instance, there is a limit of 9 on Trustees; there is also a limit of 11 on SPRC, counting Lay Leader and a Lay Member of Annual Conference.

3. Pay attention to Disciplinary **conflicts of interest**. Household members cannot serve on the Board together. If it cannot be avoided, the family members may need to excuse themselves from the room or not vote on issues with potential conflict of interest. Staff and family of staff cannot serve on the Board because of SPRC membership restrictions (plus it is simply good ethics!).

4. **Trustee Requirements**: At the first meeting at the beginning of each new year, the Board will elect a Trustee Chair to satisfy the corporate resolution requirement. It is recommended the Board Chair serve as the Trustee Chair, if the Board members is one of the Trustees. The Leadership Board, serving as the Trustees, is also the legal Board of Directors. All Board members who serve as Trustees must be over 18. The Trustee membership rule of minimum 1/3 laymen and 1/3 lay women remains in effect. The Pastor cannot be a Trustee.

5. Even though the restructuring occurs, **ministry teams** are still needed and in place. Fewer people on the Board means more people are available to do ministry. Simplifying structure is the combining of the four administrative teams of the Council, Trustees, Finance and SPR Committees. The nurture, outreach, and witnessing ministries continue their disciple-making work.

Resource from *Mission Possible 3+*, by Kay Kotan and Blake Bradford. Market Square Publishing, 2021. Permission to copy for use with *Mission Possible 3+*.

6. The concept of a Leadership Board is **designed to increase accountability and alignment** for the whole church towards its holistic mission, not be a place for ministry representatives to negotiate "turf." Members of the Board only represent and lead the whole church, not a particular interest group or ministry.

7. While the Leadership Board **may designate specialists** (such as finance specialists) from the membership of their Board, the whole Board, in toto, serves as the finance committee, Trustees, etc., not just the designated specialists.

8. The small number of governance officers on the Leadership Team **requires huge trust and congregation-wide accountability.** It is HIGHLY RECOMMENDED that you describe your future Charge Conference as being "The Leadership Board, Nominations Committee, and all clergy who hold their charge conference in the congregation." And it would also greatly help build trust, accountability, and transparency if your governing documents adopt a requirement that asks the district superintendent to convene all Charge Conferences as Church Conferences to allow all professing members to vote on matters. This allows the larger congregation to have a say in nominations and hold the Leadership Board accountable in the Board's role as the Charge Conference's executive committee.

9. Churches on **multi-point charges** will particularly need to take care to support and respect the organizational structure and ministry of one another's churches.

R-6: Leadership Board Nominations Interest Form

This application and recommendation form is adapted from the "Interest Form" created and used by the nominating committee of Camp Hill United Methodist Church of Camp Hill, Pennsylvania, to recruit and interview applicants to serve on their Unified Leadership Council.

The first year, you may need to use a mix of this interest form and some method of receiving recommendations from church members to create a pool of possible leaders. As your congregation grows in its experience of the benefits of a simplified, accountable leadership structure and more disciples are unleashed for ministry, those gifted for governance leadership will be more readily identified. You may wish to use this interest form alongside your leadership development process.

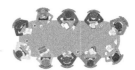

Leadership Board INTEREST FORM

Anytown United Methodist Church

First Name: _____ Last Name: _____

Preferred Phone Number: _____

Preferred Email Address: _____ _____

Please write a brief paragraph about your family & vocational life (approx. 3 full sentences):

Please share a little about your spiritual journey & what you are currently most passionate about in ministry. Please limit the story to one paragraph (approx. 4 full sentences):

Please share why you feel called to be a part of the Leadership Board in one brief paragraph (approx. 3 full sentences):

Which worship service do you typically attend? ☐ 9:00am Traditional ☐ 11:30am Contemporary

Are you part of a Sunday School Class or Wesleyan Small Group for discipleship? If so, which one?

☐ Gathering   ☐ Cornerstone   ☐ Celebration Choir
☐ New Beginning   ☐ Genesis   ☐ 20/30 Group
☐ College & Career   ☐ Forum   ☐ Journey Group
☐ Other: _____

Are you willing to serve a three-year term (January 2022 – December 2024)?   ☐ Yes   ☐ No
If no, what length of time would you be willing to serve? _____

Are you available for a leadership retreat on _(DATE)_ ?   ☐ Yes   ☐ No

Please fill out this Interest Form completely and return to the church office or the welcome desk by (DATE).

R-7: Sample Nominations Interview Questions

Thank you for your interest in offering yourself to serve in ministry on the Leadership Board. Our time together will help the Committee on Nominations and Leadership Development members better discern the most faithful steps in connecting the needs of the church's leadership to those who have offered themselves for consideration to serve.

1. Could you start by sharing with us where or how God is working with you currently as a maturing disciple?

2. How are you currently being faithful to your membership covenant through your prayers, presence, gifts, service, and witness?

3. What is it that has brought you to discern that you are being called into church leadership in this season of your life?

4. What excites you most about the possibility of serving on the Leadership Board and why?

5. What concerns/scares you most about the possibility of serving on the Leadership Board and why?

6. As you know, the church (has made the decision or) has adopted the simplified, accountable structure. What is your understanding of what simplification of the structure means? How would you describe accountable leadership?

7. The Leadership Board has a big responsibility to lead the church in its mission of making disciples. This is likely to stir up emotions and passions of the various leaders around the table when decisions are made - and rightly so! How will you feel if the Leadership Board makes a decision that you do not personally agree with? (follow-up question) Will you be able to support the decision both publicly and privately? How will you do that?

8. To sit in the Leadership Board Chair is a very different position than sitting in the pew. This means that some of the conversations and comments that might be appropriate as a congregant might not be appropriate for a board member to say. For example, a board member would not say anything negative about the pastor or other staff members regardless of how the board member felt personally. The board member is an advocate, encourager, supporter, and carrier of the mission and vision of the church. How would you handle a situation when one of your friends or family members who also attend church wanted you to share information, provide your opinion, or allow him/her to talk negatively about clergy or staff? (The current leadership covenant could be offered as a guide for the type of expectations board members would have. Ask candidates to review and provide any questions, feedback, or concerns.)

9. The board meets monthly for about 90 minutes, has an annual overnight strategic planning retreat scheduled on (date), and has an expectation that leaders will come to the meeting having reviewed a packet of information and reports prior to the meetings. From time-to-time, you may be placed on a work team for short-term projects to assist the board in their work. Are you willing and prepared to make this type of commitment for a three-year period?

10. If you were to serve on the Leadership Board, what would be your hope for your leadership ministry while serving? What would you like to accomplish or see happen?

11. What question should we have asked that we didn't?

12. What questions do you have for us?

R-8: Sample Nominations Report

2022 Anytown First UMC Leadership

- Anytown United Methodist Church is governed according to the denomination's prescribed structure as found in the *United Methodist Book of Discipline.* All *Book of Discipline* and congregational policy references to the Church Council, Board of Trustees, Staff/Pastor Parish Relations Committee, Endowment Committee, and Finance Committee shall be understood to refer to the Leadership Board. Where years are listed, they represent the final year of an individual's term.

- The Nominations Committee has undertaken a careful and discerning process of preparing the slate below for approval by Church Conference. The committee's aim is to match persons with open positions according to the following considerations:

  ¤ Maturity as a Disciple of Jesus Christ

  ¤ Alignment with the church's mission: "Making Disciples of Jesus Christ for the Transformation of the world"

  ¤ Length of membership tenure at Anytown UMC, with a balancing of experience in leadership with welcoming and engaging new leaders

  ¤ Actively fulfilling member expectations (*UM Discipline* ¶217): prayers, presence, gifts, service, and witness

  ¤ Past history of leadership in small groups, classes, ministry teams, and committees

  ¤ Balance and diversity of the committee, particularly with age, gender, and areas of involvement

  ¤ Ability to fulfill board requirements, the Board Covenant, and attend meetings

- As part of our Intentional Leadership Pathway, In YEAR, a class of "Preparatory Members" was created who will serve one year with voice, but without vote in order to prepare those who may subsequently be elected to serve a three-year voting term. In the event of a vacancy, the preparatory may be asked to complete a term.

Resource from *Mission Possible 3+,* by Kay Kotan and Blake Bradford. Market Square Publishing, 2021. Permission to copy for use with *Mission Possible 3+.*

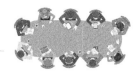

Anytown First UMC Charge Conference

- The Charge Conference includes the members of the Leadership Board, the Nominations Committee, pastors appointed to the congregation, and all active and retired clergy who have designated our congregation as their home Charge Conference.

- In order to "encourage broader participation by members of the church, the Nominations Committee recommends that Anytown FUMC request that any annual or called Charge Conference be convened as a Church Conference to extend the vote to all professing members of the congregation (2016 BOD ¶248).

- The Leadership Board serves as the incorporated institution's board of directors and serves as the executive committee of the Charge Conference.

Leadership Board

RECOMMENDED Version with NINE on the Board:

Class of 2022
John Jones, T/F/SPR
Carol Clark, T/F/SPR/LM
Yolanda Youngperson, F/SPR/Y

Class of 2023
Jennifer Jackson, T/F/SPR/C
Ben Black, T/F/SPR/LL
Larry Lewis, T/F/SPR

Class of 2024
Sue Smith, T/F/SPR/UMW
David Dent, T/F/SPR/UMM
Debbie Duncan, T/F/SPR

Version with ELEVEN voting on the Board
(Includes separate Lay Leader and Lay Member of AC who are not disciplinary term-limited)

Class of 2022
John Jones, T/F/SPR
Yolanda Youngperson, F/SPR/Y
Mary Miller, T/F/SPR

Class of 2023
Jennifer Jackson, T/F/SPR/C
Larry Lewis, T/F/SPR
Reggie Roberts, T/F/SPR/Treasurer

Class of 2024
Sue Smith, T/F/SPR/UMW
David Dent, T/F/SPR/UMM
Debbie Duncan, T/F/SPR

Preparatory Member
Andrea Anderson (non-voting)

Ex-Officio Members:
Lay Leader: Ben Black, F/SPR/LL
Lay Member of AC: Carol Clark, F/SPR/LM

Key
T – Trustee (a minimum of five and a maximum of nine, and includes at least 1/3 men and at least 1/3 women)
SPRC – Staff Parish Relations Committee, (a minimum of three and a maximum of nine, not including the Lay Leader and Lay Member to Annual Conference who are members)
F – Finance
LM – Lay Member to Annual Conference (Ex Officio on SPRC)
LL – Lay Leader (Ex Officio on SPRC)
C-Chair
UMM-United Methodist Men
UMW-United Methodist Women
Y-Youth (Note: members under 18 cannot be an elected Trustee)

Notes:
- At January meeting, Leadership Team will elect a Trustee Chairperson, which may be the Leadership Board Chairperson.
- Leadership Team may assign team members as Primary Contacts for matters pertaining to building maintenance, personnel, financial matters, or other areas of responsibility, but the Leadership Team operates as a single body encompassing the responsibilities of SPRC, Finance Committee, Endowment Committee, and Trustees.

Resource from *Mission Possible 3+*, by Kay Kotan and Blake Bradford. Market Square Publishing, 2021. Permission to copy for use with *Mission Possible 3+*.

Committee on Nominations and Leadership

Chairperson is the Appointed Senior Pastor (max 9 members, not including the pastor)

Class of 2022
Carl Clark
Belle Brady

Class of 2023
Rollie Rich
Gene Galloway

Class of 2024
Sally Smith
Rob Roberts

Child Enrichment Weekday Ministry Advisory Board

Anytown FUMC's tuition-based ministries provide Christian care and education for children throughout the year. The team provides advisory support for our state-licensed ministries for children and relates as a ministry team with the Lead Pastor (or designee), and is subordinate the Leadership Board of the congregation, according to *UMC Book of Discipline* ¶256.2.c. Since Anytown FUMC's weekday ministry shares the IRS employer ID number and nonprofit incorporation status with the church as a subordinate entity, the Anytown FUMC recommends all the Advisory Board members and chair for election by the Charge Conference. Non-members of FUMC, such as parents, may be elected to the Advisory Board, but the chair, selected by the Nominations Committee, must be a member. A majority of Advisory Board members must be professing members of Anytown FUMC.

> *¶256.2.c. Weekday Ministry Board – The term weekday ministry applies to any regularly planned ministry for children. When appropriate, one or more weekday ministry boards may be organized to oversee the weekday ministry programs of the congregation. The board's membership should be mostly professing members of the congregation, with parent, church staff, and weekday ministry staff representatives. The board will set policies consistent with the congregation's policies, state mandates, and sound business practices. The board will guide weekday ministries as appropriate opportunities for faith development, mission outreach, Christian education, evangelism, and safety. They will advocate for inclusion of children from various socioeconomic, cultural, and racial/ethnic backgrounds. Weekday ministry board(s) accountability should be placed within the local church organizational structure with consideration to the group responsible for the congregation's education ministry.*

Chairperson: Mary McMillan   **Treasurer:** Chosen by Committee   **Secretary:** Chosen by Committee

Class of 2022	Class of 2023	Class of 2024
Roland Rogers	Angela Atkins	Jeremy James
Suzy Simmons	Regina Rogers	Frankie Fulbright

Ex-Officio Members (with vote):

- Director of Child Enrichment Ministries
- Director of Faith Development
- Senior Pastor
- Associate Pastor

Resource from *Mission Possible 3+*, by Kay Kotan and Blake Bradford. Market Square Publishing, 2021. Permission to copy for use with *Mission Possible 3+*.

NOTES for readers:

1. We have included a sample of a non-independent childcare ministry to the nominations report because these entities are often a source of questions. If your congregation's childcare ministry is a separately incorporated 501(c)3, then a different kind of governing relationship must be explicitly negotiated and outlined. Take care to update any existing policies and by-laws so that the Leadership Team is defined as the executive committee of the congregation's Charge Conference and the body with which the separately incorporated child care ministry relates on matters such as rent, use of shared space and staffing, ownership of furnishings and property, relationship with the pastor and church ministries, and expectations concerning church membership representation on their independent 501(c)3 board (including who gets to choose the representatives).

2. Similarly, some churches have independently incorporated Local Church Foundations (*UM Discipline* ¶2535) instead of endowment committees. Since this arrangement creates a separately incorporated body, care will need to be taken to relate the governing board of the foundation to the congregation's Leadership Board and charge conference. This may require approving amendments to the bylaws of the foundation.

Resource from *Mission Possible 3+*, by Kay Kotan and Blake Bradford. Market Square Publishing, 2021. Permission to copy for use with *Mission Possible 3+*.

R-9: Sample Church Conference Resolution for Structure Transition

The Committee on Nominations and Leadership Development moves the Charge/Church Conference adoption of a resolution to modify our organizational plan of governance, utilizing the simplified, accountable structure:

Resolution to Change Congregational Organizational Plan to Simplified, Accountable Governance Structure

WHEREAS, ¶247.2 of the *2016 Book of Discipline for the United Methodist Church* allows alternative models of governance[†]; and

WHEREAS, the simplified, accountable leadership structure is utilized as an alternative model throughout the denomination and fulfills the provisions[††] of ¶ 243 of the *2016 Book of Discipline for the United Methodist Church;* and

WHEREAS, the Church Council of _____United Methodist Church prayerfully voted on (date) to explore the simplified, accountable structure for local church governance; and

WHEREAS, the congregation provided feedback concerning a potential change in governance structure on multiple occasions; and

WHEREAS, the congregation was motivated to convert for reasons of efficiency, alignment with our mission and vision, accountability, and missional focus; and

WHEREAS, the Church Council, Committee on Nominations and Leadership Development, [the task force on governance], and the pastor, after months of discernment, have crafted an alternative organizational for _____United Methodist Church and offered this proposal to the district superintendent for approval; and

WHEREAS, the district superintendent approved the alternative organizational plan on (date); and

NOW, THEREFORE, BE IT RESOLVED THAT:

1. On January 1, 20__ the Disciplinary authority and various responsibilities of the Church Council, Staff Parish Relations Committee (SPRC), Finance Committee, Endowment Committee, and Board of Trustees, will be combined into a single body called the Leadership Board.[†] Existing elected leadership of all classes of all constituent committees that make up the new Leadership Board will conclude their terms of service on December 31, 20__, as the church transitions to the new organizational plan.

2. The Committee on Nominations and Leadership Development of _____United Methodist Church is directed to submit a list of officers and members of a simplified, accountable structure known as the Leadership Board and a Committee on Nominations and Leadership Development, divided into appropriate three-year classes, as outlined in the *Discipline*, for election by the Charge Conference. All members of the Leadership Board and the Charge Conference will be professing members. The Chair of the Board of

Resource from *Mission Possible 3+,* by Kay Kotan and Blake Bradford. Market Square Publishing, 2021. Permission to copy for use with *Mission Possible 3+.*

Trustees will be elected from among the voting Trustee members of the Leadership Board in the first board meeting of each year, in accordance with the *Discipline*, and s/he may be the Leadership Board Chair.

3. On January 1, 20___, the Charge Conference of _____ United Methodist Church will be composed of the members of the Leadership Board, appointed clergy (ex-officio), together with retired ordained ministers and retired diaconal ministers who elect to hold their membership in our charge conference, Lay Members of Annual Conference, the Lay Leader, Treasurer and Finance Secretary (if non-staff), and the elected membership of the Committee on Nominations and Leadership Development.

4. The Lay Member of Annual Conference and Lay Leader are ex officio members of the Leadership Board, if not already elected into a membership class of the Leadership Board.

5. All Disciplinary requirements and qualifications for each of the constituent committees (Church Council, SPRC, Finance Committee, and Board of Trustees) will continue with the combined Leadership Board, including Trustee age of majority qualifications and SPRC household membership limitations.

6. All references to the Church Council, Board of Trustees, SPRC, and Finance Committee, in all existing church policies, as of December 31, 20___, shall be understood to refer to the Leadership Board beginning January 1, 20___.

7. The Board of Trustees is directed immediately to make appropriate amendments to the congregation's bylaws to reflect the new plan for organization and submit an update to the Secretary of State's office in a manner defined by state law for nonprofit corporations.

8. In service to our common mission to make disciples of Jesus Christ for the transformation of the world, all existing ministry teams will be accountable to the Pastor and Leadership Board in administrative matters and in fulfillment of ¶243.[††] The Weekday Child Care Ministry Advisory Board (¶ 256.2c) will be amenable to the Leadership Board in all matters, and is responsible for regular reporting to the Board. Alternative: If the Weekday Child Care Ministry is not a separate 501c3, this Advisory Board will be a ministry team and accountable directly to the Pastor.

9. The Leadership Board will abide with existing financial, child protection, building use, and personnel policies along with the inaugural Guiding Principles. The board will create a Leadership Board Covenant. The Leadership Board is empowered to amend these policies, principles, and covenant. The Leadership Board shall share updated Guiding Principles with the charge conference annually.

APPROVED, (date)

_____   _____
Secretary, Charge Conference   Presiding Elder

[†]¶247.2 *The Charge Conference, the district superintendent, and the pastor, when a pastor has been appointed (see ¶205.4), shall organize and administer the pastoral charge and churches according to the policies and plans herein set forth. When the membership size, program scope, mission resources, or other circumstances so require, the charge conference may, in consultation with and upon the approval of the district superintendent, modify the organizational plans, provided that the provisions of ¶243 are observed. Such other circumstances may include, but not be limited to, alternative models for the conception of a local church, such as coffee house ministries, mall ministries, outdoor ministries, retirement home ministries, restaurant ministries, and other emergent ways in which people can gather in God's name to be the church.*

[††]¶243. *Primary Tasks – The local church shall be organized so that it can pursue its primary task and mission in the context of its own community – reaching out and receiving with joy all who will respond; encouraging people in their relationship with God and inviting them to commitment to God's love in Jesus Christ; providing opportunities for them to seek strengthening and growth in spiritual formation; and supporting them to live lovingly and justly in the power of the Holy Spirit as faithful disciples.*

In carrying out its primary task, it shall be organized so that adequate provision is made for these basic responsibilities: (1) planning and implementing a program of nurture, outreach, and witness for persons and families within and without the congregation; (2) providing for effective pastoral and lay leadership; (3) providing for financial support, physical facilities, and the legal obligations of the church; (4) utilizing the appropriate relationships and resources of the district and annual conference; (5) providing for the proper creation, maintenance, and disposition of documentary record material of the local church; and (6) seeking inclusiveness in all aspects of its life.

R-10: Charge Conference Nominations Form

20____ Nominations – Simplified, Accountable Structure

Church

The use of this Simplified Structure is allowed by ¶247.2 of the *2016 Book of Discipline* with district superintendent approval. Indicate (ROLE) which member is serving as Chair (C), Lay Leader (LL), Lay Member to Annual Conference (LMAC), & Trustee Chair (TC). It is HIGHLY recommended that the board chair serve as the liaison to the DS for purposes of HR (DS). By Discipline, the "Trustee Chair" is elected by the "Trustees" (simplified structure for your church) at their first meeting of every year, so please contact your District Office to update or confirm your church's leadership record following the election.

The following persons will serve as the governing board, fulfilling the Disciplinary roles and responsibilities of Church Council, Trustees, Finance, and Staff/Pastor-Parish Relations Committee.

Term to Serve	Person's Name	Phone Number	Person's Email	Role C, LL, LMAC, DS, TC, UMW, UMM, UMY
Class of 2022				
Class of 2023				
Class of 2024				

Ex Officio Members MAY be elected with vote, but not serving as "Trustees" or voting on trustee-related business unless also part of the nine board members above. If the representatives from UMM, uMW, & UMY are part of the nine board members, you do NOT need to also include their names below. Simply note this affiliation with the appropriate code of UMW, UMM, or UMY.

UM Women Rep. (UMW)	
UM Men Rep. (UMM)	
UM Youth Rep. (UMY)	Youth under 18 cannot serve as Trustees

COMMITTEE ON NOMINATIONS AND LEADERSHIP DEVELOPMENT

¶258.1 – The committee is composed of not more than nine persons in addition to the pastor and lay leader. It shall include at least one young adult, and may include one or more youth.

Pastor (Chairperson) and Lay Leader		
Class of 2022	**Class of 2023**	**Class of 2024**

Resource from *Mission Possible 3+*, by Kay Kotan and Blake Bradford. Market Square Publishing, 2021. Permission to copy for use with *Mission Possible 3+*.

R-11: Sample Leadership Board Covenant Items

In addition to the list below, you may wish to add other covenantal elements that define the roles and authority of each board member individually and collectively, such as boundaries about making demands upon staff and staff time without consulting the pastor, matters of conflicts of interest, and the limits of personal authority as Leadership Board members.

- Leadership Board members are encouraged to invest in conversations and decisions with vigor and passion. However, once the Leadership Board has come to a decision, each Leadership Board member will openly and publicly support the decision of the Leadership Board whether the individual member personally agrees with the decision. We are a Leadership Board with a unified voice.

- Leadership Board members are expected to be present at all Leadership Board meetings unless ill or out of town. Members can be tied into meetings via speaker phones or video chat if needed. If members miss more than three meetings per year, the Leadership Board Chair will converse with the Leadership Board member to see if their seat needs to be vacated and filled by someone who can be more active.

- Leadership Board members are expected to attend the annual strategic ministry planning retreat. Members understand this is a foundational piece of the Leadership Board's work and every effort should be made to be fully present for the entire retreat.

- Leadership Board members will review the meeting packet prior to meetings coming fully prepared and ready to participate.

- Leadership Board members are role models for the congregation. Therefore, members will model mature discipleship by being present in worship at least three times per month, tithing or moving toward a tithe, have an active prayer life, serve in mission three times per year, be active in a ministry team, be in a faith development group, and openly share their faith with others in the secular world.

- Leadership Board members will be on time for meetings, silence cell phones, be fully present, and immerse themselves in the meeting without distractions in respect for others' time and commitment.

- Leadership Board members will encourage and support our pastor(s) and fellow board members.

- Leadership Board members will hold ourselves, the pastors, and other Leadership Board members accountable for their leadership roles and responsibilities. This includes allowing others to hold the board members collectively and individually accountable.

- Leadership Board members understand that conflict and disagreements are natural in any community, including the church. As a board, we will approach matters of disagreement with transparency and maintain our missional focus as a Leadership Board. When approached by a person or group concerning a matter of disagreement or conflict, we will follow the path laid out by Jesus on Matthew 18 by encouraging the concerned party to go directly to the individual, to volunteer to go with the concerned party as a witness, or to invite the concerned party to address the full leadership or an assigned work team to address the issue. At no time will we support secret meetings that undermine the integrity or authority of the pastor or Leadership Board.

- Leadership Board members understand that as a leader, comments or conversations about personnel (pastor or staff) is inappropriate with anyone at any level and is to be avoided. Members are expected to be supportive and encouraging publicly. Concerns are to be processed with the collective Leadership Board only.

- Leadership Board members carry, support, and promote the mission and vision of the church at all times.

- Leadership Board members hold one another in prayer and invest in their board prayer partner through daily prayer and minimum weekly interaction.

R-12: Sample Guiding Principles

Topics and Focus Areas for Guiding Principle Consideration

- Mission, vision, core values of the church

- Identification of the board's role, powers, responsibilities, and authority, in regards to the *Book of Discipline*

- Clear distinction for the role of governance for the board - not management

- The Leadership Board will ensure there is a current organizational chart reflective of the current decision-making process and chain of command at all times.

- The Leadership Board is to provide transparent and routine communication to keep the congregation informed of missional effectiveness and resource alignment.

- Financial approval policies for staff/ministry team leaders, the pastor, and the building maintenance team

- Hiring, terminating, and evaluating authority of the pastor and other paid staff

- References or inclusion to church wide policies for the following areas:

  - Building and equipment usage policies (for example, facility rental policies for members, internal ministry groups, outside non-profit groups or for-profit businesses)

  - Safe sanctuary policies for child protection

  - Employee handbook

  - Building safety

  - Technology usage and safety

  - Counters' policies and procedures

- How decisions will be made by the Leadership Board: parliamentary rules of order, such as the usage of Robert's Rules of Order, the consensus method, or other variations.

- Include how to edit or add a guiding principle

- Official record keeping practices and access to records of meetings and executive session minutes

Resource from *Mission Possible 3+*, by Kay Kotan and Blake Bradford. Market Square Publishing, 2021. Permission to copy for use with *Mission Possible 3+*.

- Role and function of the building maintenance team

- Authority and responsibility of the treasurer

- Relationship of Nominations and Leadership Development to the Leadership Board

- Boundaries that state how individual board members may not make demands on staff time outside formal board requests.

- How daycare and/or preschool relate to the church, pastor, and Leadership Board in terms of supervision of personnel and accountability (There is a huge legal and governance difference between childcare ministries that operate under a church's ministry (operate under the church's legal umbrella) and childcare ministries that exist as a separate but related 501(c)(3). These differences will impact how you write your guiding principle defining the relationship as well as how they appear on the organization chart.)

- Defining public meetings vs executive sessions (such as personnel matters when the board is operating as the congregation's S/PPRC).

Guiding Principles Catalogue

The following guiding principles are offered to you as guide lines or thought-starters. These are not intended to be a complete set of building principles. In fact, you will find a few of the guiding principles are contradictory to one another. This is intentional and is offered to remind churches of the importance around clarity around specific principles. Guiding principles are intended to be a permission-giving tool to eliminate waiting on decisions or permission as a bottle-neck to ministry flow. Guiding principles provide healthy boundaries and macro rather than micro decision-making. Please do not cut and paste these (or other churches') guiding principles. Every church has its own unique setting, so special care and attention in this work will prove to pay dividends for years to come.

- All references to the Church Council, Board of Trustees, Staff/Pastor Parish Relations Committee, Endowment Committee, and Finance Committee, in all congregational policies as of _____, and in all references in the *Book of Discipline* of the United Methodist Church, shall be understood to refer to the Leadership Board beginning _____.

- Once the budget is approved, those responsible (i.e., staff and team leaders) for the various ministry areas have the authority to spend their budget to align with the objectives for their ministry area approved by the pastor. No further approval is needed to access the budget in their area of responsibility. *

- The pastor is responsible for reviewing line items within ministry areas with the appropriate staff or team leaders for accountability from the staff and to the board.

- Any member of the Building Maintenance Team has the authority to purchase supplies for building maintenance and improvement up to $_____ without approval. The Building Maintenance Team leader can authorize purchases for building maintenance and improvement up to $_____. Purchases up to $_____ can be approved by the pastor (executive pastor or business manager). Any purchases over $_____ need Leadership Board approval unless the expenditure is already approved in a capital expenditure line item in the approved budget. *

- Any expenditure over $_____ will require three bids. Preference will be given to hire local companies offering competitive bids within ___% of other bids. If the expenditure is already approved in the budget and meets the previous criteria, there is no further approval needed. The ministry team leader or staff member responsible for the purchase will provide documentation of the bids to the Leadership Board for purposes of a paper trail only. *

- *The treasurer must be consulted concerning any single purchase or expenditure over $_____ for purposes of cash flow. The treasurer does not approve or deny purchases but rather confirms large purchases will not create cash flow issues.

- The pastor has the authority to hire and release employees using the church's employee policies and procedures in the ___ UMC Employee Handbook. When terminating an employee, the pastor will invite a board member to sit in on the exiting conversation for purposes of liability protection. The pastor has the responsibility to supervise, discipline, and evaluate staff performance as outlined in the ___ UMC Employee Handbook.

- The authority to hire and terminate employees of the church shall be vested in the Leadership Board. The pastor shall have the authority to interview and recommend candidates to fill open staff positions. The Board shall have the sole authority to determine the number of staff positions, approve job descriptions for each staff member and set the salary paid to each staff member. The Leadership Board delegates to the pastor the authority to supervise, discipline, and manage paid staff.

- The pastor will review all paid staff annually using the approval evaluation process in the employee manual dated _____. Paid staff will review unpaid staff/team and leaders annually using the same evaluation process.

- The Weekday Child Care Advisory Board (BOD ¶ 256.2.c) is fully amenable and accountable to the Leadership Board and shall submit an annual budget and recommended policy changes to the Leadership Board. The director of weekday ministries is supervised by the pastor.

- The board recognizes and approves the Building Usage Policies dated _____.

- The board recognizes and approves the Building Security and Key Policies dated _____.

- The board recognizes and approves the Financial Controls Policies dated _____.

- The board recognizes and approves the ____ UMC Personnel Policies date _____.

- All meetings of the Leadership Board shall be open to the public, with the exception of any meeting or portion of a meeting in which a personnel matter or a matter of legal negotiations is considered. In those cases, the Board will transition into executive session. Minutes of executive session agenda items concerning personnel matters will be kept separately as part of the "S/PPRC" files.

- Leadership Board members are nominated by a separate and independent Committee on Nominations and Leadership Development, chaired by the pastor, and elected by the Charge Conference as described in the BOD. The Nominations Committee will be responsible for developing new leaders and equipping them for future Leadership Board positions.

- Due to Leadership Board's serving as the congregation's Staff-Parish Relations Committee, no immediate family member of the pastor or other paid staff person may serve as a member of the board. Due to serving as the congregation's Board of Trustees, only Leadership Board members over the age 18 will have voting privileges in matters of property, incorporation, legal matters, contracts, insurance, investments, or other matters described in the BOD ¶s 2525-2551.

- The Lead Pastor is the Leadership Board's only link to church ministry and programming. The Lead Pastor has complete authority and accountability for all staffing, including hiring, evaluating, firing, and consideration of raises. The Council will never give instructions to persons who report directly or indirectly to the Lead Pastor. The Council will view Lead Pastor performance as identical to church performance so that organizational goals will be viewed as the Lead Pastor's performance.

- Compensation for the Lead Pastor and all appointed clergy will be determined by a Charge/Church Conference. Recommendations for the Lead Pastor's compensation will be made by the Leadership Board (as part of their SPRC duties) to the entire Church Council for consideration before the Charge/Church Conference. Recommendations for other appointed clergy compensation will be made by the Lead Pastor in consultation with the Leadership Board to the entire Church Council for consideration before the Charge/Church Conference. Decisions about increases in the Lead Pastor's compensation will be based primarily on the following three criteria: 1. Council's review of Lead Pastor's effectiveness in reaching established goals. 2. Needs of the church for a Lead Pastor with the skill sets necessary for reaching established goals. This will be determined in relationship to the compensation packages of churches of similar or larger size in the Annual Conference. 3. Possible cost of living increases. However, it is understood that the primary criteria for compensation will always be (a) the Leader Board's review of the Lead Pastor's performance.

- The Lead Pastor shall not cause or allow any activity, decision, or organizational circumstance that is unlawful or in violation of commonly accepted business practices and professional ethics. Furthermore, the Lead Pastor shall not cause or allow any activity, decision, or organizational circumstance that is a violation of the current *Book of Discipline,* Standing Rules of the Annual Conference, or the express direction of the resident bishop and/or district superintendent of the annual conference.

R-13: Leadership Board Meeting Agenda

First United Methodist Church
Leadership Board Meeting
Date _____

Our Mission: To make new disciples of Jesus Christ for the transformation of the world.

Our Vision: Each of us at FUMC is on a journey to grow closer to God, to be more like Jesus, and to be filled with the Holy Spirit. No matter where you are in your walk with Christ, you are invited to journey and grow with us, through the power of the Holy Spirit, so that we can fulfill God's commission.

Core Values: Excellence, evangelism, engagement, equipping, expansion and encouragement.

Time	Item	Leader
6:00pm	Opening Prayer	Jennifer Jackson, Chair
6:00pm	Spiritual Formation	David Dent
6:15pm	Leadership Equipping	Carol Clark
6:30pm	Review of New People	Pastor Taylor
6:35pm	Goal Review and Accountability Conversation	Pastor Taylor
6:50pm	Packet and Consent Calendar Items	
6:55pm	Leadership Opportunities	Jennifer Jackson
6:55:	Item #1	
7:05:	Item #2	
7:15:	Item #3	
7:25	Communication	
7:30	Closing Prayer	Debbie Duncan

Next Meeting is (date) _____

Resource from *Mission Possible 3+*, by Kay Kotan and Blake Bradford. Market Square Publishing, 2021. Permission to copy for use with *Mission Possible 3+*.

R-14: Online Report/Request for Action Form for Leadership Board

Update/ Action Request for __(DATE)____

Please submit this form to the church office 10 days prior to Leadership Board Meeting,
so it can be added to the agenda

❏ **For Information Only**   ❏ **Needs Action from Leadership Board**

Committee or   ❏ Facilities Team   ❏ Worship Planning Team

Ministry Team: ❏ Ministry Team/Task Group:_____   ❏ Staff:_____

(Staff should coordinate with pastor before submitting)

Committee Chair/Team Leader Contact:

Name: _____   Email: _____   Phone: _____

ISSUE / PROPOSAL:

Use this section to explain the actions, key strategies, and/or challenges with which
the committee or team is faced. Include proposed solutions or strategic plans.

FINDINGS / RATIONALE:

Explain how the proposed action helps the congregation
fulfill its mission and impact the mission field.

FUNDING IMPLICATIONS? ❑ None beyond budgeted Annual Fund

❑ Yes; See below for costs and funding plan

Financial Stewardship in a congregation requires advance planning, teamwork, and discernment of priorities. Fundraising beyond the Annual Fund can be delicate work.

Please include in this section the financial implications of the proposal, and fundraising plans if Designated Funds or additional support is required.

ACTIONS TAKEN BY COMMITTEE / TEAM:

Our congregation seeks to empower committees and ministry teams to do ministry and take action, within the guiding principles, strategic goals, and administrative policies of the congregation. Use this section to outline the actions planned or already taken by the Committee/Team under its own authority.

ACTIONS REQUIRING Leadership Board APPROVAL:

This includes: Proposed changes in Policy or Guiding Principles, actions requiring Fiduciary or Mandated Duties, actions requiring changes in the Budget, and proposals that would change a congregational strategic goal.

Resource from *Mission Possible 3+,* by Kay Kotan and Blake Bradford. Market Square Publishing, 2021. Permission to copy for use with *Mission Possible 3+.*

R-15: Leadership Board's Annual Rhythm Checklist and Reference Chart

Checklist for Planning your Leadership Rhythm

- Establish your leadership rhythm and tweak it as necessary
- Always plan at least one season ahead (bonus points for planning a year ahead!)
- Conduct at least one strategic planning leadership retreat annually
- Evaluate mission, vision and progress on goals monthly

Annual Rhythm Reference Chart for the Leadership Board

Month	Focus
January	Elect "trustee" chair, covenant, roles/responsibilities, commissioning service for out-going and in-coming Leadership Board members during worship
February	Easter plans, statistical trends, facility improvement plans
March	Town hall meetings with feedback
April	Deep financial dive, stewardship campaign planning, serve together
May	Ensure policies, procedures, and guiding principles are up to date
June	Deep dive into goals to identify any needed shifts
July	Possible new pastor arrival, Town Hall
August	Final retreat preparations, staff evaluations completed by pastor, feedback from cottage meetings if a new pastor has been appointed
September	Strategic ministry planning retreat conducted, nominations working on discerning new leadership for upcoming year
October	Clergy evaluation, staff retreat, staff budget requests, clergy appreciation
November	Finalize budget, charge conference, new leader training
December	State of the church town hall, clergy consultation

R-16: Suggested Strategic Ministry Planning Steps and Timeline

Month	Action Step
August	Inform new leaders of retreat dates
August	Assign/select prayer partners for retreat
September	Strategic ministry planning retreat led by third party
September/October	Staff retreat led by pastor
October/November	Budget requests to Board from staff via pastor based on goals
December	Meeting and strategic planning retreat dates set for next year
January	Reservations at retreat center for September retreat
February	Recruit third party leader to lead retreat
March-August	Board chair and pastor work with the retreat leader to assure effective and efficient retreat experience including team building, missional evaluations, setting spiritual and leadership formation for upcoming year, SMARTER goals for upcoming year, and other relevant deeper strategic and generative work.
Use *Strategy Matters* as a complete strategic ministry planning retreat resource and guide	

R-17: Simplified, Accountable Structure (SAS)

Frequently Asked Questions for the District Superintendent

1. Where can I find information on simplified structure in the *Book of Discipline?*

¶ 247.2 in the 2016 edition

2. Which positions can be combined for one person on the Board to hold?

Most all positions can be combined as long as the minimum number is elected. The Lay Leader, Lay Member to Annual Conference, S/PPR Chair and Trustee Chair must be designated, but could all be the same person.

3. Is there an absolute minimum number for the Board?

Nine is the standard and recommended minimum. Very small congregations may be able to have a Board of six, composed of two individuals in each three-year class.

4. Does the pastor have a vote?

No. Because the Leadership Board's work switches roles quickly from Disciplinary committee to committee, we recommend that the pastor not vote, in order to preserve clarity and unity in the Board. If a matter comes up that depends on one vote of the pastor, that is probably a sign that more conversation and discernment is needed.

5. Can family members serve together on the Board?

Per the Book of Discipline, family members cannot serve on the Board together. If it cannot be avoided, the family members may need to excuse themselves from the room or not vote on issues with potential conflict of interest. Staff and family of staff cannot serve on the Board.

6. Should staff (paid and unpaid) serve on the Board?

No

7. Are the Financial Secretary and Treasurer required to be on the Board?

No, but they can be. The recommendation and best practice is for them not to be on the Board and instead to be thought of as more of a staff position.

8. Which position on the Board serves as the liaison to the district superintendent for Staff/Pastor Parish Relations Committee purposes?

It is recommended that the Board Chair serves as the S/PPRC liaison to the DS.

9. Are there still three-year terms and classes?

Yes. One third of the Board will roll off each year.

Resource from *Mission Possible 3+,* by Kay Kotan and Blake Bradford. Market Square Publishing, 2021. Permission to copy for use with *Mission Possible 3+.*

10. Is the Board self-nominating?

No. There is still a requirement that there be a separate Committee on Nominations and Leadership Development to nominate the Board Members to the Charge Conference each year.

11. How long can a person serve on the Board? Board members serve a three-year term.

Since all members are serving as S/PPR, Trustees and Finance, it is recommended they roll off after each three-year term. After being off the Board for a year, the person can roll back onto the Board if elected.

12. Are UMM, UMW, and UMYF representatives required to be on the Board?

If the church has these chartered groups, a member of that group may serve if requested on the Board as a leader of the local congregation (not to report about their group).

13. How many must be present to take an official vote? What requires an official vote?

A quorum is described as whoever is present. (Note of exception: in rare matters that require the Trustees to function as a legal body, a majority of Board members who are Trustees must be present.) Simple majority of Board members attending approves a motion.

14. How is the Trustee Chair elected or appointed as required by the corporate resolution?

At the first meeting at the beginning of each new year, the Board will elect a "trustee chair" to satisfy the corporate resolution requirement. It is recommended the Board Chair serve as the trustee chair. Please note that all members of the Board who will serve in the role as a trustee must be of legal age (18+ in most states).

15. If a church moves to the simplified, accountable structure, how does ministry happen?

Even though the restructuring occurs, ministry teams are still needed and in place. Fewer people on the Board means more people are available to do ministry. Simplifying structure is the combining of the four administrative teams of the Council, Trustees, Finance and S/PPR Committees. The only change for ministry teams is that the Nominations Committee is no longer responsible for identifying and nominating leaders and members for ministry teams.

16. What kind of approval is needed from the DS to move to the simplified structure?

The DS must approve a modified organizational structure. We highly recommend two points of DS contact before moving forward: First, the Pastor and Church Council Chair (and perhaps also the Lay Leader) request permission to begin discernment and study. We also highly recommend a SAS Coach be deployed to help the church in this Discernment Phase. After the congregation discerns and discusses the matter, then the Church Council votes on whether or not to make a formal request to move to SAS. Upon a favorable vote, the pastor, church council chair, and lay leader write a letter to the DS seeking formal approval permission to move to the SAS structure along with a Church Conference to consider moving to the modified organizational structure.

17. What kind of approval is needed from the congregation to move to the simplified structure?

We highly recommend a two-step approval process: First, the Church Council requests formal DS permission and a Church Conference, with every professing member able to vote, to consider moving to the modified organizational structure. A Resolution will need to place all committee authority into the new Leadership Board and call on Nominations to recommend potential board members. Then, a called or annual Charge Conference in which the Nominations Committee offers up an initial slate of nine board members, divided into three classes.

18. Must the SAS Board members be professing members of the church?

Yes. By Discipline, all Board Members will need to be professing members of the church because some of the constituent committees require professing membership, with a Discipline-recommended minimum of 1/3 being laywomen and 1/3 being lay men.

19. What size church is too small or too large for SAS?

While 247.2 was written primarily for small churches who had difficulty finding enough people to fill all the "slots" in a committee structure, it was some of our largest churches that first discovered the power and efficiency of SAS. Churches with an average worship attendance under 50 may already be doing a de facto simplified structure which may or may not include accountability. Large Churches that worship in the thousands have discovered the need for SAS as they seek to counteract ministry silos and mission drift. Congregations from 50-500 in worship will quickly discover the power of SAS in unleashing more laity for ministry and focusing the church on Christ's mission.

20. Who can attend the meetings?

Congregation members are always invited to attend the meetings, but do not have voice or vote. When the Board needs to move to executive session to address S/PPRC matters or to consider legal negotiations (such as buying or selling property), these church members will need to be excused.

R-18: Requirements for initial DS consultation

Initial Consultation with Your District Superintendent

Share your motivations and reasons (your WHY) for a potential structure change.	
List the names and roles of lay officers involved in the discussion up to this point.	
Share which Disciplinary administrative committees you believe will be incorporated into the governing Leadership Board. While this may, of course, change as your church leadership wrestles with the possibilities and options, the DS may have particular recommendations or requirements so that your church's structure may be approved.	☐ Church Council/Administrative Board ☐ Council on Ministries ☐ Staff-Parish Relations Committee ☐ Board of Trustees ☐ Finance Committee ☐ Endowment Committee ☐ Other_____ ☐ Other_____ ☐ Other_____
Share your possible timeline for the structure change. Use the Discernment Steps.	Discernment Steps: _____ Consultation with the DS: _____ Contact SAS Certified Coach: _____ Congregational Vote: _____ Nominations Work: _____ Charge Conference Elections: _____ New Board Begins Service: _____

Resource from *Mission Possible 3+*, by Kay Kotan and Blake Bradford. Market Square Publishing, 2021. Permission to copy for use with *Mission Possible 3+*.

R-19: Recommendation for District Governance Simplification

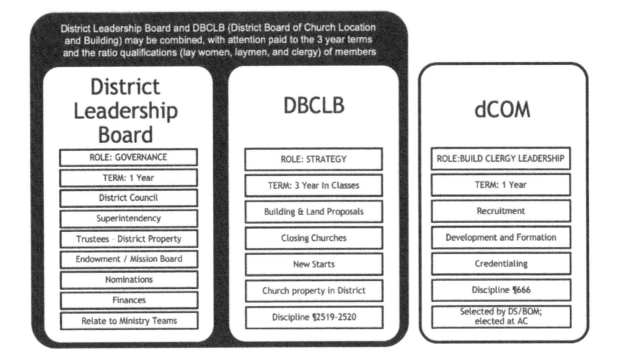

District Leadership Board

- District Lay Leader (four-year quadrennium term)

- Two Lay Women (Trustees)

- Two Lay Men (Trustees)

- Two Clergy (Trustees)

- Two At-Large Members (We recommend a Finance Steward or Treasurer and a District Ministry Team Liaison)

- Two Members selected by DS

- Any Non-Voting Advisory Members as needed (There may be ex officio officers that your conference requires, or that would prove helpful in your context such as disaster response coordinators.)

Resource from *Mission Possible 3+*, by Kay Kotan and Blake Bradford. Market Square Publishing, 2021. Permission to copy for use with *Mission Possible 3+*.

R-20: SAS for Conferences

A Conference Leadership Team:

- Chair: Conference Lay Leader (in collaboration with the Bishop)

- Twelve people: 1/3 laywomen, 1/3 laymen, 1/3 clergy with 1/5 appointed by Bishop

  - Include first lay and clergy delegates elected to General Conference

  - Directors of Congregational Development, Leadership Development, Connectional Ministries, and Administrative Services

  - Chair of Board of Ordained Ministry,

  - Chair of Cong Development Team

  - Chair of Leadership Development Team

  - Chair of Connectional Ministries Team

Note: Conference Staff Directors and Bishop are non-voting members.

A model using three Conference Ministries Teams

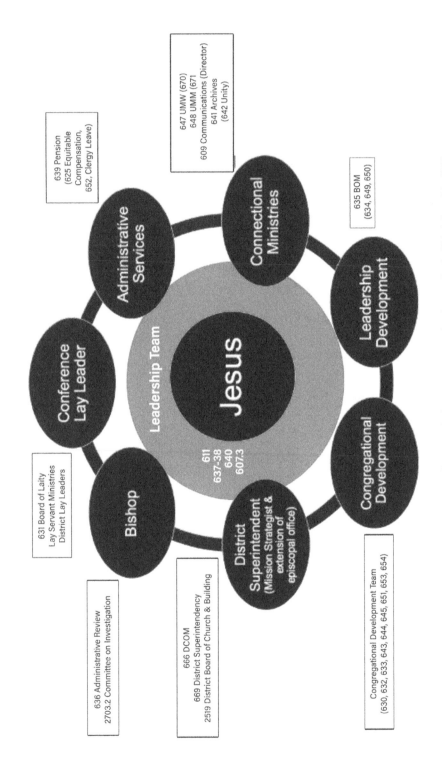

639 Pension
(625 Equitable Compensation,
652, Clergy Leave)

647 UMW (670)
648 UMM (671
609 Communications (Director)
641 Archives
(642 Unity)

635 BOM
(634, 649, 650)

Administrative Services

Connectional Ministries

Leadership Development

Conference Lay Leader

Leadership Team

Jesus

611
637-38
640
607.3

Congregational Development

Bishop

District Superintendent
(Mission Strategist & extension of episcopal office)

631 Board of Laity
Lay Servant Ministries
District Lay Leaders

636 Administrative Review
2703.2 Committee on Investigation

666 DCOM
669 District Superintendency
2519 District Board of Church & Building

Congregational Development Team
(630, 632, 633, 643, 644, 645, 651, 653, 654)

All numerical references correspond to the 2016 Book of Discipline of the UMC

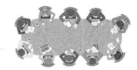

A model using a combined Connectional Ministries Team

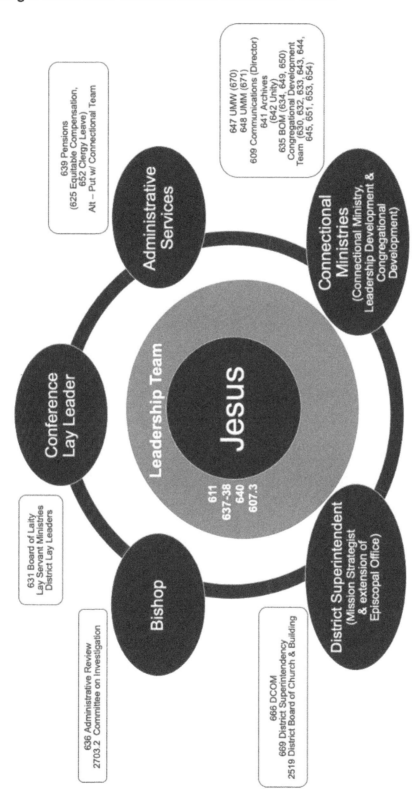

All numerical references correspond to the 2016 Book of Discipline of the UMC

647 UMW (670)
648 UMM (671)
609 Communications (Director)
641 Archives
(642 Unity)
635 BOM (634, 649, 650)
Congregational Development
Team (630, 632, 633, 643, 644, 645, 651, 653, 654)

639 Pensions
(625 Equitable Compensation,
652 Clergy Leave)
Alt – Put w/ Connectional Team

Administrative Services

Connectional Ministries
(Connectional Ministry,
Leadership Development &
Congregational
Development)

Conference Lay Leader

Leadership Team

Jesus

611
637-38
640
607.3

631 Board of Laity
Lay Servant Ministries
District Lay Leaders

Bishop

District Superintendent
(Mission Strategist
& extension of
Episcopal Office)

636 Administrative Review
2703.2 Committee on Investigation

666 DCOM
669 District Superintendency
2519 District Board of Church & Building

Resource from *Mission Possible 3+,* by Kay Kotan and Blake Bradford. Market Square Publishing, 2021. Permission to copy for use with *Mission Possible 3+.*

R-21: Creating a Conference-wide Approach to Simplified, Accountable Structure

1. Start with accountable leadership at all levels: conference staff, coaches, congregations, pastors, district superintendents

2. Create conference-wide consistency and common SAS language (preferably through SAS Coach Certification)

    a. SAS Certified Coaches have on-going access to learning and best practices

    b. SAS Certified Coaches is a national group sharing, supporting, and equipping specifically for SAS

    c. Having Certified SAS Coaches ensures your conference has the most updated information, resources, and think-tank for simplified, accountable structure

    d. Having Certified SAS Coaches provides a partner for DS's to assist in discernment, equipping and implementing with consistency and the latest best practices

    e. Having Certified SAS Coaches will provide a team of equipped coaches to walk alongside churches in their discerning, equipping, implementing initially and on-going which ensures the best chance of a healthy transition.

3. Maintain clear expectations for congregations seeking to utilize SAS

    a. Ensure adherence to BOD (term limits, qualifications, conflicts of interest, membership)

    b. Ensure existence of separate and independent Nominations Committees that relate to the charge conference

    c. Emphasize that all the Disciplinary expectations and authorities of the included committees are invested in the new Leadership Board. No one should ever say, "we got rid of all committees"

    d. Recommend Leadership Board Chair also serve as the liaison to the DS

    e. Expectation for equipping ALL SAS Churches' New Leaders - this means SAS equipping would need to be offered annually by a Certified SAS Coach

Resource from *Mission Possible 3+,* by Kay Kotan and Blake Bradford. Market Square Publishing, 2021. Permission to copy for use with *Mission Possible 3+.*

4. Create clear expectations for district superintendents to maintain alignment

   a. DS's Trained in the most current SAS recommendations (For instance, we no longer recommend SPRC or finance "representatives" as part of our board training.)

   b. Take churches using the SAS model into consideration during the appointment process. If a pastor is not willing and/or able to lead and be held accountable and to hold staff accountable, extreme caution should be demonstrated. Consider another appointment or at the very least provide a Certified SAS Coach during the first year of the appointment for the purposes of equipping, supporting, encouraging, and accountability.

   c. A willingness to tell churches "NO" regarding SAS as the best faithful step for a congregation when the church is not ready, it's not the right season to transition, has unresolved conflict, or unwilling to practice accountable leadership.

   d. Create a conference-wide system for district superintendents to consider requests from congregations seeking to begin discernment and approval of SAS

   e. Deploy a conference-wide Charge Conference Nominations Form specifically for congregations that use SAS

   f. In assessment and consultation materials, support alignment of pastoral goals and congregational goals with conference strategic goals

5. Conference Cabinets and Developers should create and manage a SAS Coaching System

   a. Encourage collaboration between the coaches and the district superintendents

   b. Coach Report Precedes Coach Payment for Accountability

   c. Have Coach Review SAS Nominations Form

   d. Create List of Churches Implementing Well for Others to Talk to and "Sit In" on their SAS Meetings (clergy & laity)

   e. Have an evaluation process for SAS Coaches to ensure local congregations and leaders are being provided the resources needed and congregations are truly living into the SAS model

Resource from *Mission Possible 3+,* by Kay Kotan and Blake Bradford. Market Square Publishing, 2021. Permission to copy for use with *Mission Possible 3+.*

R-22: Shifts Made in SAS

Below is a quick list of the shifts made in the past decade in structuring, implementing and understanding simplified, accountable structure. Often those who have not kept up on the model are unaware of these best practices or shifts. Therefore, some less than optimum practices continue and are often shared in additional settings perpetuating the unhealthy practices, using no longer recommended approaches, and missing newly discovered approaches for a more sustainable and effective leadership structure with accountability. This is one of many reasons why on-going training is important – even if a clergy or lay person has had prior training.

- **Shift in Practice:** No More Representatives or Specialists– Instead use Work Teams

- **Shift in Terminology:** Stop using "single board" structure or "one-board" model

- **Shift in Size:** We recommend nine Board Members, not nine to thirteen

- **Shift in Training: Creation of Three Phases - Discernment, Equipping, Implementation**

- **Shift in Chair Responsibilities:** Board Chair should be Lay Leader, DS Liaison (S/PPRC), and Trustee Chair

- **Shift in Leadership Preference:** From secular experience to mature disciples

- **Shift in Nominations Committee Role:** equipping, application/interview, intentional leadership development

- **Shift in Priorities:** Communication is key

- **Shift in Resourcing:** A growing, shareable toolbox and certified SAS coach cohort has been created

R-23: Best Practices to Eliminate Common SAS "Gaps"

The lists below identify the common gaps in implementation of the simplified, accountable structure in local churches. They are divided into the three areas which are the most difficult areas of change and development when implementing SAS: accountability, adaptive change, and leadership. Certified SAS Coaches are trained to help develop good practices to eliminate these gaps when working with leaders.

Accountability Gaps:

- Developing and enforcing the Leadership Covenant
- Holding one another accountable at all levels
- Unified voice
- Practicing Appropriate Confidentiality
- Governance Mode
- Shift from congregant to leader
- Coaching investment

Adaptive Change Gaps

- Communication
- Agenda
- Incompatible Room Set Up
- Strategic Ministry Planning followed by Staff/Ministry Team Leaders Retreat
- Move from reporting to generative and strategic priorities

Leadership Gaps

- Hard conversations
- Pastor over or under leading
- Developing and enforcing Guiding Principles
- Leadership Selection
- BOD Issues: term limits, relatives, separate nominations
- Establishing forwarding thinking rhythms
- Establish on-going SAS training

R-24: Initial Consultation with Your District Superintendent to study a ¶ 247.2 Modified Organizational Plan

Share your motivations and reasons (your WHY) for a potential structure change	
List the names and roles of lay officers involved in the discussion up to this point.	
Share which Disciplinary administrative committees you believe will be incorporated into the governing Leadership Board. While this may, of course, change as your church leadership wrestles with the possibilities and options, the DS may have particular recommendations or requirements so that your church's structure may be approved.	❑ Church Council/Administrative Board ❑ Council on Ministries ❑ Staff-Parish Relations Committee ❑ Board of Trustees ❑ Finance Committee ❑ Endowment Committee ❑ Other_____ ❑ Other_____ ❑ Other_____
Share your possible timeline for the structure change. Use the Discernment Steps.	Discernment Steps:_____ Consultation with the DS: _____ Contact SAS Certified Coach: Congregational Vote: _____ Nominations Work: _____ Charge Conference Elections:_____ New Board Begins Service:_____

R-25: Formal Request to the DS to use a ¶247.2 Modified Organizational Plan

1. A request for approval of a modified organizational plan, based on ¶247.2 of the *Discipline*	
2. A listing of the committees that will be combined in the new Leadership Board	☐ Church Council/Administrative Board ☐ Council on Ministries ☐ Staff-Parish Relations Committee ☐ Board of Trustees ☐ Finance Committee ☐ Endowment Committee ☐ Other_____ ☐ Other_____ ☐ Other_____
3. A brief overview of the discernment process used by the congregation to come to their recommendation.	Discernment Team study: Initial Consultation with the DS: Congregational Feedback Methods: Work with SAS Certified Coach:
4. A copy of the resolution that will be used to transition to the new structure	See the Resources Section for a sample resolution
5. A request for further consultation and feedback with the district superintendent, as the superintendent feels necessary.	
6. A request to convene a charge conference as a ¶248 Church Conference in order to encourage the broadest support and participation of the congregation for the change.	

R-26 Brief Overview of Simplified, Accountable Structure

In the United Methodist Church (UMC), our polity has historically called for four administrative committees to care for the "business" of the church. Those four committees are the Trustees Committee, Finance Committee, Pastor-Parish Relations Committee, and the Church Council. These committees usually consist of 6-12 people serving three-year rotating terms. In addition to these generalities, each committee has its particular nuances and requirements as outlined in our *UMC Book of Discipline* (book that constitutes the law, polity, and doctrine of the United Methodist Church). While the structure and numbers vary from church to church, the average congregation has somewhere between 25 to 75 members tied up in serving on these four administrative committees.

While the predecessor bodies that constitute our denomination have approved a *Book of Discipline* for 200 years, the first edition of the *United Methodist Book of Discipline* originated in 1968 when the UMC was formed through the union of the Evangelical United Brethren Church and the Methodist Church. In 1968 the church's primary responsibility was to receive the continuous flow of people coming in the door from a church-centric culture and make them official members. Designed for continuity and stability, the legacy committee structures we inherited were simply not designed for the complexity and rapid changes of our modern era. In the 21st Century, simply adding names to the membership roll is not the primary responsibility of the administrative committees since culture is no longer church-centric (in fact the church is counter cultural) thus resulting in the church needing to structure differently for a shifting time and focus.

In the latest edition (2016) of the *Book of Discipline* ¶247.2, the church, with approval of the district superintendent, is provided the opportunity to restructure in order to be more missionally focused. While the *Book of Discipline* describes in great detail how the four administrative committees are formed, this latest paragraph is quite general and flexible in nature. In working with hundreds of churches and thousands of leaders over the past decade (plus), we (Kay and Blake) have continuously massaged, tweaked, and improved a Simplified, accountable structure model for local congregations to adopt. This model has now found its way into churches across the country in multiple conferences. It is now referred to the simplified structure model generally accepted by district superintendents, cabinets, and bishops (with some districts and conferences requiring their own particular nuances).

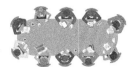

This paragraph in the *Discipline* was introduced for the primary benefit of small churches who were struggling to have enough people to fill the four administrative committees as required by the traditional structure. However interestingly enough, it was the larger churches who were some of the early adopters. They quickly identified the efficiency and effectiveness in the model.

We are often asked about the effectiveness of simplified, accountable structure for the various size churches in the various church settings (rural, suburban, urban). In our experience, this model can (and does) work in any size church. Of course, there are nuances in the various settings, but the overall number of board leaders and accountability are static. The nuances occur in such things as the structure of staff and ministry teams according to church size, whether the church has a daycare or preschool, and how to operate in a multi-point charge. Further nuances occur in the guiding principles, leadership covenants, and the nominations process. The bottom line is that a simplified, accountable structure can work for any size church in any setting.

To simplify church structure, the four administrative committees (trustees, finance, staff-parish relations, and council) cease to exist as we know them, and they are replaced by one new Leadership Board of nine people with three year terms. This new board is nominated by the Committee on Nominations and Leadership Development and voted on by either the church or charge conference. Rather than holding four separate meetings of the four previous administrative committees, there is now one board meeting where the leaders are able to practice a healthier and more holistic approach with missional focus and direction. Technically, and in fulfillment with the requirements of the *Discipline*, all four committees still exist, but they exist as a single unified Leadership Board, with all of their responsibilities, qualifications, and authority of each administrative committee located in the simplified board. The new Leadership Board is the Church Council, and it is also the Trustees, which is the Finance Committee, and is the Staff Parish Relations Committee.

When simplifying the structure, accountability must be a deeply integrated and highly accepted component of simplification. Without accountability, simplification is not recommended! When transitioning to accountable leadership, the new Leadership Board shifts from managing the church to governing the church. This is a significant shift that should not be minimized or glossed over. While simplifying is a technical shift, accountability is an adaptive shift which takes longer and is a harder turn to make for most churches. Thus, this is not the "easy fix" some churches might think or even desire.

Accountable leadership changes not only the agenda, but also the conversations, focus, and priorities at the table. The nominations process is adapted, too, in this model. The role of the pastor will likely need to shift and sometimes staff roles, too. While the new Leadership Board governs in the model of accountable leadership, the pastor leads, the staff (paid and unpaid ministry leaders) equips and coordinates ministry, and the congregation is released to be in ministry.

The primary purposes and benefits of simplified, accountable leadership are …

- Removes bottlenecks in the decision-making process (i.e. time, energy, resources, multiple committees/layers, silos, disjointed focus and priorities, etc.)

- Systems, procedures, and policies in place that are flexible and adaptable

- More people released and available for ministry

- Leadership Board responsible for church's faithfulness to The Great Commission (making disciples)

- Leadership Board aligns church resources to the mission and vision

- Guiding Principles in place for efficiency and permission-giving within healthy boundaries

- Leaders are held accountable at all levels

- Leadership Board is responsible for focusing on the areas of stewardship, strategic alignment, generative future-focus, and accountable leadership

- Missional focus, priority, and alignment are non-negotiables

Mission Possible by Kay Kotan and Blake Bradford lays out the three phases of leading with the simplified, accountable structure (discerning, equipping, implementing) in detail, along with tools and samples to ease the transition and encourage clarity as your congregation begins operating with this powerful and effective model of leadership.

More from Kay Kotan
and Blake Bradford

marketsquarebooks.com

New from Kay Kotan

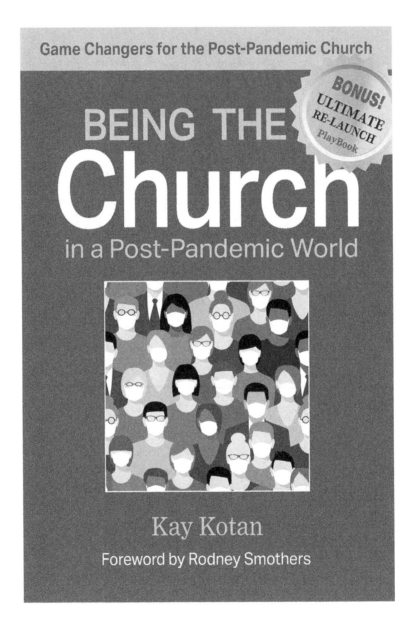

Game Changers for the Post-Pandemic Church

BONUS!
ULTIMATE
RE-LAUNCH
PlayBook

BEING THE
Church
in a Post-Pandemic World

Kay Kotan

Foreword by Rodney Smothers

marketsquarebooks.com

More Books by Kay Kotan & Friends

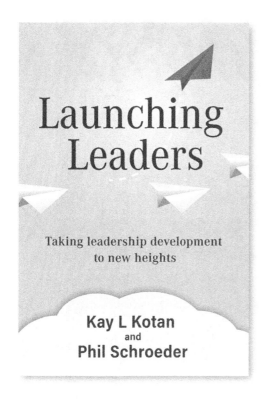

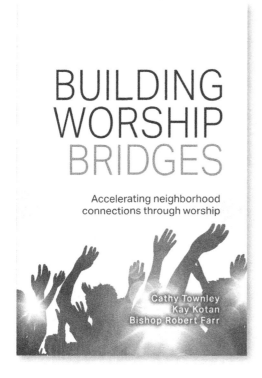

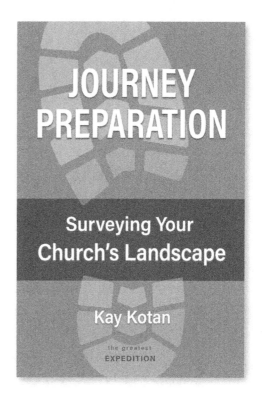

marketsquarebooks.com

Made in the USA
Monee, IL
01 August 2023

40281032R00164